THE SURVIVOR MANUAL

Books by Mark Burnett

Survivor: The Ultimate Game
Survivor II: The Field Guide

THE SURVIVOR MANUAL

Based on U.S. Armed Forces Survival Techniques

Introduction by
MARK BURNETT

St. Martin's Griffin
New York

www.stmartins.com

A John Boswell Associates, Inc. book

No copyright is claimed in any United States government works included in this book.

ISBN 0-312-28421-7

First published under the title *The U.S. Armed Forces Survival Manual*

First St. Martin's Griffin Edition: October 2001

10   9   8   7   6   5   4   3   2   1

✸ INTRODUCTION ✸

What does it take to be a survivor? If you've watched the first two seasons of our television show, *Survivor,* you know some of the answers. To survive—to *win*—an enormous amount of physical prowess and mental acumen is necessary. The most successful contestants are canny and able to strategize, to form alliances and to change the "rules" of those alliances when necessary. They know both how to collaborate and when to go lone wolf, how to husband their strength and when to exert themselves.

The book you're holding in your hands would be invaluable to any of the tribe members on *Survivor.* Especially in the earliest rounds of the game, you can watch contestants sizing each other up in several key areas: personality, character, and raw skills. If Jenna had known how to catch and cook a fish, could she have lasted to a later round on *Survivor I?* If Marilyn had known how to start that fire she worked so hard at in *Survivor II,* would she have been removed so early? What a contestant knows how to do—or what he doesn't—marks him immediately. Contestants who don't have basic survival skills can't be useful to the other tribe members or to themselves: They have one less chip to play.

A superficial observation might be that society has become too civilized to need basic survival skills like finding drinkable water or knowing how to safely stow food without a refrigerator. But when I look at the news, I see the natural world impinging on our constructed society scores of times a day: Drivers are trapped in blizzards, tornadoes play havoc with housing and the water supply, strains in the system mean that whole regions do without power and electricity. And I've always believed that the best test of a person is how they react, how they manage, what they know how to do when all creature comforts have been stripped away and they're left one on one against the elements. I've made it a point in my life to put myself up against the toughest odds again and again. Otherwise I think its hard to know what you're really made of. And that's what *Survivor* is all about.

The Survivor Manual is the real deal. In this handbook, you'll find a treasure trove of useful if not crucial information—simple, detailed instructions on everything from building a shelter to foraging for food, bandaging a fracture to identifying poisonous snakes, orienteering to constructing a raft. Learn these skills—know them cold—and you'll not only be able to face anything nature throws at you, but will have the confidence that can come only from truly being able to survive under any circumstances.

—Mark Burnett

❂ FOREWORD ❂

For centuries, Americans have taken great pride in their self-sufficiency. It is one of the cornerstone values upon which this country has thrived.

But twentieth century technology has made self-sufficiency more and more difficult to attain. In this age of specialization, it is far easier to find an expert to perform the task at hand. As a result we have become less and less capable of taking care of ourselves.

With this in mind, the editors set out to gather the latest information available on survival technique and thought. With research assignments, it is very rare that one can go to a single authoritative source for the information one is seeking. This book is an exception to that rule. There is no greater authority in the world on the subject of survival than the four branches of the United States Armed Forces.

Most of the material contained in this volume has been collected and culled from an array of brochures, pamphlets, and articles published by the Government Printing Office for use by American military personnel throughout the world. This is the same source material provided to our ground troops and Special Forces during World War II, to the Marines in Korea, and to the Green Berets and Navy Seal units in Vietnam. It is material that is regularly updated and revised, from information provided by soldiers and sailors who have actually been called upon to use it. It is practical, specific material that represents the most current and modern thinking on effective survival action technique.

The editors' task, therefore, was to collect, collate, and arrange this material into one cohesive, clear, accurate, accessible volume that would be suitable for civilian as well as military use. Today—when international air travel has made flight over remote and isolated areas a commonplace occurrence, when wilderness hiking and camping are more popular than ever, when ownership of recreational and off-road vehicles, boats, and private planes is at an all-time high—it is the kind of information that everyone should have at his or her fingertips.

The editors, John Boswell and George Reiger, both former Naval officers, are graduates of the U.S. Navy's SERE (Survival, Evasion, Resistance, and Escape) School. Boswell is a writer, editor, and literary agent who has worked in the publishing business for nine years. Reiger, the recipient of the Vietnamese Armed Forces Medal of Honor, was one of the first military advisors in Vietnam, and later served as an official translator at the Paris Peace Talks. He is a former editor of *Popular Mechanics,* Conservation Editor of *Field and Stream,* and the author of nine books on outdoor and wilderness subjects.

The editors would like to express their appreciation and thanks to: The Government Printing Office; the Office of the Adjutant General, Department of the Navy; Headquarters, U.S. Marine Corps; and the Directorate of Administration, Department of the Air Force, for their help and assistance in facilitating the search for the material contained in *The U.S. Armed Forces Survival Manual.*

✪ CONTENTS ✪

CHAPTER SIX   Basic Survival Skills

Travel • Shelter • Environmental Hazards • *Reptiles* • *Sea Urchins, Sea Biscuits, Sponges, and Anemones* • Health Hazards • Water • Food • *Seaweeds* • *Other Edible Plants* • *Invertebrates* • *Mollusks* • *Worms* • *Arthropods* • *Echinoderms*   237

CHAPTER ELEVEN   Survival Under Unusual Conditions

Emergency Procedures for Plane Crash • *On Land* • *On Sea* • Nuclear Attack • *Immediate Action* • *Radiation* • Natural Disasters • *Preparation (Floods, Tornadoes, Hurricanes, Earthquakes, Tidal Waves, Lightning, Forest Fires)* • *After a Disaster*   267

CHAPTER ONE

The Psychology of Survival

No one can ever be fully prepared for a survival situation. If you are lucky, you may have access to a survival kit, a rifle, or an axe. If you are smart, you are already well versed in the skills and techniques that will be described in this manual. But no matter how lucky or skillful you might be, to find yourself suddenly isolated in a desolate area of the world is a shock to the entire human system—emotionally and mentally, as well as physically. It is important to understand the psychology of survival as well as its techniques.

THE WILL TO SURVIVE

Track and field athletes talk of "The Bear" that haunts middle- and long-distance runners. After going some distance the runner, in a matter of a few yards, will break stride, will pull up out of the running crouch, and will perceptibly begin to slow. Overcome with pain or cramps or fatigue, he has lost the will to win.

The same phenomenon often occurs in survival situations, only the stakes are far greater than winning or losing a track event. There are reported incidents of people who have been rescued and treated for all maladies, and who have then died in the hospital. They had lost the will to live. The experiences of hundreds of servicemen isolated during World War II, Korea, and Vietnam combat prove that survival is largely a matter of mental outlook. The will to survive is the most important factor. Whether you are with a group or alone, emotional problems resulting from shock, fear, despair, loneliness, and boredom will be experienced. In addition to these mental hazards, injury and pain, fatigue, hunger, or thirst tax the will to live. If you are not prepared mentally to overcome all obstacles and to expect the worst, the chances of coming out alive are greatly reduced.

WHERE THE MIND LEADS . . .

Interviews with thousands of survivors of World War II German prison camps have demonstrated the amazing resiliency of the human body when guided by the human spirit. Our bodies are highly complex machines, yet even when subjected to the most harsh and degrading conditions, the will to live can sustain the living process. The body's demands for energy from food sources can, over a period of time, be reduced to practically zero. Survivors of German concentration camps have reported that life, even under inhuman circumstances, was worth living. In many cases, this spirit alone was credited for their survival.

PREPARATION

Proper preparation can give the survival victim a strong psychological edge toward overcoming his or her survival situations. While no one *expects* to be in such a situation, one can *anticipate* certain conditions that dramatically increase the possibility. If you are preparing to go on a camping or hiking trip or to ride in a small plane or boat, the odds of finding your life *in extremis* are increased.

The following tips are not only sound advice but, if followed, offer strong psychological support under survival conditions:

1) Prepare a Survival Kit (see Appendix II) and take it along on any trip that offers even the most remote possibility of being stranded or isolated.
2) If you own or are a regular traveler in a small plane, pleasure boat, or recreational vehicle, keep a copy of this manual in your glove compartment or tool box.
3) If you hike or camp, take along a copy of this manual in your backpack or knapsack.

4) Commit to memory as much of the information in the book as possible. Knowledge of survival techniques builds confidence and confidence will lead to control of the survival environment.

PANIC AND FEAR

Almost everyone who has ever found himself lost, isolated, and cut off from civilization has experienced fear—fear of the unknown, fear of pain and discomfort, fear of one's own weaknesses. Under such conditions fear is not only normal—it is healthy. Fear heightens one's senses and attunes one to potential dangers and hazards. Fear is the natural surge of adrenalin, present in all mammals, that acts as a defense mechanism against hostility or the unknown.

But fear must be harnessed and properly channeled or it can lead to panic. Panic is the most destructive response to a survival situation. Energy is wasted, rational thinking is impaired or destroyed altogether, and positive steps to one's survival become impossible. Panic can lead to hopelessness, which can begin to break down one's will to survive.

Several positive mental steps can be taken to make fear an ally and panic an impossibility. As mentioned above, preparation and knowledge of survival techniques instill confidence and lead to control of one's self as well as one's environment. In addition, it is important to *occupy your mind immediately* with an analysis of the situation and the survival tasks at hand. It will help you to remember the word S-U-R-V-I-V-A-L and to use it as a memory device. The interrelated survival tips keyed to the individual letters of the word will provide you with an initial survival checklist. More important, it focuses the mind on the tasks at hand, sublimating fear and the danger of panic.

S-U-R-V-I-V-A-L

Size Up the Situation—Am I injured? What emergency first-aid measures must I take? What is the injury status of others in my group? What are the immediate dangers? Is there anything immediately preceding my present situation that tells me where I am or how best to survive? Am I near water? Food? What are the weather and terrain conditions? What is there around me that can aid my survival?

Undue Haste Makes Waste—Do not scurry about without direction or purpose. Until you are fully aware of your situation it is important to conserve energy. Under survival conditions energy is precious and time (except in medical emergencies) of less importance. Do not engage in any physical activity until you have a plan and specific tasks to perform. Wasted activity can foster a sense of helplessness that can ultimately lead to panic.

Remember Where You Are—Most likely you will be required to forage and to travel some distance from your initial location. Familiarity breeds security, and there is little that is more defeating in a survival situation than to "lose" your focal point or base camp. Note your surroundings, unusual topographic features, etc., and make a mental picture of them. When leaving your base camp, mark your path so that you can always retrace your footsteps. No matter how stranded or isolated you may be, you are "somewhere." Knowing where you are, even if only in reference to your immediate surroundings, increases your chances of being rescued.

Vanquish Fear and Panic—Reminding oneself consciously of the debilitating force of fear and panic can diminish their danger. Take an "attitude check" and objectively analyze the results.

Improvise—No matter where you may find yourself there will be something, probably several things, within your immediate range of activity that will aid in your survival. The more inventive and creative you are, the more comfortable your circumstances will become. You must alter your frame of reference. A tree no longer is a tree but becomes a potential source of food, fuel, shelter, and clothing.

Familiarize yourself with your surroundings. Like an optical illusion, the mind will miraculously transform objects of nature into instruments of survival.

Value Living—The urge to survive is basic in man and animal, and underlies most cultural and technological revolutions throughout history. Under extreme conditions the will to survive can be severely tested. If the will is lost, it renders all knowledge of survival techniques useless.

Do not take unnecessary risks. You are the key to your own survival, and foolish gambles resulting in injury or some form of incapacitation limit your effectiveness.

Act Like the Natives—In many areas of the world remote from civilization you may discover human inhabitants. Primitive natives and tribal groups are usually not hostile; however, approach them with caution. They know the country: available water, shelter areas, food, the way back to civilization. Be careful not to offend them. They may save your life. To enlist native help, use these guides:

1) Let the natives make the initial contact. Deal with the recognized headman or chief to get what is needed.
2) Show friendliness, courtesy, and patience. Do not show fright; do not display a weapon.
3) Respect their local customs and manners.
4) Respect their personal property.
5) Most tribal cultures are male-dominated. As a general rule, try to avoid direct contact or communication with the female members of the tribe.
6) Learn from the natives about woodcraft and getting food and drink. Seek their advice concerning local hazards.
7) Avoid physical contact without seeming to do so.
8) Paper money is usually worthless, but coins—as well as matches, tobacco, salt, razor blades, empty containers, or cloth—may be valuable bartering items.
9) Leave a good impression. Others may need this help.

Learn Basic Skills—This volume will tell you how to perform basic skills. But learning is doing. The more you repeat basic tasks and skills, the more adept you will become at performing them.

Survival is a positive mental attitude toward yourself and your surroundings. By memorizing, then analyzing, the survival tips keyed to the letters of the word, you will have already established a direction for your survival actions and some worthwhile tasks to perform.

LONELINESS AND BOREDOM

These are the stepsisters of fear and panic. Unlike the latter they do not come upon one suddenly and savagely, but quietly and unexpectedly, usually after all the basic survival tasks have been performed and the basic survival needs—water, food, shelter, and clothing—have been provided for. Loneliness and boredom can lead to depression and undermine the will to survive.

The psychological antidote for loneliness and boredom is the same as for fear and panic: Keep the mind occupied. Set priorities and tasks that will minimize discomfort, enhance the possibility of rescue, and provide for survival over an extended period of time. Consider unexpected yet possible emergencies as contingency operations and devise plans and tasks to deal with them.

Set a schedule. A schedule not only provides a form of security; it occupies the mind with the business at hand.

Set large tasks, such as building a "permanent" shelter, and establish tasks that must be repeated every day, such as keeping a diary.

Loneliness and boredom can only exist in the absence of affirmative thought and action. In a survival situation there is always plenty of work that needs to be done.

SURVIVAL IN GROUPS

Group dynamics can be both a help and a hazard to individual survival. Obviously, there are more hands to perform the necessary tasks, and contact with another human being can be psychologically supportive. Still, a chain is as strong as its weakest link, and the survival difficulties encountered can be multiplied by the number of people encountering them. Group survival also introduces an additional potentially destructive factor: dissension. Dissension must be avoided at all costs.

As individual reactions to survival situations become automatic, so must those of the group. Groups (such as squads or platoons) that work together and have leaders that fulfill their responsibilities have the best chance for survival. If there is no designated leader, elect one. If your group considers the following factors, the odds of returning to friendly control are greatly improved:

1) Organize group survival activities.
2) Recognize one leader. The leader should delegate individual duties and keep the group appraised of overall survival activities.
3) Develop a feeling of mutual dependence within the group.

4) When possible, the group should make decisions under the direction of the leader. Otherwise, no matter what the situation, the leader must make the decisions, and his orders must be followed.

Finally, know that the greatest test of your will and stamina will occur after you are *almost* rescued—when you see the plane or ship, but no one aboard sees you. You will feel an inevitable backlash of depression and despair. But don't succumb. Where there is one aircraft, there will be more. If it is flying a search pattern, it means someone is looking for you. Now is the time to direct your energy and survival techniques toward being seen *next time*. And there will be a next time.

The theme of survival is: **Never give up.**

CHAPTER TWO

Finding Direction with a Map and a Compass

Knowing or finding out where you are is literally the first step toward successful survival. Every year people get lost—and some perish—because they had no map or were unable to utilize effectively the maps they did have.

The simplest way to avoid this risk is to know where you are at all times on your journey. Although you are not likely to have maps covering all the terrain for every trip you make—especially trips abroad where reliable maps are often difficult to obtain—you can remain generally oriented by knowing the direction in which you were going and the country in or over which you are moving.

If you are abandoning a ship or aircraft at sea and time permits, try to find out your latitude and longitude, the difference in bearing between true and magnetic norths, heading to the nearest land, prevailing wind direction, prevailing ocean current (if any), and direction and distance to the nearest shipping lanes.

If you are a passenger on a commercial liner (air or ocean), the captain and his crew will automatically take command of the survival effort. They may not feel you should "worry" about such information. Point out to them that something could happen to them, and that the more people there are with essential information regarding location and possible paths of rescue, the more likely it is that everyone will survive.

If you are on a pack trip or safari with a guide, ask him to keep you up to date on where you are and where you are going. Review maps with him regarding your daily progress; something could happen to your guide, leaving you without his special knowledge of the local region.

MAP READING

Most people would claim to know how to read a map—and those people would be partially right. But a map can provide the reader with a wealth of information that is not readily apparent to the uneducated eye. In fact, map reading can be a difficult, often fascinating field of study, far too complex to cover here in any great detail. What is presented here is a basic explanation of maps; the map's relationship to geographic coordinates, or lines of latitude and longitude; and the simple use of a map with a compass.

Both the Army and the Navy offer map-reading courses to their personnel (some lasting eight weeks, an indication of just how complex this seemingly simple subject can be). Much of the text material used in these courses is available to the public. For further information on map reading, write the Office of Information, Dept. of the Navy, Washington, D.C. 20350, or the Office of the Chief of Information, Dept. of the Army, Washington, D.C. 20310, or request a copy of "Map Reading" (Dept. of the Army, FM 21-76) from the Government Printing Office.

WHAT IS A MAP?

The purpose of a map is to permit you to visualize a portion of the earth's surface much as a bird flying overhead sees the ground (see fig. 2-1). Of course, given changing angles and distances, not even a bird sees all ground features in their true proportions, positions, and shapes. Thus, a mapmaker must focus on those details that pertain to a map reader's special interests and needs.

For example, a truck driver is not at all interested in having a map with such details as individual buildings, or water depths of the various rivers he crosses. If the roads on his map often seem larger and wider than the towns they pass through, the truck driver accepts such unreality because the map better serves his needs that way.

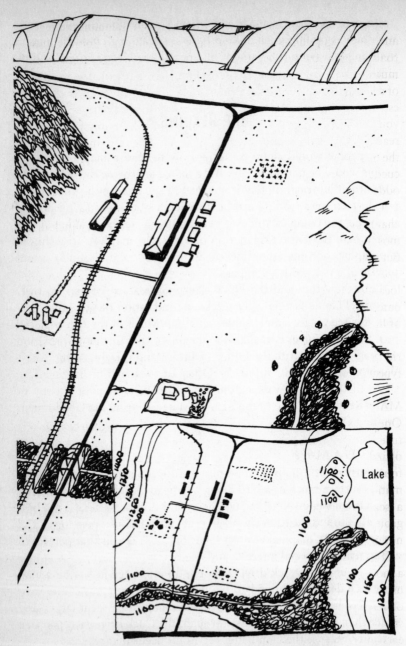

Fig. 2-1   A "Bird's-Eye" View of the Ground
and a Map (inset) of the Same Area

Road maps—These are more correctly called "planimetric maps," and they are useful mostly for getting from Point A to Point B along a road or highway. In a survival situation, however, they are certainly much better than no maps at all. Road maps are oriented to the points of a compass, which can help you in determining direction to the nearest water supply or populated area. By using the distance, or bar, scale you can also estimate how far you are from the point you wish to reach. Most important, you can determine direction and distance to the nearest road or highway, thus increasing your chances of being rescued. If lost, seek out a crossroad or intersection, which doubles your odds of encountering a car or truck.

Charts—These are "navigational maps" featuring water depths, channel locations, and buoys or other markers. Since they include almost no shore-based features, they are of no use for a land expedition—but vitally important for coastal or sea travel.

A different kind of *chart* is used by aircraft pilots; it features the location of airports, forbidden overflight areas, and Loran coordinates. While essential to the pilot's particular task, such information is of little additional use to the survivor.

Topographic maps—These maps show all the features of planimetric maps, plus land shapes and elevations. They are the most useful type of map to have in a survival situation.

MARGINAL INFORMATION

One would not attempt to put together an unassembled piece of furniture without first reading the instructions. Maps also come with a set of instructions. These instructions, called marginal information, are found boxed together on all topographic maps. The marginal information will explain the map's symbols, indicate distances, and provide a scale for converting distances on the map to distances over the ground (see fig. 2-2). The information gained from these marginal notes can be instrumental in your survival.

To facilitate the identification of features on the map by providing a more natural appearance and contrast, topographic symbols are also usually printed in different colors, with each color identifying a class of features. The colors vary with different types of maps, but on a standard large-scale topographic map, the colors used and the features each represents are:

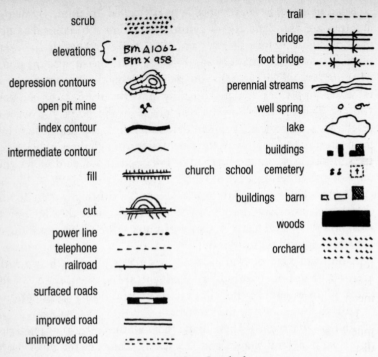

Fig. 2-2   Map Symbols

Black—the majority of cultural or manmade features.
Blue—water features such as lakes, rivers, and swamps.
Green—vegetation such as woods, orchards, and vineyards.
Brown—all relief features such as contours.
Red—main roads, built-up areas, and special features.

Elevations are depicted with brown contour lines. The elevation is found by following one of the heavier lines (called "contour lines") until a number breaks its continuity. That number is either in feet or meters, and every point on that same line is the same number of feet or meters above sea level. The contour line is usually every fifth line going up the side of a hill. There will be a note at the bottom of the map indicating whether the number is in feet or meters, and the elevation distance between the lines, called the "contour interval."

At the bottom of every topographic map is a *graphic (bar) scale* (see fig. 2-3). This provides the map reader with a precise definition of scale

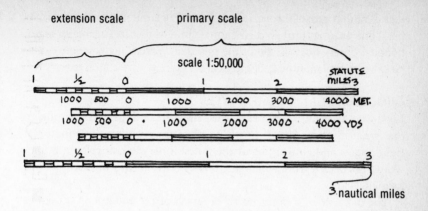

Fig. 2-3   Graphic Bar Scale

for all major natural features. For example, if the map says its scale is 1:50,000, that means one unit of measure on the map in feet, yards, or meters is equal to 50,000 of the same units of measure on the ground.

In addition, the graphic scale will usually have graded bars in yards, miles, and meters, so that by taking a straight edge and matching the distance between two points on the map with one of the bars in the graphic scale, you can determine the real distance between those two points. For short distances, the graphic bar usually includes subdivided distances to the left of the *primary scale,* known as the *extension scale.*

Topographic maps for the United States are available from the U.S. Geological Survey. For areas east of the Mississippi, write to the U.S.G.S. in Washington, D.C. 20244. For regions west of the Mississippi, write U.S.G.S. Federal Center, Denver, CO 80225. The quickest way to get maps of Alaska is to write U.S.G.S., 520 Illinois Street, Fairbanks, AK 99701. The National Forest Service also produces excellent topographic maps of areas under its jurisdiction, and they can be obtained either from regional offices of the Forest Service or directly from the service headquarters in Washington, D.C. 20250. Topographic maps of Canada are available from the Map Distribution Office, Department of Mines and Technical Service, Ottawa, Ontario.

Similar services are available in many other nations. However, while English-speaking nations base their geographical coordinates on a prime meridian that passes through Greenwich, England, other countries may use a line passing through their capital cities or the site of a major astronomical observatory as the prime meridian. Before giving some examples, let us explain how geographical coordinates are conceived.

GEOGRAPHICAL COORDINATES

If we were to draw a set of east–west rings around the earth parallel to the equator, and a set of north–south rings crossing the equator at right angles and converging at the poles, a network of reference lines would be formed from which any point on the earth's surface could be located.

The distance of a point north or south of the equator is known as its *latitude*. The rings around the earth parallel to the equator are called parallels of latitude or simply *parallels*.

Beginning map readers are sometimes confused by the fact that lines of latitude run east–west, but north–south distances are measured between them. A second set of rings around the globe at right angles to the lines of latitude and passing through the poles are known as meridians of *longitude*, or, simply, meridians. In the same way, lines of longitude run north–south, but east–west distances are measured between them.

Geographic coordinates are expressed in angular measurement. Each circle is divided into 360 degrees. Each degree is divided into 60 minutes, and each minute into 60 seconds. The degree is symbolized by °, the minute by ′, and the second by ″. Starting with 0° at the equator, the parallels of latitude are numbered to 90° both north and south. The extremities are the North Pole at 90° north latitude and the South Pole at 90° south latitude.

Latitude can have the same numerical value north or south of the equator, so the direction N or S must always be given. Starting with 0° at the prime meridian, longitude is measured both east and west around the world. Lines east of the prime meridian are numbered to 180° and identified as east longitude; lines west of the prime meridian are numbered to 180° and identified as west longitude. The direction E or W must always be given. The line directly opposite the prime meridian, 180°, may be referred to as either east or west longitude. For example, the "x" in fig. 2-4 represents a point located at 39 North Latitude and 95 West Longitude. In written form latitude is always expressed first; therefore this location would read 39°N 95°W.

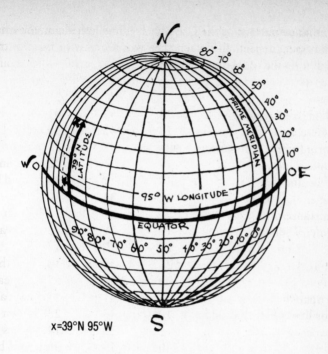

x=39°N 95°W

Fig. 2-4   Latitude and Longitude

The values of geographic coordinates, being in units of angular measure, will mean more if they are compared with units of measure with which we are more familiar. At any point on the earth the ground distance covered by 1 degree of latitude is approximately 111 kilometers (69 miles); 1 second is equal to approximately 30 meters (100 feet).

The ground distance covered by 1 degree of longitude at the equator is also approximately 111 kilometers (69 miles), but it decreases as one moves north or south until it becomes zero at the poles. For example, 1 second of longitude represents about 30 meters (100 feet) at the equator, but at the latitude of Washington, D.C., 1 second of longitude is approximately 24 meters (78 feet).

As mentioned earlier, the maps made by some nations do not have their longitude values based on a prime meridian passing through Greenwich, England. Below are prime meridians used by other nations. When these maps are obtained in the United States, a note usually appears in the marginal information giving the difference between the Greenwich meridian and the one used on the map. To convert the maps from these nations to the Greenwich Prime Meridian, you must add or subtract (depending on whether you are east or west of the Greenwich line) the following distances:

	°	′	″	
Amsterdam, Netherlands	4	53	01	E
Athens, Greece	23	42	59	E
Batavia (Djakarta), Indonesia	106	48	28	E
Bern, Switzerland	7	26	22	E
Brussels, Belgium	4	22	06	E
Copenhagen, Denmark	12	34	40	E
Djakarta, see Batavia				
Ferro, Canary Islands	17	39	46	W
Helsinki, Finland	24	57	17	E
Istanbul, Turkey	28	58	50	E
Lisbon, Portugal	9	07	55	W
Madrid, Spain	3	41	15	W
Oslo, Norway	10	43	23	E
Paris, France	2	20	14	E
Pulkovo, U.S.S.R	30	19	39	E
Rome, Italy	12	27	08	E
Stockholm, Sweden	18	03	30	E
Tirane, Albania	19	46	45	E

MAP ORIENTATION

To find where you are on a map, carefully study your surroundings. Are there any hills or peaks, streams or rivers, manmade structures like barns, towers, or railroads nearby? Pick two such prominent features and then relate them to the map. Although all maps are held so that they can be read with the north side of the map at the top, turn the map until the topographic features are in accordance with your location. The direction you are facing or want to go can now be determined from the geographical coordinates found on the map. This is called *map orientation.*

DIRECTIONS

Directions are expressed in everyday life as right, left, straight ahead, etc., but the question arises, "To the right of what?" Map readers require a method of expressing a direction that is accurate, adaptable for use in any area of the world, and has a common unit of measure. Directions are expressed as units of angular measure, and there are several systems used. However, the most commonly used unit of angular measure is the degree, with its subdivisions of minutes and seconds.

The *grad* is a unit of measure found on some foreign maps. There are 400 grads in a complete circle (a 90° right angle equals 100 grads). The grad is divided into 100 centesimal minutes (centigrads) and the minute into 100 centesimal seconds (milligrads). This unit of measure is used with the metric system.

In order to measure anything, there must always be a starting point or zero measurement. To express a direction as a unit of angular measure, there must be a starting point or zero measure and a point of reference. These two points designate the base, or reference line. There are three base lines: true north, magnetic north, and grid north. Those most commonly used are magnetic and grid; the magnetic when working with a compass, and the grid when working with a military map.

True north is a line from any position on the earth's surface to the North Pole. All lines of longitude are true north lines. True north is usually symbolized by a star.

Magnetic north is the direction to the North Magnetic Pole, as indicated by the north-seeking needle of a magnetic instrument. Magnetic north is usually symbolized by a half arrowhead.

Grid north is the north that is established by the vertical grid lines on the map. Grid north may be symbolized by the letters GN or the letter y.

The most common method of expressing a direction is by using *azimuths*. An azimuth is defined as a horizontal angle, measured in a clockwise manner from a north base line. When the azimuth between two points on a map is desired, the points are joined by a straight line and a protractor is used to measure the angle between grid north and the drawn line. This measured angle is the *grid azimuth* of the drawn line. When using an azimuth, the point from which the azimuth originates is imagined to be the center of the azimuth circle.

Types of azimuths take their names from the base line from which they have been measured; true azimuths from true north, magnetic azimuths from magnetic north, and grid azimuths from grid north. Therefore, any given direction can be expressed in three different ways: a grid azimuth if measured on a topographic map, a magnetic azimuth if measured by a compass, or a true azimuth if measured from a meridian of longitude.

A *back azimuth* is the reverse direction of an azimuth. It is comparable to doing an "about-face." To obtain a back azimuth from an azimuth, add 180° if the azimuth is 180° or less, or subtract 180° if the azimuth is 180° or more. The back azimuth of 180° may be stated as either 0° or 360°.

A *declination diagram* is placed on most large-scale maps to enable the user to orient the map properly. The diagram shows the interrelationship of magnetic north, grid north, and true north. On medium-scale maps declination information is shown by a note in the map margin. Declination is the angular difference between true north and either magnetic or grid north.

THE MAGNETIC COMPASS

The hand-held magnetic compass is the most commonly used and simplest instrument for determining and measuring directions and angles. It comes in a variety of styles, from simple pocket or wrist models to more complex orienteering (Slyva) or lensatic models. All styles are useful for basic navigation, and all should be equipped with some sort of cover to protect the lens from damage.

The Slyva model is attached to a transparent rectangular piece of plastic which has ruled edges and a large arrow (the so-called direction-of-travel arrow) printed on it.

The lensatic compass has a hinged metal tab equipped with a small magnifying lens, which enables you to read small degree marks in taking bearings. The protective cover for this compass is provided with a keyhole-type sight for lining up landmarks.

For basic orientation and map reading, any magnetic compass will work so long as it is accurate to begin with, and kept that way by always using it away from steel or iron objects or outside areas with noticeable deposits of magnetite, a type of iron ore.

Since all magnetic compasses point to magnetic north, not true north, all maps carry a correction (called *declination*) between the true reference points, which naturally varies from point to point throughout the world.

For example, in the United States, the true north bearing overlaps the magnetic north bearing on a line running roughly from Michigan's Upper Peninsula, through Chicago, south to the tip of Florida. Anywhere east or west of this line, you must compensate for true north by adding or subtracting the required number of degrees indicated on your map. While such compensations are usually not necessary for short hikes, in the case of a prolonged expedition in, say, the Pacific Northwest, (where magnetic compass bearings are in some places more than 20° east of true north), appropriate adjustments between map and compass are crucial.

For about fifty cents, you can buy an *isogonic* or declination chart of the United States (Chart No. 3077) from the U.S. Coast and Geodetic Survey, Distribution Division C44, Washington, D.C. 20235.

Military or Lensatic Compass

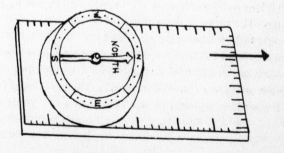

Orienteering or Slyva Compass

Fig. 2-5   The Compass

Using a map and compass is simple, for it involves no more than keeping track of where you are and of where you plan to go. Even if your path is blocked by a marsh or swamp not clearly indicated on the map, by making three right angle courses around the obstacle you will find yourself both on the other side and back on the same heading as you were before toward your preselected objective.

Rarely will you have to hike for any great distance without being able to see some distant landmark which coincides with a feature on your map. Only in deep woods or jungle is your ability to use reference points hampered. Then it may be necessary to climb the tallest available tree to check for distant mountain ranges or other features. Incidentally, it is difficult, even from the top of the jungle canopy, to distinguish rivers and streams from the surrounding jungle, due to the uniform height and dense growth of such heavily forested areas. For that reason and many others, once you locate a jungle river, stick with it as a source of water, food, and basic orientation.

Triangulation is nothing more than putting yourself on a map with the help of two reference points, if you are not near either one of these points. Take a compass bearing on point A and then one on point B. Transfer these bearings to your map, as illustrated (see fig. 2-6), and where the two lines intersect—that's where you're standing.

The only time careful coordination between map and compass is crucial is when you are plotting a zigzag course across rugged terrain. Then it is necessary after each leg on a given bearing to transfer the number of steps you have taken onto the map by assuming that your average stride is about 30 inches. The graphic bar at the bottom of the map will help simplify the conversion of steps to yards, meters or miles. However, you *must* determine the closest possible approximation to your position before you can head off on another bearing.

So long as your objective is a large feature such as a road crossing at right angles to your general direction of travel, pinpoint accuracy is not essential. However, if you are trying to find a cabin in deep woods or a particular ridge among many, an error of a few yards in the beginning can put you thousands of yards off target several miles downrange. Therefore, treat each leg of any compass course with as much precision as possible.

Don't overestimate your progress on rugged ground. Although you may be able to jog a mile in eight minutes or walk a mile in fifteen min-

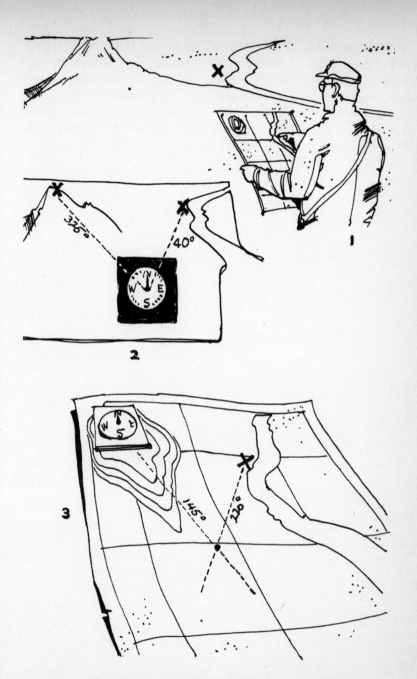

Fig. 2-6   Determining Your Location by Triangulation

utes, you will be lucky to average a mile an hour if you are wearing a heavy back pack and moving over mountains and fallen timber. This is another reason to use a map and compass and to keep track of your pace. Many people will hike rigorously from a campsite in the morning only to return exhausted in the afternoon. They may correctly approach the campsite but turn away when only a few hundred yards from the clearing—convinced they have already walked too far.

CHAPTER THREE

Finding Direction Without a Map or a Compass

You may find yourself without a map or a compass, or in an iron-ore-rich or polar part of the world where the use of a magnetic compass can do more harm than good. If you are above 60° latitude in the Northern Hemisphere, and unless you know where you are and are positive that by following a nearby river downstream, you will reach a friendly village, the U.S. and Canadian Departments of Defense strongly urge all distressed people in survival situations to stay where they are and wait for rescuers to find them. The presence and location of all aircraft and ground parties in polar regions are reported to and monitored by a variety of domestic and foreign government agencies, and any irregularities or calls for help are quickly converted into search-and-rescue missions.

However, under other circumstances or in other parts of the world, you may want to attempt to move toward civilization rather than wait for civilization to come to you. Important to that effort is not getting lost a second time—i.e., knowing how to retrace your steps to the point of departure and how to move purposefully and precisely in the direction in which you wish to go. Advice on crossing rough terrain and maintaining direction will be offered in the next chapter. But before starting out (and at regular intervals during your journey), you must first determine direction. The fundamental step in establishing direction is locating the four points of the compass. There are several ways to do this without a compass.

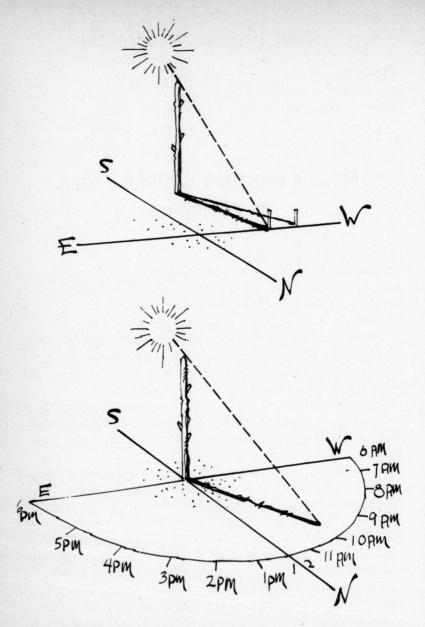

Fig. 3-1   Determining Direction and Time of Day:
Shadow-Tip Method

FINDING DIRECTION DURING THE DAY

THE SUN

Remember that the sun rises in the east (but rarely *due* east) and sets in the west (but rarely *due* west). The sun rises slightly to the south of east and sets slightly to the north of west, and the declination or angle of variance is different with different seasons. Remember, however, that direction is relative to one's purpose. If you must reach a specific point or location, you must align your direction with true or magnetic north or south. But if your purpose is simply to maintain a direction, the sun's arc is the best constant point of reference. Try to check your direction at least once a day using one of the following methods.

The Shadow-Tip Method for Determining Direction

1) Place a stick or twigless branch into the ground at a fairly level spot where a distinct shadow will be cast. Mark the spot where the shadow will be cast. Mark the spot where the shadow tip strikes the ground with a stone, twig, or pebble.

2) Wait until the shadow tip moves a few inches. If you are using a 3-foot stick, about 15 minutes should be sufficient. The longer the stick, the faster the shadow will move. Mark the new position of the shadow tip in the same way as the first.

3) Draw a straight line through the two marks to obtain an *approximate* east–west line. The first shadow tip is always toward the west; the second shadow tip mark is always toward the east—*any time of day and anywhere on earth.*

4) A line drawn at right angles to the east–west line at any point is the *approximate* north–south line, which will help orient you to any desired direction of travel.

Inclining the stick to obtain a more convenient shadow, in size or direction, does not impair the accuracy of the shadow-tip method. Thus, a traveler on sloping ground or in highly vegetated terrain need not waste valuable time looking for a sizable level area. A flat dirt spot the size of your hand is all that is necessary for shadow-tip markings, and the base of the stick can either be above, below, or to one side of it. Also, any stationary object (the end of a tree limb or the notch where branches join) serves just as well as an implanted stick, because only the shadow *tip* is marked.

Time of Day Using the Shadow-Tip Method   Being able to establish time of day is important for such purposes as keeping a rendezvous, carrying out prearranged concerted action by separated persons or groups, estimating the remaining duration of daylight, and so forth. Shadow-clock time is closest to conventional clock time at midday, and the spacing of the other hours, compared to conventional time, varies somewhat with the locality and the date.

To find the time of day, move the stick to the intersection of the east–west line and the north–south line, and set it vertically in the ground. The west part of the east–west line indicates 6 a.m., and the east part is 6 p.m., *anywhere on earth.*

The north–south line now becomes the noon line. The shadow of the stick is an hour hand in the shadow-clock, and with it you can estimate the time using the noon line and the 6 o'clock line as your guides. Depending on your location and the season, the shadow may move either clockwise or counterclockwise, but this does not alter your manner of reading the shadow-clock.

The shadow-clock is not a timepiece in the ordinary sense. It makes every day twelve unequal "hours" long, and always reads 6 A.M. at sunrise and 6 P.M. at sunset. However, it does provide a satisfactory means of telling time in the absence of properly set watches.

If you have a watch, the shadow-clock can be used to "store up" the direction you obtained by using the shadow-tip method. Merely set your watch to shadow-clock time and then use the "watch method" described below. This avoids the ten to fifteen minute wait required to complete a shadow-tip reading for true direction, and thereby permits you to take as many instantaneous readings as are necessary to avoid "circling." After traveling for an hour or so, take a check shadow-clock reading and reset your watch if necessary. The direction obtained by this modified watch method is the same as that obtained by the regular shadow-tip method using a stick. That is, the degree of accuracy of each method is identical.

DIRECTION, USING A WATCH

A watch can be used to determine *approximate* true north or south, as shown (see fig. 3-2). In the north temperate zone only, the hour hand is pointed toward the sun. A south line can be found midway between

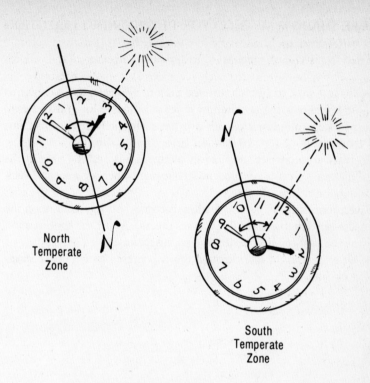

North
Temperate
Zone

South
Temperate
Zone

Fig. 3-2   Determining Direction Using a Watch

the hour hand and 12 o'clock. If on daylight saving time, the north–south line is found midway between the hour hand and one o'clock. If there is any doubt as to which end of the line is north, remember that the sun is in the east before noon and in the west in the afternoon.

The watch may also be used to determine direction in the south temperate zone; however, the method is different. The 12 o'clock hour dial is pointed toward the sun, and halfway between the "12" and the hour hand will be a north line. If on daylight saving time, the north line lies midway between the hour hand and "1." The temperate zones extend from latitude 23½° to 66½° in both hemispheres.

The watch method can be in error, especially in the lower latitudes, and may cause "circling." To avoid this, make a shadow-clock and set your watch to the time indicated. After traveling for an hour take another shadow-clock reading. Reset your watch if necessary.

EQUAL SHADOW METHOD FOR DETERMINING DIRECTION

This variation of the shadow-tip method (see fig. 3-3) is more accurate and may be used at all latitudes less than 66° at all times of the year.

1) Place a stick or branch into the ground *vertically* at a fairly level spot where a distinct shadow at least 12 inches long will be cast. Mark the shadow tip with a stone, twig, or other means. This must be done 5 to 10 minutes before noon (sun time).
2) Trace an arc using the shadow as the radius and the base of the stick as the center. A piece of string, a shoelace, or a second stick may be used to do this.
3) As noon approaches the shadow becomes shorter. After noon the shadow lengthens until it crosses the arc. Mark the spot as soon as the shadow tip touches the arc a second time.
4) Draw a straight line through the two marks to obtain an east–west line.

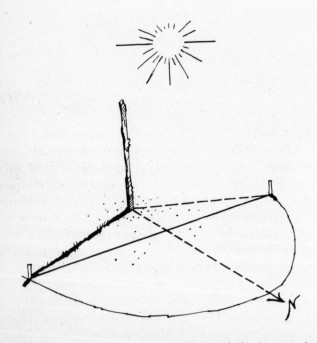

Fig. 3-3   Determining Direction: Equal Shadow Method

Northern Hemisphere

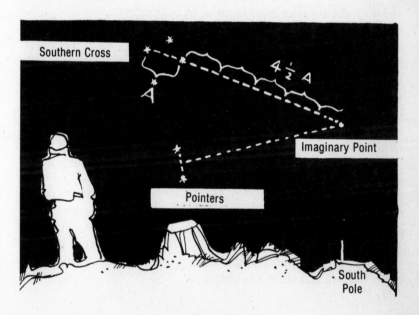

Southern Hemisphere

Fig. 3-4 Determining Direction at Night

Although this is the most accurate version of the shadow tip method:

- *It must be performed around noon.*
- In order to complete the procedure, the observer must watch the shadow and complete step 3 at the exact time the shadow tip touches the arc.

FINDING DIRECTION AT NIGHT

At night the stars may be used to determine the north line in the Northern Hemisphere or the south line in the Southern Hemisphere. To find the North Star, look for the Big Dipper. The two stars at the end of the bowl are called the "pointers." The North Star is in a straight line out from the "pointers" (at about five times the distance between them). The Big Dipper rotates slowly around the North Star and does not always appear in the same position.

The constellation Cassiopeia can also be used. This group of five bright stars is shaped like a lopsided "M" (or "W" when it is low in the sky). The North Star is straight out from the center star, about the same distance as from the Big Dipper. Cassiopeia also rotates slowly around the North Star and is always almost directly opposite the Big Dipper. This position makes it a valuable aid when the Big Dipper is low in the sky, or possibly out of sight because of vegetation or high terrain features.

South of the equator, the constellation Southern Cross will help you locate the general direction of south and, from this base, any other direction. This group of four bright stars is shaped like a cross that is tilted to one side. The two stars forming the long axis, or stem, of the cross are called the "pointers." From the foot of the cross, extend the step four and a half times its length to an imaginary point. This point is the general direction of south. From this point, look straight down to the horizon and select a landmark.

DEAD RECKONING

Before moving from where you are in a survival situation, remember that keeping a record of your time underway is as important as maintaining a given direction. A log or detailed diary is essential not only to successful dead reckoning navigation, but to survival in general. For many centuries, mariners have used dead reckoning to navigate their ships when they are out of sight of land or during bad weather, and it is just as applicable to navigation on land.

Movement on land must be carefully planned. One's starting location and destination should be known or approximated, and—if a map is available—carefully plotted, along with any known intermediate features along the route. These intermediate features, if clearly recognizable on the ground, serve as invaluable checkpoints. If a map is not available, the plotting is done on a blank sheet of paper. A scale is selected so that the entire route will fit on one sheet. A north direction is clearly established. The starting point and destination are then plotted in accurate relationship to each other.

If the terrain permits, the ideal course is a straight line from starting point to destination. This is seldom possible or practicable. The route of travel usually consists of several courses, with an azimuth, or angle stated in degrees, established at the starting point for the first course to be followed. Distance measurement begins with the departure, and continues through the first course until a change in direction is made. A new azimuth is established for the second course and the distance is measured until a second change of direction is made, and so on. Records of all data are kept and all positions are plotted.

For determining distance over land, a "pace" is the best unit of measure. A pace is equal to one natural step, approximately 30 inches. Usually, paces are counted in hundreds, and hundreds can be kept track of in many ways: make notes in a record book; count on your fingers; place small objects such as pebbles into an empty pocket: tie knots in a string; or use a mechanical hand counter. Distances measured this way are only approximate, but with practice can become very accurate. It is important that any person who might find himself in a survival situation predetermine the length of his average pace. This is done by measuring the length of ten average paces (in feet, inches, etc.) and dividing that length by ten. In the field, an average pace must often be adjusted because of the following conditions:

Slopes—The pace lengthens on a downgrade and shortens on an upgrade.

Winds—A headwind shortens the pace, a tailwind increases it.

Surfaces—Sand, gravel, mud, and similar surface materials tend to shorten the pace.

Elements—Snow, rain, or ice cause the pace to be shortened.

Clothing—Heavy clothing shortens the pace; the type of shoe affects traction and therefore the pace length.

Stamina—Fatigue affects the length of the pace.

STEERING MARKS

A steering mark is any well-defined object on the ground in the direction of travel, toward which a navigator may steer. It is easier to follow these than to steer continuously by compass.

Steering marks by day Naturally, steering marks are easier to find during daytime marches. Such objects as lone trees or buildings, timber corners, and shapes on the horizon are good examples. Even a cloud formation or wind direction may be used if checked periodically by any of the celestial direction-finding methods discussed.

Steering marks by night By night the stars are usually the single source of steering marks. Because of the rotation of the earth, the positions of the stars are continually changing and compass checks on azimuth are necessary. The length of the safe period between checks depends on the star selected. A star near the north horizon serves for about a half hour. The pole star is an ideal steering mark since it is less than 1° off true north, but above latitude 70° it is too high in the sky to be useful. When moving south, azimuth checks should be made every 15 minutes to be safe. When traveling east or west, the difficulty of staying on azimuth is more likely to be caused by the star climbing too high in the sky or losing itself behind the western horizon than it is by the star changing direction angle. In all of the above cases, it is necessary to change to another guide star when the first becomes useless. South of the equator, the above general directions for using north and south stars are reversed.

CHAPTER FOUR

On the Move

If, as mentioned in the previous chapter, you suddenly find yourself lost, isolated, or the victim of a plane crash, it is better to stay where you are.

If, however, certain conditions (see Chapter Six) warrant that you are better advised to travel, or if you are forced to leave your base camp in search of food and water, there is much you should know about moving through the wilderness.

Your selected route of travel depends upon your situation, needs, weather conditions, and the nature of the terrain. Whether a ridge, stream, valley, dense forest, or mountain range is selected, be sure it is the *safest*, rather than merely the easiest way.

RATE OF TRAVEL

Plan and accomplish each day's travel so that enough time and energy are left to establish a secure and satisfactory campsite. Rest and sleep are extremely important during travel.

The rate of travel will be determined by a number of factors, including: climatic conditions, e.g., temperature, sun, wind, rain, snow, etc.; your physical condition; the terrain (angle of slope and type of footing); time and distance requirements (Must a certain place be reached by a prescribed time?); the amount of equipment carried (carry only what is essential); and food and water requirements. Hunt and gather food during travel. This should reduce the need to undertake special travel to fulfill food requirements.

ORIENTEERING

Unless you are traveling through dense forest or over the open sea, you can sometimes use distant mountains for orientation to help guide you on your trek. One prominent peak may provide a reference point for up to a week. However, beware of the illusion of seeing a peak and assuming you are still moving in a given direction when you are actually wandering at a tangent to your course and away from rescue. Follow a straight line, one that you can always backtrack, by lining up two landmarks—trees or rocks—and then lining up a third landmark beyond the second. Mark the landmarks—blaze trees or pile up rocks in a distinctive way—as you move along, always picking another landmark *in a straight line* as you approach your next-to-last reference point.

Follow a route parallel to a ridgeline, but directly below it. Game trails are frequently on top of ridges, and may be used as travel lanes. You also find less vegetation and frequent vantage points for locating landmarks.

Using a stream as a route or as a guide is of particular advantage in strange country because it provides a fairly definite course and generally leads to populated areas; it is a potential food and water source, as well as a route for travel by boat or raft. Be prepared, however, to ford, detour, or cut through the thick vegetation lining the stream. If following a stream in mountainous country, look for falls, cliffs, and tributaries as checkpoints. In flat country, streams usually meander, are bordered by swamps, and are thick with undergrowth. Travel on them provides little opportunity to locate landmarks.

Following a coastline is a long, roundabout route; but a coastline is a good reference area from which to get your bearings, and it also provides a probable source of food.

TYPES OF TERRAIN

TRAVEL THROUGH DENSE VEGETATION

With practice, movement through thick undergrowth and jungle can be done effectively by cautiously parting vegetation. Long sleeves worn down will help avoid cuts and scratches.

Avoid scratches, bruises, and loss of direction and confidence by developing "jungle eye." Disregard the pattern of trees and bushes directly to the front. Focus the eyes beyond your immediate front, and rather than looking AT the jungle, look THROUGH it. Stop and stoop occasionally and look along the jungle floor.

Keep alert by moving slowly and steadily in a dense forest or jungle, but stop periodically to listen and take your bearings. Use a machete to cut through dense vegetation, but do not cut unnecessarily. Noise carries a long distance in the woods, and can be reduced by stroking upward when cutting creepers and bush. A stick or staff can be used to part the vegetation, to reduce the possibility of dislodging biting ants, spiders, or snakes. DO NOT grab at brush or vines when climbing slopes; they may have irritating spines or sharp thorns.

Many jungle and forest animals follow well-established game trails. These trails wind and crisscross but frequently lead to water or clearings. Make sure the trails lead in the desired direction of travel by checking your bearings frequently.

In many countries, electric and telephone lines run for miles through sparsely inhabited countryside. Usually the right-of-way is sufficiently clear to afford easy travel. When guiding or traveling along these features, care must be taken when approaching transformer and relay stations, which may be protected by hostile guards.

TRAVEL IN MOUNTAINOUS TERRAIN

Travel in the mountains or other rugged country can be dangerous and confusing unless you know a few tricks. What looks like a ridgeline from a distance might be a series of ridges and valleys. In extremely high mountains, a snowfield or glacier that appears to be continuous and easy to traverse might cover a sheer drop of hundreds of feet. In jungle mountains, trees growing in valleys formed by streams reach great heights, and their tops are at about the same level as trees growing on the valley slopes and hilltops where the water is scarce; this forms a tree line that from a distance appears level and continuous. Mountain travel consumes a great deal of energy and should be avoided when you have suitable alternate routes.

Follow valleys or ridges in mountainous terrain. To save time and energy during mountain walking, keep the body weight directly over the feet by placing the soles of your shoes flat on the ground. If small steps are taken and your movement is slow, but steady, this is not difficult.

Travel may be up or down a steep slope or cliff. Before starting, pick your route carefully, making sure it has places for hand- or footholds from top to bottom. Try out every hold before placing weight on it, and keep your weight evenly distributed. Heed the following hints:

1) Unless necessary, do not climb on loose rock.
2) Move continuously, using the legs to lift your weight and the hands to keep your balance. Try to maintain three points of contact; only move one hand or one foot at a time.
3) Be in a position to go in either direction at any time without danger.
4) In climbing down, face out from the slope as long as possible. This is the best position from which to choose routes and holds.
5) Rappel when descending steep slopes, if an easier route for descent is not available.

Equipment for Descending Slopes   When traveling in mountainous country, or over snow or ice, make an effort to acquire or improvise a sturdy rope and ice axe. The job of descending steep slopes will be difficult or even impossible without them. If available, use parachute suspension lines and obtain a sturdy pole as a substitute for an ice axe.
Hasty Rappel   Anchor the rope around a tree or rock, allowing the ends to hang evenly. Facing slightly sideways to the anchor, place the double rope across your back and under your arms. The hand nearest the anchor is the guiding hand, and the lower hand does the braking. To stop, bring the braking hand across the front of your body, locking the rope. At the same time, turn to face toward the anchor point. After reaching the bottom, pull one strand of the doubled rope to retrieve it. Use this rappel only on moderate pitches or on very long, gentle slopes. Its main advantage is that it is quick and easy to use, especially when the rope is wet.

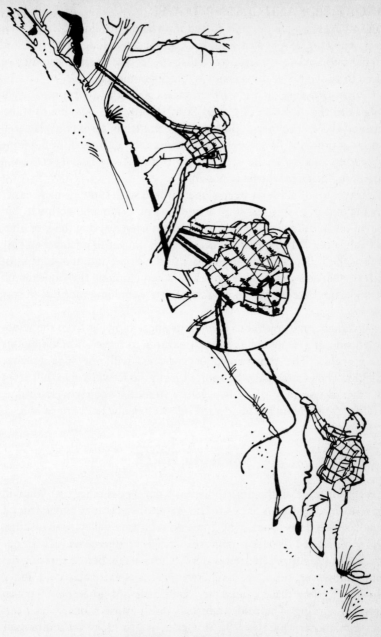

Fig. 4-1   Hasty Rappel

SNOWFIELDS AND GLACIER TRAVEL

The quickest way to descend a steep snowfield is to slide down on your feet, using an ice axe or a stout stick about 5 feet long as a brace and to dig into the snow to stop any falls. The ice axe or stick also may be used to probe for deadly crevasses (cracks in the ice).

When traveling on a glacier, crevasses generally are found at right angles to the direction of glacier flow. Usually it is possible to travel around them since they seldom extend completely across the glacier. If snow is present, the greatest caution must be exercised, and a rope should be used to secure each party member. Avoid heavily crevassed areas and glaciers whenever possible.

Travel up or across a steep slope covered with snow is made easier by kicking steps into the slope while moving diagonally across it. But be on the alert for avalanches, especially during a spring thaw or after a fresh snow. When moving where there is danger of avalanches, stay out of the valley, away from the base of the slope, and, if a slope must be crossed, cross as high as possible. When climbing the slope, climb straight up. If caught in an avalanche, use swimming motions to stay on top.

Overhanging projections formed by snow blowing from the windward side of a ridge are additional hazards to travel in mountainous snow fields. The projections, or cornices, will not support your weight. They can usually be spotted from the leeward side, but from windward you may see only a gently rounded, snow-covered ridge. Follow the ridge on the windward side well below the cornice line.

CROSSING WATER

Except for travel in the desert, there is a good possibility that you will have to ford a stream or river. The water obstacle may range from a small, ankle-deep brook that flows down a side valley to a rushing, snow- or ice-fed river. A person who knows how to cross such an obstacle can use the roughest of waters to advantage. Before entering the water, however, check the temperature. If it is extremely cold and a shallow fording place cannot be found, it is not advisable to try to cross by fording. The cold water may easily cause shock, which can cause temporary paralysis. In this case, try to make an improvised bridge by felling a tree over the stream or building a simple raft.

Before attempting to ford, move to high ground and examine the river for:

1) Level stretches where it breaks into a number of channels.
2) Obstacles on the other side that might hinder travel. Pick a spot on the opposite bank where travel will be easier and safer.
3) A ledge of rocks that crosses the river, indicating the presence of rapids or canyons.
4) Any heavy timber growths. These indicate where the channel is deepest.

When selecting a fording site, keep the following points in mind:

1) When possible, choose a course leading across the current at about a 45° angle upstream.
2) Never try to ford a stream directly above or close to a rapids, waterfall, or deep hole.
3) Always ford where you would be carried to a shallow bank or sandbar should you lose your footing.
4) Try to avoid rocky places, since a fall can cause serious injury; however, an occasional rock that breaks the current and provides a handhold may help.

METHODS OF CROSSING WATER

Wading Before entering, remove your socks and put your shoes back on. Do not risk having your feet cut by sharp rocks or sticks. Use a stout pole for support. Brace it on your upstream side to help break the current. The pole can also be used to test for potholes.

Swimming Use the breast, back, or side strokes. They are less exhausting than other techniques, and will allow you to carry small bundles of clothing and equipment while swimming. If possible, remove clothing and equipment and float it across the river. Wade out until the water is chest deep before swimming. If the water is too deep to wade, lower yourself slowly to minimize the possibility of snags and falls due to obstacles hidden under the water. In deep, swift water swim diagonally across the stream with the current.

Swimming in rapids or swift water is not as great a problem as might be expected. In shallow rapids, get on your back with your feet pointing downstream; keep your body horizontal and your hands alongside your hips. Use your hands much like a seal moves his flippers. In deep rapids, swim on your stomach and aim for shore when possible. Avoid currents that converge; you can be sucked down and held under by the effect of the confluence.

Swimming Aids　If unable to swim, you can ford a river by using certain swimming aids. These include:

Clothing—Either of these methods provides a serviceable pair of water wings:

1) If you are already in the water, take off your trousers; knot each leg and button the fly. Grasp the waistband on one side and swing the trousers over your head from back to front so that the waist opening is brought down hard on the surface of the water. Air is trapped in each leg.
2) If you are out of the water, take off your trousers; knot each leg and button the fly. Hold the trousers in front of you and jump into the water (after making sure the water is deep enough to avoid injury). Again, air is trapped in each leg.

Empty tins, gas cans, and boxes—Lash together as a buoyant, but use only when crossing slowly moving water.

Logs or planks—Before deciding to use a log or raft, test its ability to float. This is especially important in the tropics because many tropical trees, particularly the palm, sink even when the wood is dead.

Rafts—Rafting rivers is one of the oldest forms of travel and is often the safest and quickest method of crossing a water obstacle—once the raft has been built. However, building a raft under survival conditions is tiring and time-consuming, even when you have proper equipment and help. If absolutely necessary, or if you plan to take the raft all the way downriver, proceed. It may be your most effective course of action.

Spruce trees that are found in polar and sub-polar regions make the best rafts. However, any dry wood, or bamboo in the tropics, will do. Before incorporating a log into the raft, roll it into the water to make sure it floats.

A raft can be constructed without spikes or rope if you have an axe and a knife. Consider a suitable raft for three men to be 12 feet long and 6 feet wide.

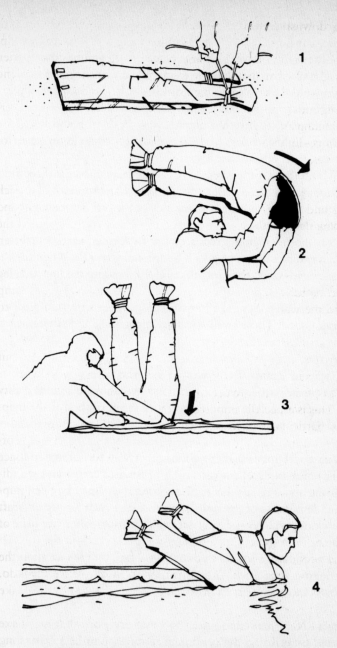

Fig. 4-2 Making "Water Wings" From Pants

Building a Notched Raft

1) Build the raft on two skid logs placed so they slope downward to the bank. (You may be able to manhandle one log at a time, but you won't be able to budge a finished raft.) Smooth the skid logs with an axe so the raft logs lie evenly on them.
2) Cut four offset inverted notches, one in the top and bottom of both ends of each log. Make the notches broader at the base than at the outer edge of the log.
3) To bind the raft together, drive through each notch a three-sided wooden crosspiece about a foot longer than the width of the raft. Connect all the notches on one side of the raft before connecting those on the other.
4) Lash the overhanging ends of the two crosspieces together at each end of the raft to give it additional strength. When the raft enters the water, the crosspieces swell, binding the logs together tightly.
5) If the crosspieces fit too loosely, wedge them with thin pieces of dried wood. These swell when set, tightening and strengthening the crosspieces.

Other Types of Rafts   Even with an axe, the type of woodwork required to construct the kind of raft described above demands a great deal of time and skill. A simple and more rapid method is the use of "pressure bars," lashed securely at each end, to hold your logs together:

1) With a tarpaulin, shelter half, or other waterproof material, you can build an excellent raft using brush as a frame and stuffing.
2) In northern regions during the winter, rivers may be open in the middle because of the swift current. Cross such a river on an ice block raft which can be cut off from the frozen shore ice using an axe or even sometimes a pole (if there is a crack in the ice). The size of the raft should be about 6 by 9 feet, and the ice should be at least 1 foot thick. A pole is used to move the ice block raft across the open part of the river.

Crossing a River   Crossing a deep and swift river on a raft may be accomplished by utilizing the pendulum motion of surface waters at a

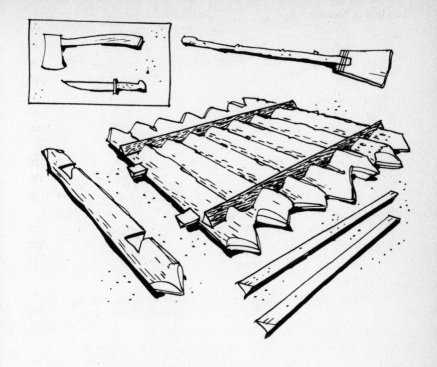

Notched Raft

Pressure Bar Raft

Fig. 4-3   Types of Log Rafts

Fig. 4-4 Crossing a River Using Pendulum Action

bend in the river. This method is useful when several men have to cross. However, the following requirements must be met:

1) The raft must be angled to the direction of the current.
2) The rope from the anchor point must be seven to eight times as long as the width of the river.
3) The rope's attachment to the raft must be adjustable, to change the raft's angle of drift so it can return to the starting side.

Determining Width of a River Before crossing a body of water it can be helpful to know the distance to the opposite shore. This can easily be determined by studying fig. 4-5 and following these simple steps:

1) Select a rock, tree, or other object on the opposite bank and position yourself directly across from it.
2) Estimate the approximate half-width of the river and pace off that distance in either direction along the bank (i.e., perpendicular to your line of vision in step 1). Count your paces.
3) Mark that point with a rock or stake and continue walking along the bank.

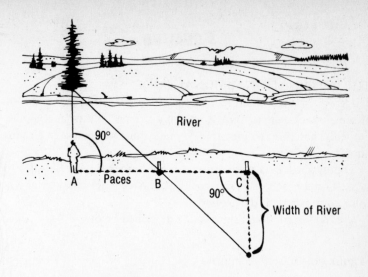

Fig. 4-5   Determining the Width of a River

4) When you have walked the same number of paces as you did in step 2, stop. Mark this second point with a rock or stake.
5) Turn and walk directly away from the bank (i.e., perpendicular to the line you have just walked). Continue walking until the object on the opposite bank and the first marker are, when looking over your shoulder, both directly in your line of sight. Stop.
6) The distance between your second marker and your present position equals the width of the river.

CROSSING QUICKSAND, BOGS, AND QUAGMIRES

These obstacles are found most frequently in tropical or semitropical swamps. Pools of muck are devoid of any visible vegetation and usually will not support even the weight of a rock. If you cannot detour such obstacles, attempt to bridge them by using logs, branches, or foliage. If none are available, cross the obstacle by falling face downward with your arms spread. Start swimming or pulling your way through, keeping your body horizontal. Use the same method for crossing quicksand.

SIGNALING

THE INTERNATIONAL SIGNAL CODE

There is always a chance of being air rescued, but one man—or a group—is not easy to spot from the air, especially when visibility is limited. Therefore, be prepared to make your whereabouts and needs known to rescuers.

Tramp out letters in the snow or use branches to spell out a message. If on a beach, use large rocks or seaweed. Select material whose color contrasts with the ground.

Use the international signal code described below:

Message	Symbol
Require doctor, serious injuries	I
Require medical supplies	II
Unable to proceed	X
Require food and water	F
Require firearms and ammunition	⋁⋁
Require map and compass	□
Require signal lamp with battery and radio	¦
Indicate direction to proceed	K
Am proceeding in this direction	↑
Will attempt takeoff	▷
Aircraft seriously damaged	⌐
Probably safe to land here	△
Require fuel and oil	L
All well	LL
No	N

46

Yes

Not understood

Require engineer

OTHER METHODS OF SIGNALING

1) Produce smoke by making a large fire and piling enough damp vegetation on to smother it.
2) Signal by waving your undershirt, shorts, or trousers, or by spreading them against a contrasting background.
3) Flash a beam of light from a mirror or other shiny material. Improvise a mirror from a ration tin or belt buckle. Punch a cross-hole in the center of the reflector. Reflect sunlight from the

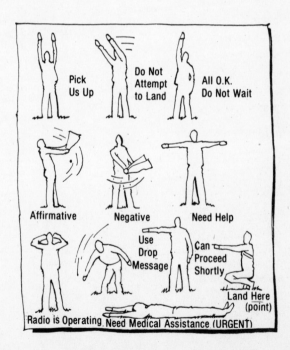

Fig. 4-6 Ground-to-Air Body Signals

mirror to a nearby surface, slowly bring it to eye level, and look through the sighting hole. A bright spot of light can be seen on the target. Continue sweeping the horizon even though no ships or planes are sighted. Mirror flashes can be seen for miles even on hazy days.

4) If an air rescue is possible, know the ground-to-air body signals (see fig. 4-6).

5) Use a spruce torch for night signaling. Select a tree with dense foliage. Place dry timber in the lower branches to light the tree. Insure that the fire is not likely to get out of control and endanger your safety, or anyone else's.

CHAPTER FIVE

First Aid

Sickness, disease, and injury are immediate and ongoing concerns to anyone in a survival situation. This chapter will cover first-aid measures for effectively dealing with the ordinary and extraordinary illnesses and injuries that one may encounter in remote and isolated areas of the world. First-aid information on weather-related injuries will be found in Chapters Six through Ten.

BASIC HYGIENE

Protection against disease and sickness involves making habits of many simple practices which can be grouped under the general heading of good personal hygiene. Immunizations will help protect against a few of the more serious diseases to which one might be exposed—smallpox, typhoid fever, tetanus (lockjaw), typhus, diphtheria, cholera, plague, and yellow fever. They will not protect against the much more common diseases like diarrhea, dysentery, colds, and malaria. The only means of preventing these is keeping physically fit and keeping disease germs out of your body. Applying the following rules will go a long way toward keeping you on your feet.

KEEP CLEAN
Body cleanliness is the first defense against disease germs. A daily shower with hot water and soap is ideal. If this is impossible, keep

hands as clean as possible, clean under the fingernails, and sponge the face, armpits, crotch, and feet at least once a day.

Keep clothing, especially underclothing and socks, as clean and dry as possible. If laundering is impossible, shake out clothing and expose to sun and air daily.

When available, use a toothbrush regularly. Soap or table salt and soda make good substitutes for toothpaste; and a small green twig, chewed to a pulpy consistency at one end, will serve as a toothbrush. Rubbing with a clean finger is another method. This method also massages the gums. After eating, rinse your mouth if potable water is available.

GUARD AGAINST INTESTINAL SICKNESS

Common diarrhea, food poisoning, and other intestinal diseases are the most common and often the most serious diseases to guard against. They are caused by eating or drinking contaminated food, water, or other beverages. To guard against these diseases:

1) Keep the body, particularly the hands, clean. Keep the fingers out of the mouth. Limit the handling of food with the hands.
2) Insure the potability of drinking water by the use of water treatment tablets or by boiling for 1 minute.
3) Wash and peel all fruit.
4) Do not keep food for long periods following preparation.
5) Sterilize eating utensils, preferably by boiling in water.
6) Keep flies and other vermin off your food and drink. Keep the camp clean.
7) Adopt strict measures for disposing of human waste and garbage.

Vomiting may be caused by heartburn, indigestion, gastritis (irritation of the lining of the stomach), ulcer, food poisoning, and gastrointestinal allergy (intake of a certain food or substance that the body rejects).

In a survival environment, food poisoning and gastrointestinal disease should be considered as probable causes for vomiting.

If poisoning is suspected, drink huge amounts of water (warm water, if possible) and induce further vomiting.

Diarrhea is the primary manifestation of disease of the intestine. Diarrhea can become serious, even fatal, if you become dehydrated. If diarrhea is accompanied by fever, pus, or blood, this may indicate a bacterial or parasitic infection rather than a viral infection, and is much more serious. Bacterial and parasitic infection can be avoided by good personal hygiene.

If vomiting or diarrhea occurs, rest and stop eating solid food until the symptoms ease. Take fluids, particularly potable water, in small amounts at frequent intervals. As soon as it can be tolerated, resume eating semi-solid food. Normal salt intake should be maintained.

Food and water ingested into the body immediately preceding vomiting and diarrhea should be considered the probable source. These items should be avoided in the future.

GUARD AGAINST HEAT INJURY

In hot climates, develop a tan by gradual exposure to the sun. Strenuous exertion in the hot sun may cause a heat stroke. The lesser illnesses caused by heat can be prevented by consuming enough potable liquids and salt to replace losses through perspiration. Avoid overeating, as this may also induce heat injury. For specific heat-related hazards see Chapter Seven ("Survival in the Tropics") and Chapter Eight ("Survival in Desert Areas").

GUARD AGAINST COLD INJURY

When exposed to severe cold, conserve body heat by every possible means. Take particular care of the feet, hands and exposed areas of the body. Keep socks dry and use any available material—including rags, paper, moss, grass and leaves—to improvise protective covering. For specific cold-related hazards, see Chapter Nine ("Survival in Cold Climates").

TAKE CARE OF YOUR FEET

Dirty or sweaty socks will cause foot deterioration. If a clean extra pair is not available, wash out those that you are wearing. If you have an extra pair, put the washed pair inside the shirt next to the body. They should dry in a short time. If possible, wear woolen socks; they absorb perspiration. Socks may be frozen and then beaten to remove dirt, perspiration, salts, and moisture.

Blisters are dangerous because they may become infected. Such infections can limit travel and may, if they become severe, result in immobilization. If your shoes fit well and if you dry them after crossing wet ground, change your socks frequently, use foot powder (if available), and massage or gently rub your feet, you should have little trouble with blisters.

Should a blister develop, wash the area frequently with water to avoid infection. If the blister is about to break, you can puncture it near its edge with a sterilized pin or needle and press out the fluid. If the blister is in no danger of breaking, do not puncture. Place padding on the area to reduce pressure and chafing. Padding can be fashioned from a sterilized piece of clothing.

SICKNESS AND DISEASE

Disease may be the worst enemy in your struggle for survival. Although it is not necessary to know a great deal about diseases, you should know about their presence in certain areas, how they are transmitted, and how to prevent them.

Most diseases are caused or transmitted by parasitic plant and animal organisms such as ticks and mites that enter the body, multiply, and set up a series of disturbances. If you know about the carriers responsible for a particular disease, you are better able to avoid contracting the disease by keeping the transmitting agents away from your body.

SMALLER FORMS OF LIFE
Forms of life, such as insects, can be more dangerous and uncomfortable than even a scarcity of food and water; however, their greatest danger is in their ability to transmit weakening and often fatal diseases through their bites.

Disease-transmitting agents require certain environmental conditions, such as proper amount of sunlight, ideal temperatures, and suitable breeding sites, to exist and multiply. Because of these factors, you have only a limited number of disease-transmitting agents to guard against at any one place or time.

Frequently, the particular disease organisms which are transmitted to man must, at some time in the course of the transmitting agent's life, pass through more specific hosts. If the hosts are absent, the disease organism does not exist in the area and cannot be transmitted regardless of how many potential transmitting agents are present. Man is a specific host in the case of malaria.

Mosquitoes and Malaria   Mosquito bites are not only unpleasant, they can lead to death. Mosquitoes are found throughout the world. In some areas of the Arctic and temperate regions during the late spring and early summer, they are more numerous than at any time in the tropics. Tropical mosquitoes, however, are much more dangerous because they transmit malaria, yellow fever, dengue fever, encephalitis, and filariasis.

Take every precaution against mosquito bites by following these rules:

1) Camp on high ground away from swamps.
2) Sleep under mosquito netting if available. Otherwise, use any available material.
3) Smear mud on your face, especially before going to bed.
4) Wear all clothing, especially at night.
5) Tuck the pants into the tops of your socks or shoes.
6) Smoke, as a last resort, can be used to reduce exposure to mosquitoes. A "smudge pot" can be made by igniting dry bark covered with water-soaked bark, green leaves and saplings, moss, animal dung or toadstools. Toadstools burn slowly and a smoldering piece, burning end out, can be strung around one's neck.
7) Kerosene, gasoline, or alcohol acts as a repellent to almost all forms of pests and insects.

Flies   Like mosquitoes, flies vary in size, breeding habits, and in the discomfort or danger they can cause. The protection used against mosquitoes generally is effective against flies.

Fleas   These small wingless insects can be extremely dangerous in some areas because they can transmit plague to man after feeding on plague-ridden rodents. If you use a rodent as food in suspected plague areas, hang up the animal as soon as it is killed and do not handle it until it becomes cold. Fleas will leave a cold body. To protect yourself wear tight-fitting leggings or boots. Fleas drown in water. A thorough washing will remove most fleas. If you suspect your shelter is flea-infested, wash and scrub it out thoroughly. Fleas will evacuate a wet place.

Ticks   These flat oval pests are distributed throughout the world and are especially prevalent in the tropics and subtropics. They are carriers of tick relapsing fever and tick typhus. The two types of ticks are the hard, or wood tick, and the soft tick. Ticks burrow into the skin, leaving their back ends exposed. Do not try to pull off a tick with the fingers if other means are available: The head will break off in the skin and leave a sore.

To remove a tick apply any of the following to the tick's exposed end: oil; moistened tobacco; heat from a match, cigarette, or hot ember; hot water. Also, expose the skin to the smoke of a green wood fire. The tick will back out of the skin and can then be removed from the body.

Mites, Chiggers, and Lice   These very small insects are common in many areas of the world, and their ability to irritate is entirely out of proportion to their size. Chiggers are immature stages of certain mites, which bore into the skin and cause itching and discomfort. People particularly susceptible to these bites may become ill. In some parts of the world, chiggers transmit scrub typhus. The human itch mite may cause various skin diseases, such as scabies or Norwegian itch. Secondary infection as a result of scratching may result. Chiggers can be removed by bathing in salt water. Also, chiggers and mites can be repelled by wearing clothing that has been repeatedly exposed to fire smoke until the smoke odor has permeated the clothing.

Native villages usually are infested with lice. Try to avoid huts and personal contact with the natives. If bitten by a louse, try not to scratch, because you will spread the louse feces into the bite. It is through infection with louse feces that man contracts such diseases as epidemic typhus and louse-borne relapsing fever. If you do not have any louse powder, boiling your clothing will rid it of lice. If this is not possible, expose the body and clothes, particularly clothing seams, to direct sunlight for a few hours to remove the lice. After exposure to these insects, wash yourself, preferably with soap. If soap is not available, the sediment or sand from stream bottoms is an acceptable substitute. Frequently inspect the hairy portions of the body for lice.

Bees, Wasps, and Hornets   The stings of an aroused swarm of bees, wasps, or hornets may be dangerous, even fatal. If you are attacked, plunge through dense brush or undergrowth.

A bee loses its sting in the wound; it should be removed to avoid infection; but wasps and hornets can sting perpetually. To ease pain, apply mud, moistened clay, moist tobacco, or wet salt to the sting. If available apply ammonia or a paste of baking powder. These remedies also work for bites or stings from scorpions, centipedes, and caterpillars.

Spiders Except for the black widow or hourglass, and the brown or recluse, spiders in general are not particularly dangerous. Even the tarantula is not known to bite with fatal or even serious effects. The black widow, however, along with tropical members of the same family, should be avoided as their bites cause severe pain, swelling, and even death. All of these spiders are dark and marked with white, yellow, or red spots. Acute abdominal cramps may follow the bite of one of these spiders and may continue intermittently for a day or two. It is possible to mistake the pain for acute indigestion or even appendicitis.

Scorpions The sting of this unusually small animal is painful but seldom fatal. Some of the larger species, however, are more dangerous, and their sting may result in death. Scorpions are found in widely separated areas and may constitute a real danger, since they hide in clothing, shoes, or bedding. Shake out your clothes before putting them on. If stung, use cold compresses or mud. In the tropics apply coconut meat. Some of the venom can be removed by applying a hollow reed over the sting and pressing firmly into the skin for several minutes, causing the poison and a little blood to run out.

Centipedes and Caterpillars Centipedes are numerous in the tropics, and some of the larger species can inflict painful bites. They seldom bite man, however, except when they cannot escape. Like the scorpion, they are not dangerous except when they have taken shelter in an article of clothing that is about to be worn. Centipedes and caterpillars sometimes cause severe itching and inflammation when brushed against. Caterpillars can also cause painful blisters. In addition, death in extremely weak adults has been attributed to almost simultaneous contact with several of the so-called "electric caterpillars" found in Central and South America.

Leeches These blood-sucking animals are found in widely separated areas of Borneo, the Philippines, Australia, the South Pacific, and various parts of South America. They cling to blades of grass, leaves, and twigs and fasten themselves to passing individuals. Bites cause discomfort and loss of blood, and may be followed by infection. Remove leeches by touching them with a lighted cigarette, match, or moist tobacco, or by using insect repellent.

Flukes or Flatworms These parasites are found in sluggish fresh water in parts of tropical America, Africa, Asia, Japan, Formosa, the Philippines, and other Pacific islands. There is no danger of flukes in salt water. Flukes penetrate the skin of those who come in contact with them either by drinking or bathing in infested waters. They feed on blood cells, and their eggs escape through the bladder or intestine. Proper wearing of the uniform will help avoid exposure.

Hookworm Common in the tropics and subtropics, the hookworm larvae enters through bare feet or any other exposed skin that is in contact with the ground. There is no danger from hookworms in wilderness areas away from human habitation.

FIRST AID FOR SNAKEBITES

Almost all snakes bite. If the snake is non-poisonous, the bite should be washed and cleaned and medically treated as a small puncture wound.

Unless you are an expert in snake identification, treat all snakebites as poisonous. Follow these steps:

1) Remain calm, but act swiftly.
2) Within practical limits, immobilize the affected part in a position below the level of the heart.
3) Place an improvised, lightly constricting band (tourniquet) 2 to 4 inches closer to the heart than the site of the bite, and reapply the constricting band ahead of the swelling if it progresses up the arm or leg. The constricting band should be placed tightly enough to halt the flow of blood in surface blood vessels, but not tightly enough to stop the pulse (arterial flow).
4) If it can be accomplished within one hour, make a single cut (with a knife, razor blade, or any available sharp-edged instrument) over each fang mark. The cuts must not be more than ½-inch long and ⅓-inch deep and should be made through the skin parallel to the bitten part.
5) Apply suction to the wound. If a snakebite kit is available, use its suction pump. If none is available, apply suction by mouth, spitting out the blood and other fluids frequently. Snakebite poison is not harmful in the mouth unless there are cuts or sores in the mouth. Even so, the risk is not great. Suction should be kept up for at least 15 minutes before loosening the tourniquet.

6) If after 15 minutes you feel no intense dryness and tightness of the mouth, headaches, pain, or swelling of the bitten area, the bite is non-poisonous.

7) If poisonous, continue treatment as stated in (step 5) above.

BASIC LIFESAVING FIRST-AID MEASURES I:
LACK OF OXYGEN

Human life cannot exist without a continuous intake of oxygen. Lack of oxygen rapidly leads to death. First aid, therefore, involves knowing how to open the airway and restore breathing and heartbeat.

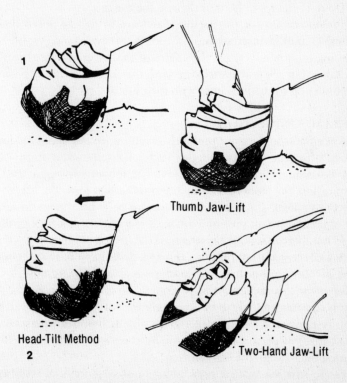

Thumb Jaw-Lift

Head-Tilt Method
2

Two-Hand Jaw-Lift

Fig. 5-1   Opening the Airway

ENLARGING AIRWAY PASSAGE

Head-Tilt Method   Immediately place the person on his back with his neck extended and his head in a chin-up position. If a rolled blanket, poncho, or similar object is available, place it under his shoulders to help maintain this position; but do not waste time obtaining such materials. *Seconds count!* The head-tilt method is effective in many cases.

Jaw-Lift Method   If the head-tilt method is unsuccessful, adjust the jaw to a jutting out position. This positioning moves the base of the tongue farther away from the back of the throat, thus enlarging the airway passage to the lungs. It may be accomplished by either the thumb jaw-lift method or the two-hand jaw-lift method.

Thumb jaw-lift—This is ordinarily the method of choice for adjusting the jaw unless the nature of the injury prevents its use. Place your thumb in the person's mouth, grasp the lower jaw firmly, and lift it forward. Do not attempt to hold or depress the tongue.

Two-hand jaw-lift—If the person's jaws are so tightly closed that the thumb cannot be inserted into the mouth, the two-hand jaw-lift is used. Using both hands, grasp the angles of the lower jaw just below the ear lobes. Lift the jaw forcibly forward; then open the lips by pushing the lower lip toward the chin with the thumbs.

ARTIFICIAL RESPIRATION

If the injured person does not promptly resume adequate spontaneous breathing after the airway is open, artificial respiration must be started. Be calm. Think and act quickly! The sooner you begin artificial respiration, the more likely you are to succeed in restoring breathing. If you are in doubt as to whether or not he is breathing, do not waste valuable seconds; give him artificial respiration, since it can do no harm to a person who is breathing. If the person is breathing, you can ordinarily feel and see his chest moving, or feel and hear air being expelled by putting your hand or ear close to his mouth and nose.

If the person has no heartbeat, you must also give him closed-chest heart massage immediately. If two persons are available, one can give artificial respiration while the other gives closed-chest heart massage. If you are the only person available, you must perform both measures, alternating them as later described.

There are two primary methods of administering artificial respiration: the mouth-to-mouth and the chest-pressure arm-lift. The mouth-to-mouth method is the preferred one; however, it cannot be used if the person has a crushed face.

Mouth-to-Mouth Resuscitation Method In this method of artificial respiration, you inflate the person's lungs with air from your lungs. This can be accomplished by blowing air into his mouth. The mouth-to-mouth resuscitation method is performed as follows:

1) With the injured person lying on his back, position yourself at the side of his head. Place one hand behind the neck to maintain the head in a face-up position, with the head tilted back as far as possible.
2) Pinch the nostrils together with the thumb and index finger of your other hand and let this same hand exert pressure on the forehead to maintain the backward head tilt. (The nose can also be sealed by pressing your cheek firmly against it.)
3) Take a deep breath and place your mouth (in an airtight seal) around the person's mouth. (If the injured person is an infant or small child, cover both his nose and mouth with your mouth, sealing your lips against the skin of his face.)
4) Blow into the mouth forcefully to cause the person's chest to rise. (In infants and small children you should need to blow only small puffs of air from your cheeks, rather than deep breaths from your lungs.) If the chest rises, this indicates that sufficient air is getting into the person's lungs. Then proceed to the next steps.

If the chest does not rise, take corrective action immediately by adjusting the jaw and blowing harder, making sure that air is not leaking from around your mouth or out of the person's pinched nose.

If the chest still does not rise, move the person's head to one side and clear his airway with your fingers. To do this, open his mouth and run your fingers down the inside of the lower cheeks, over the base of the tongue, and into the throat. Move your fingers across the back of the throat with a sweeping motion to remove any vomitus, mucus, or foreign bodies.

If the airway is still not clear, roll the person onto his side; then, using the heel of your hand, deliver sharp blows between the person's shoulder blades to dislodge the foreign body from the airway. Immediately inflate his lungs, using mouth-to-mouth resuscitation.

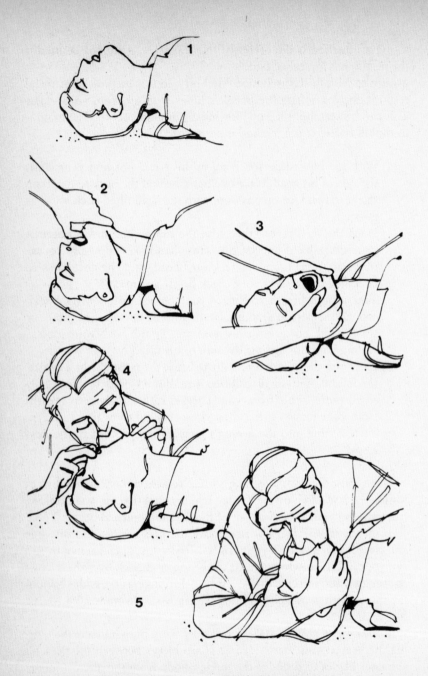

Fig. 5-2   Mouth-to-Mouth Resuscitation

5) When the person's chest rises, remove your mouth from his mouth and listen for the return of air from his lungs (exhalation). If his exhalation is noisy, elevate his jaw more.

6) After each exhalation of air from the person's lungs, pinch his nose again and blow another deep breath into his airway. Adequate ventilation should be insured on every breath by seeing the person's chest rise and fall and by hearing and feeling the air escape during exhalation. The first four breaths should be full, quick breaths (except in infants and small children), without allowing time for full lung deflation between breaths. Thereafter, repeat the mouth-to-mouth resuscitation procedure at the rate of approximately once every 5 seconds. Continue mouth-to-mouth resuscitation until the person regains consciousness, or for at least 45 minutes in the absence of all life signs. As the person starts to breathe, adjust the timing of your efforts to assist him. A smooth rhythm is desired, but split-second timing is not essential.

After a period of resuscitation, the person's abdomen may bulge. This indicates that some of the air is going into his stomach. Since inflation of the stomach makes it more difficult to inflate the lungs, apply gentle pressure to the abdomen with your hand at frequent intervals between inflations.

If your breathing has been very deep and rapid for too long a period, you may become faint, tingle, or even lose consciousness if you persist. However, if you administer only four full quick breaths, and then adjust your breathing to the rate of approximately once every 5 seconds with only moderate increase in normal volume, you will be able to continue to give artificial respiration for a long period without experiencing temporary ill effects. (If you become distressed from giving shallow breaths to an infant or a small child, interrupt your rhythm occasionally to take a deep breath.)

Mouth-to-Nose Method   This method should be used if you cannot perform mouth-to-mouth breathing because the person has a severe jaw fracture or mouth wound or his jaws are tightly closed by spasms. The mouth-to-nose method is performed in the same way as the mouth-to-mouth method except that you blow into the nose while you pinch the lips closed with one hand. It may be necessary to separate the person's lips to allow the air to escape during exhalation.

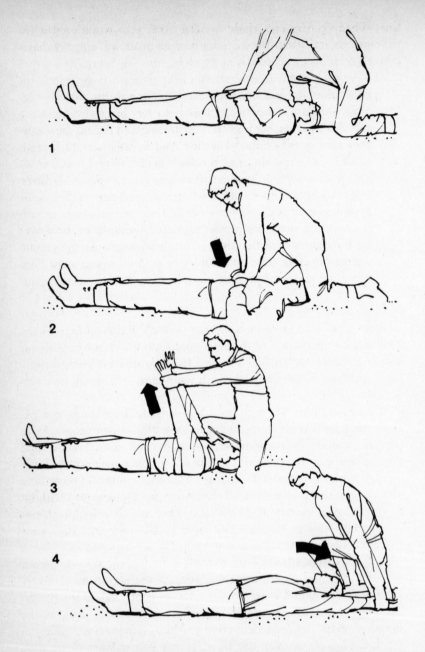

1

2

3

4

Fig. 5-3   Artificial Respiration: Chest-Pressure Arm-Lift Method

Chest-Pressure Arm-Lift Method   This method is to be used when the mouth-to-mouth method cannot be used because the person has a crushed face.

1) *Preliminary Steps.* Clear the person's airway. Position him on his back. Position the person's head with his face up and place a rolled blanket or some other similar object under his shoulders so that his head will drop back in a chin-up position. Stand at his head and face his feet. Kneel on one knee and place your other foot at the other side of his head and against his shoulder to steady it. If you become uncomfortable after a period of time, quickly switch to the other knee.

2) *Procedure.* Grasping the person's hands and holding them over his lower ribs, rock forward and exert steady, uniform pressure almost directly downward until you meet firm resistance. This pressure forces air out of the lungs.

3) Lift his arms vertically upward. Stretch them backward as far as possible. This process of lifting and stretching the arms increases the size of the chest and draws air into the lungs.

4) Replace his hands on his chest and repeat the cycle: *press, lift, stretch, replace.* Give 10 to 12 cycles per minute at a steady, uniform rate. Give counts of equal length to the first three steps. The fourth or *replace* step should be performed as quickly as possible.

5) As he attempts to breathe, adjust the timing of your efforts to assist him. Continue artificial respiration until the person regains consciousness, until you are relieved by a medically trained person, or for at least 45 minutes in the absence of all life signs.

6) *Releasing Position to Replacement.* When you become tired, release your position to another person, if available, with no break in rhythm. Continuing to administer artificial respiration, move to one side while the replacement takes his position from the other side. During the *stretch* step, the replacement grasps the person's wrists and continues artificial respiration in the same rhythm, shifting his grip to the person's hands during the *replace* step.

CLOSED-CHEST HEART MASSAGE

If a person's heart stops beating, you must give him closed-chest heart massage as well as artificial respiration immediately. *Seconds count!* Stoppage of the heart is soon followed by cessation of respiration un-

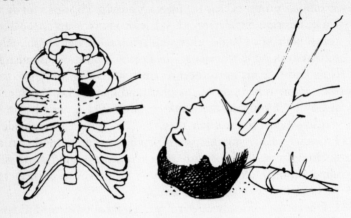

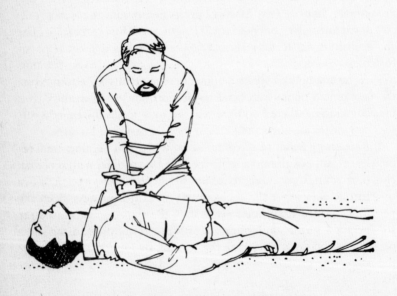

Fig. 5-4 Closed-Chest Heart Massage

less cessation of respiration has occurred first. Be calm. Think, and then act! When a person's heart has stopped, he has no pulse at all, he is unconscious and limp, and the pupils of his eyes are opened wide. To determine the presence or absence of a person's pulse, place the tips of your fingers on his neck at the side of his windpipe. If you do not detect a pulse immediately, do not waste time checking further; start heart massage and artificial respiration at once! Furthermore, if you find the person's pulse to be very weak and irregular, you must give him closed-chest heart massage and artificial respiration, since these signs indicate ineffective beats of the heart and precede heart stoppage.

Closed-chest heart massage is the rhythmical compression of the heart without surgically opening the chest. It is designed to provide artificial circulation, in order to keep blood flowing to the brain and other organs until the heart begins to beat normally again. It is not the same as open-chest heart massage, in which the chest wall is cut open and the heart itself is compressed directly by hand.

The heart is located between the breastbone and the spine. Pressure on the breastbone pushes the heart against the spine, thus forcing the blood out of the heart into the arteries. Release of pressure allows the heart to refill with blood.

Preliminary Steps   Since closed-chest heart massage must always be combined with artificial respiration, it is preferable to have two rescuers. One person positions himself at the injured party's side and performs closed-chest heart massage while the other person positions himself on the opposite side of the injured party at his head, keeping the head tilted back and administering artificial respiration. If you must administer these steps alone, alternate these methods as described below.

Prepare the person for the mouth-to-mouth method of artificial respiration. The person must always be in the horizontal position when closed-chest heart massage is performed, as there is no blood flow to the brain when the body is in a vertical position, even during properly performed closed-chest heart massage. The surface on which the person is placed *must be solid*. The floor or the ground is adequate. A bed or couch is too flexible. Elevate the legs about 6 inches while keeping the rest of the body horizontal. This will help the return of blood to the heart.

Position yourself close to the person's side and place the heel of one hand on the lower half of the breastbone. Be careful *not* to place your hand on the soft tissue of the abdomen below the breastbone and rib cage. Spread and raise the fingers of your hand so that you can apply pressure to the breastbone without pressing on the ribs. Place your other hand on top of the first. (If the injured person is a child, omit placing the second hand over the first. If he is an infant, place only the fingertips of one hand on the breastbone.)

Basic Procedure With your hands in the correct position, bring your shoulders directly over the person's breastbone, keep your arms straight, and press downward. Apply enough pressure to push the breastbone down 1½ to 2 inches. Too much pressure may fracture the person's ribs; therefore, do *not* push the breastbone down more than 2 inches. (If the injured person is a child, press the breastbone lightly with only one hand. If he is an infant, press the breastbone lightly with your fingers.)

Release the pressure immediately. The heel of the rescuer's hand should not be removed from the chest during relaxation, but pressure on the breastbone should be completely released so that it returns to its normal resting position between compressions.

Measures Applied With Two Rescuers If there are two rescuers, one performing artificial respiration and the other administering closed-chest heart massage, the person who is administering closed-chest heart massage should compress the heart *once every second* (60 compressions per minute). At this rate he does not pause for breaths to be blown into the airway. The compressions must be uninterrupted, regular, and smooth. Proper timing for 60 compressions per minute with a natural rhythm is achieved by counting aloud as follows: one 1,000, one 2,000, one 3,000, one 4,000, one 5,000. Each time the rescuer says "one," he compresses the heart; and as he says the thousand number, he releases the pressure. He repeats the same count to 5,000 throughout the entire period he is administering closed-chest heart massage.

The member of the rescue team who is performing artificial respiration quickly blows into the person's lungs after each five compressions (5:1 ratio). When the other rescuer says "5,000," this is his signal to blow a deep breath into the person's airway. The breaths are interjected without any pauses in compression. This is *important,* as any interruption in heart compression results in a drop in blood flow and blood pressure to zero.

Two rescuers can perform closed-chest heart massage and artificial respiration best when they are on opposite sides of the injured person. They can then switch positions when one becomes fatigued, without any significant interruption in the 5:1 rhythm. This is accomplished by the rescuer who is performing artificial respiration's moving to the side of the injured person's chest immediately after he has inflated the lungs. He places his hands in the air next to those of the other rescuer who continues to perform heart compression. As soon as the other rescuer's hands are properly placed, the rescuer initially performing heart compression removes his hands (usually after the count of 2000 or 3000 in the series of compressions), and the other rescuer then continues with the series of compressions. The rescuer who has been compressing then moves to the injured party's head and interposes the next breath on the count of 5000.

Measures Applied With One Rescuer   When there is only one rescuer, he must perform both closed-chest massage and artificial respiration using a 15:2 ratio. This ratio consists of 15 heart compressions followed by *2 very quick but full lung inflations*. To make up the time used for inflating the lungs, the rescuer must perform each series of 15 heart compressions at the faster rate of *80 compressions per minute*. This timing is achieved by counting aloud as follows: 1 and 2 and 3 and 4 and 5 and, 1 and 2 and 3 and 4 and 10 and, 1 and 2 and 3 and 4 and 15. After the count of "15," the rescuer blows two deep breaths into the person's airway in rapid succession (within a period of 5 to 6 seconds) without allowing full exhalation between the breaths. He repeats the same count as he continues resuscitation. Cessation of resuscitative measures must not be based upon the discomfort of the rescuer. It may be necessary to perform these lifesaving measures for a long time after the heavy effects of body discomfort and fatigue are felt. They should be continued until the victim regains consciousness, until the rescuer is relieved by a medically trained person, or for at least 45 minutes in the absence of all life signs.

BASIC LIFESAVING FIRST-AID MEASURES II: BLEEDING

Human life cannot continue without an adequate volume of blood to carry oxygen to the tissues. An important first aid measure, then, is to stop bleeding in order to prevent unnecessary loss of blood.

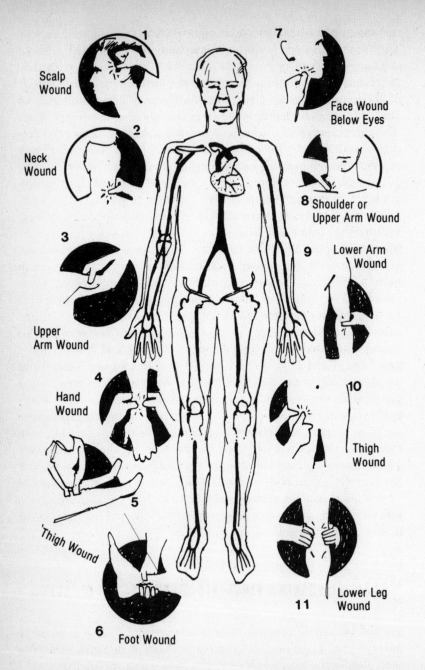

Fig. 5-5 Pressure Points for Control of Arterial Bleeding

1. Scalp Wound
2. Neck Wound
3. Upper Arm Wound
4. Hand Wound
5. Thigh Wound
6. Foot Wound
7. Face Wound Below Eyes
8. Shoulder or Upper Arm Wound
9. Lower Arm Wound
10. Thigh Wound
11. Lower Leg Wound

The open wound is the most common condition which requires your first-aid assistance. Acute loss of blood may lead to shock, and shock may lead to death.

The use of the pressure dressing is the preferred method for controlling severe bleeding. Elevation of the wounded limb and application of digital pressure should also be used, as appropriate, in conjunction with the pressure dressing. The tourniquet can be used to control bleeding from a limb. It should not be used, however, unless a pressure dressing has failed to stop the bleeding.

APPLICATION OF PRESSURE DRESSING, ELEVATION OF LIMB, AND DIGITAL PRESSURE

The application of a sterile dressing with pressure to a bleeding wound helps clot formation, compresses the open blood vessels, and protects the wound from further invasion of germs.

Examining the Wound   Before applying the pressure dressing, examine the injured party to determine whether there is more than one wound. For example, a projectile or other flying debris may have entered at one point and come out at another point. The exit wound is usually larger than the entrance wound.

Removing the Clothing   Cut the clothing and lift it away from the wound, to avoid further contamination. Tearing the clothing might result in rough handling of the injured part. Do not touch the wound; keep it as clean as possible. If it is already dirty, leave it that way. Do not try to clean it in any way.

Covering the Wound and Applying Pressure   Cover the wound with a field first-aid dressing (if available), and apply pressure to the wound by using the bandage strips attached to the dressing.

If additional pressure is required to stop the bleeding, place your hand over the dressing and press hard. Pressure from your hand may be required for 5 to 10 minutes to allow the clot to form. The clot must be strong enough to hold with the help of only the dressing and bandage strips when your hand is removed. Additional pressure can also be applied by placing a thick pad on top of the original dressing at the site of the wound and firmly securing this pad with a cravat or strip of material. Do not remove any dressings or bandages once they are placed over the wound. Apply any additional dressings over the ones in place. Removing a dressing may dislodge clots which are partially formed.

Elevating the Limb Frequently, bleeding can be lessened by raising the injured part above the level of the heart; however, direct pressure must be continued. Elevation must not be used if there is a broken bone in the injured part. Moving an unsplinted fracture causes pain, can increase shock, and may further damage nerves, muscles, and blood vessels.

Applying Digital Pressure If blood is spurting from the wound (arterial bleeding), digital pressure can be used to control the bleeding until a pressure dressing can be unwrapped and applied. Digital pressure is applied to a pressure point with the fingers, the thumbs, or the hands. A pressure point is the site at which a main artery supplying the wounded area lies near the skin surface or over a bone. By pressing at this point, the flow of blood from the heart to the wound is shut off or at least slowed down. You will have properly located a pressure point when you can feel the pulse at this point. You must feel the pulse before applying the digital pressure.

Application of a Tourniquet A tourniquet is a constricting band placed around an arm or leg to stop severe bleeding.

The tourniquet should be used *only* when pressure over the wound area, pressure over the appropriate pressure point, and elevation of the wounded part (if it is possible) fail to control the bleeding. Its use will rarely be necessary and should be avoided if possible. Use of a tourniquet has on occasion been associated with injury to blood vessels and nerves. If it is left on too long, it can cause loss of an arm or leg.

Bleeding from a major artery of the thigh, lower leg, or upper arm, or bleeding from multiple arteries (which occurs in a traumatic amputation) may prove to be beyond control by pressure. If the first-aid dressing under hard hand pressure becomes soaked with blood and the wound continues to bleed, you should apply a tourniquet.

Once a tourniquet has been applied, it must stay in place; and the victim must receive professional medical assistance as soon as possible. Do not loosen a tourniquet after it has been applied and has stopped the bleeding. Shock and blood loss can result in death.

In the absence of a specially designed tourniquet, a tourniquet may be made from strong, soft, pliable material such as gauze or muslin bandage, clothing, or kerchiefs. An improvised tourniquet is used with a rigid stick-like object. To minimize skin damage, insure that the improvised tourniquet is sufficiently wide to remain at least 1 inch in width after tightening.

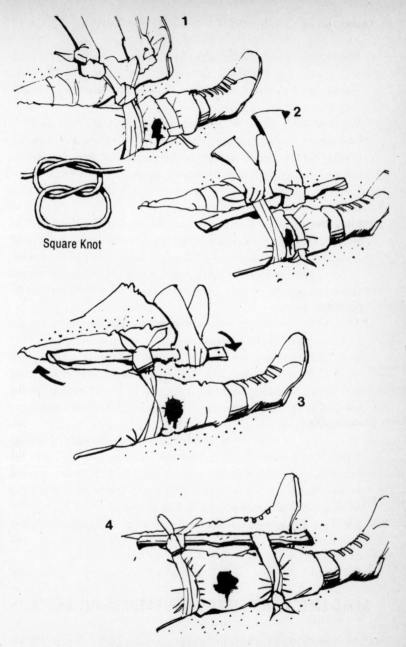

Square Knot

Fig. 5-6   Applying a Tourniquet

Then proceed as follows:

1) Place the tourniquet around the limb between the wound and the body trunk (or between the wound and the heart). Place the tourniquet 2 to 4 inches above the injury. Never place it directly over a wound or fracture.

2) When possible, place the tourniquet over the smoothed sleeve or trouser leg to prevent the skin from being pinched or twisted. Damaging the skin may deprive the surgeon of skin required to cover the amputation, thus forcing amputation of more of the limb than might otherwise be necessary. Protection of the skin reduces the pain.

3) Once the bandage is in place, pass the stick under the loop and twist to tighten. Tighten it only enough to stop blood from passing under it. If a pulse can be felt in the intact wrist or foot of the affected limb before the tourniquet is applied, stoppage of this pulse can be used as the indicator that tourniquet pressure is sufficient.

4) To detect a pulse, place two fingers (not the thumb) over the pressure point in the wrist or ankle. Do not use your thumb because the small arteries in your thumb may cause a false pulse reading. If such a pulse cannot be used as an indicator, you must rely upon your judgement of reduction of blood flow from the wound. In this case, uncover the wound temporarily to observe the blood flow.

5) After a tourniquet is properly tightened, arterial (spurting) bleeding will immediately cease; but bleeding from veins in the lower part of the limb will continue until the vessels are drained of the blood already in them. *Do not* continue to tighten the tourniquet in an attempt to stop this drainage.

6) After the tourniquet has been secured in place, dress and bandage the wound.

BASIC LIFESAVING FIRST-AID MEASURES III: SHOCK

Shock is a condition in which there is inadequate blood flow to the vital tissues and organs. Shock which remains uncorrected may result in death, even though the injury or condition causing the shock would not otherwise be fatal. Shock can result from many causes, such as loss of blood, loss of fluid from deep burns, expansion of the blood vessels, pain, and reaction to the sight of a wound or blood. First aid includes knowledge of how to *prevent shock*, since the injured person's chances of survival are much greater if he does not develop shock.

Shock may result from any type of injury. The more severe the injury, the more likely shock is to develop.

The early signs of shock are restlessness, thirst, pale skin, and a rapid heartbeat. A person in shock may be excited or he may be calm and appear very tired. He may be sweating even though his skin feels cool and clammy. As shock becomes worse, he breathes in small fast breaths or gasps even when his airway is clear. He may stare vacantly into space. His skin may have a blotchy or bluish appearance, especially around the lips and mouth.

ADMINISTERING FIRST AID

Your objective is to administer first-aid measures which will prevent shock from developing or getting worse, such as elevating the person's feet, loosening his clothing, and placing covers over and under him to prevent chilling. All of the shock control measures described in the following paragraphs help to prevent or control shock.

Maintain Adequate Respiration and Heartbeat To maintain adequate respiration and heartbeat, you may need to do nothing more than clear the upper airway, position the person to insure adequate drainage of any fluid obstructing his airway, and observe him to insure that his airway remains unobstructed. You may need to administer artificial respiration and closed-chest heart massage.

Stop the Bleeding Control bleeding by application of pressure dressing, by elevation of the part, and by use of pressure points as appropriate. Apply a tourniquet only as a last resort.

Loosen Constrictive Clothing Loosen clothing at the neck and waist and at other areas in which the clothing tends to bind the person. Loosen but do not remove boots or footgear.

Reassure the Person Take charge. Show, by your calm self-confidence and gentle yet firm actions, that you know what you are doing and that you expect him to feel better because you are helping him. Be attentive; initiate conversation only to give instructions or warnings or to obtain necessary information. If the person asks questions regarding the seriousness of his injury, reassure him. Remember, shock is a psychological as well as a physiological response.

POSITIONING THE VICTIM

The position in which a victim should be placed varies, depending upon the type of wound or injury and whether he is conscious or unconscious. Unless he has an injury for which a special position is prescribed, gently place him on a blanket or another suitable protective item in one of the following positions:

1) If he is conscious, place him on his back on a level surface with his lower extremities elevated 6 to 8 inches to increase the flow of blood to his heart. This may be accomplished by placing his pack or another suitable object under his feet. If he is placed on a litter, elevate the foot of the litter. Remember however, do not move a person who has a fracture until it has been properly splinted.
2) If the person is unconscious, place him on his side or on his abdomen with his head turned to one side to prevent his choking on vomitus, blood, or other fluid.
3) The person with a head injury should be lying so that his head is in a position higher than his body.
4) Keep the victim comfortably warm. Do not overheat the victim. If possible place a blanket, a poncho, a shelter half, or other suitable material under him. He may or may not need a blanket over him, depending upon the weather. If the weather permits, remove any wet clothing except boots or footgear before covering him.

DRESSINGS AND BANDAGES

All wounds are considered to be contaminated, since infection-producing germs are always present on the skin, on the clothing, and in the air. Furthermore, any projectile or instrument causing the wound pushes or carries germs into it. Infection results from the multiplication and growth of the germs which invade the wound or a break in the skin. The fact that a wound is contaminated, however, does not lessen the importance of protecting it from further contamination. The fewer the germs which invade a wound, the less possibility there is of infection and the greater are the person's chances for recovery. Dress and bandage a wound as soon as possible, to protect it from further contamination as well as to stop the bleeding.

DRESSINGS

Dressings are sterile pads or sterile compresses used to cover wounds. They are usually made of gauze or cotton wrapped in gauze. In the field the most widely used dressing is the field first-aid dressing with attached bandages. Other dressings available under certain conditions are gauze compresses of various sizes and small compresses on adhesive strips.

To apply a dressing, cut clothing and lift it away from the wound to avoid further contamination. Remove the dressing from its wrapper and place it directly over the wound without letting it touch anything else.

A field dressing can be fashioned from a piece of cloth or clothing. Boil the cloth immediately before using and fold into a pad large enough to cover the wound, being careful not to touch that part of the dressing that will come in direct contact with the wound.

Apply an antiseptic, if available, to that side of the dressing that will cover the wound. Antiseptics found in nature include: the sap (or balsam) of the balsam firs (puncture sap blister found on the bark); the gum of the sweet gum tree; raw turpentine from any pine tree; and the resins from cypress and hemlock trees. In the case of the cypress and hemlock, a knot from the tree can be boiled and the antiseptic resin will rise to the surface of the water. Never turn over a dressing and use it on its other side, as this side will be contaminated.

BANDAGES

A bandage may be made of gauze or muslin. It is used over a dressing to secure it in place, to close off its edges from dirt and germs, and to create pressure on the wound for control of bleeding. It is also used to support an injured part or to secure a splint to an injured part. A bandage must be applied firmly, with the ends secured in place to prevent the

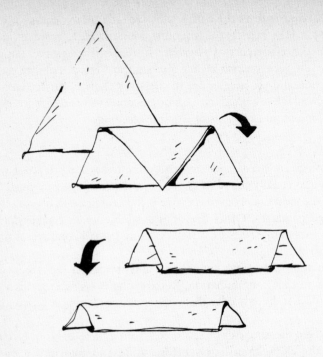

Fig. 5-7 Triangular Bandage Folded into a Cravat Bandage

bandage and dressing from slipping. It must not be applied so tightly that it stops circulation. If a knot is necessary for securing a bandage, the square knot must be used, since it will not slip.

Tailed Bandages Tailed bandages may be attached to the dressing as they are in the field first-aid dressing. The two tails are split 4 to 6 inches from the loose ends; they may be split farther as required to bandage a particular part of the body. Tail bandages may also be made by splitting a strip of gauze (4 by 36 inches) from each end, leaving the center part intact to cover the dressing, which has been placed over the injured part.

Triangular and Cravat Bandages Triangular and cravat bandages are made from the triangular piece of muslin provided in most general purpose first-aid kits. If this bandage is applied without folding it, it is called a triangular bandage. If it is folded into a strip, it is called a cravat bandage. Two safety pins are packed with each bandage.

These bandages are valuable in an emergency, since they are easily applied. They can also be improvised from a piece of shirt, sheet, kerchief, or any other pliable material of a suitable size. To improvise a triangle, cut a square of material somewhat larger than 3 by 3 feet and fold it diagonally. If two bandages are needed, cut the material along the fold.

APPLYING BANDAGES

Eyes   Even though only one eye is injured, both eyes must be bandaged. Since both eyes move together, any movement of the uninjured eye would cause the same movement and further damage to the injured eye.

Jaw   Before applying a bandage to a person's jaw, take any removable dentures (full or partial) from his mouth and put them in his pocket. In applying the bandage, allow the jaw enough freedom to permit passage of air and drainage from the mouth. To avoid bandaging the mouth completely closed, place a wad of material with a thickness of approximately ⅛ inch between the upper and lower teeth and gums. To insure that this wad of material does not fall into the mouth and block the airway, leave streamers of the material attached to the wad and tie them to the bandage.

Hands and Feet   Insure that fingers and toes are separated with absorbent material before wrapping and tying bandages, in order to prevent chafing and irritation of skin.

SEVERE WOUNDS

Certain types of wounds require special precautions and procedures. These injuries include head injuries, face and neck wounds, sucking wounds of the chest, and abdominal wounds.

HEAD INJURIES

A head injury may consist of one of the following conditions or of a combination of them: a cut or bruise of the scalp; a fracture of the skull with injury to the brain and/or the blood vessels of the scalp, skull, and brain. Usually, serious skull fractures and brain injuries occur together; however, it is possible to receive a serious brain injury without a skull fracture.

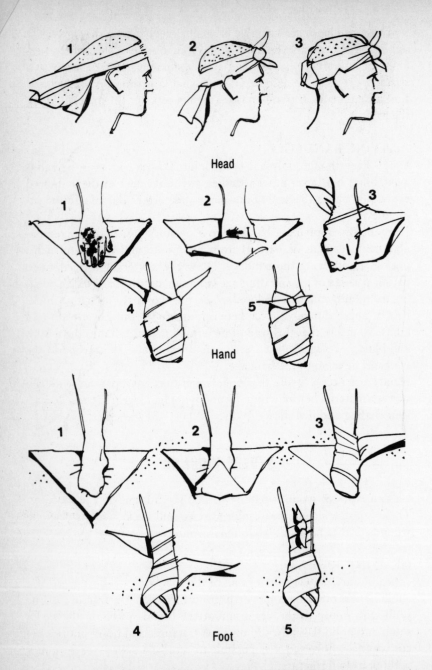

Head

Hand

Foot

Fig. 5-8 Applying a Triangular Bandage

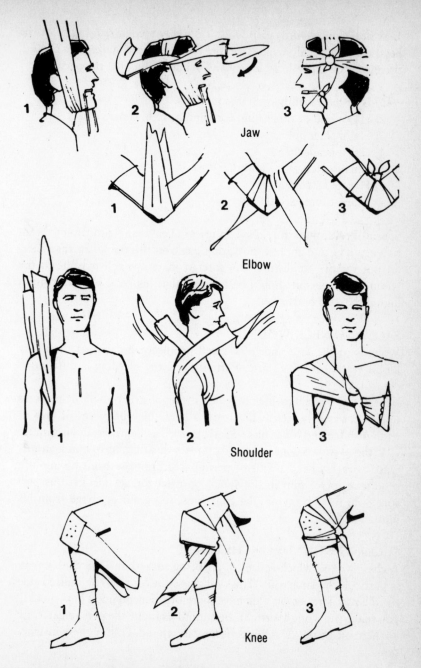

Jaw

Elbow

Shoulder

Knee

Fig. 5-9 Applying a Cravat Bandage

A head injury with scalp wound is easily recognized. Injury of the head *without* a scalp wound is more difficult to recognize. You should, therefore, suspect a head injury and act accordingly if the person:

1) Is or has recently been unconscious.
2) Has blood or other fluid escaping from his nose or ears.
3) Has a slow pulse.
4) Has a headache.
5) Is nauseated or is vomiting.
6) Has had a convulsion.
7) Is breathing very slowly.

Special Precautions for Head Injuries   Leave any protruding brain tissue as it is, and apply a sterile dressing over this tissue. Furthermore, do not remove or disturb any foreign matter which may be in the wound. The person should be lying so that his head is in a position higher than his body.

FACE AND NECK WOUNDS

Wounds of the face and neck bleed profusely, because of the many blood vessels in these parts. Furthermore, the bleeding is difficult to control.

Stop any bleeding which may be causing obstruction of the person's upper airway. Then clear his airway. There may be pieces of broken teeth or bone and loose bits of flesh, as well as dentures, in his mouth.

If the person is conscious and chooses to sit up, have him lean forward with his head down to permit free drainage from his mouth; otherwise, place him in the shock position for an unconscious person, even though he may be conscious, to permit drainage from his mouth.

SUCKING WOUNDS OF THE CHEST

A chest wound which results in air being sucked into the chest cavity is particularly dangerous. This will cause the lung on the injured side to collapse. The person's life may, therefore, depend upon how quickly you make the wound airtight. Be sure to examine the person carefully so that you do not miss a second or exit wound. Follow these instructions:

1) Have the person forcibly exhale (breathe out), if possible, and hold his breath while you seal the wound.

2) Seal the wound airtight by applying a piece of plastic or foil (or whatever thin, non-porous material is available) directly over the wound. Apply the first-aid dressing over the seal and have an assistant or the injured person exert pressure on the dressing with his open hand while you secure the bandages attached to the dressing around his body. (Note: If petrolatum gauze is available, it should be applied directly over the wound.)

3) Apply a strip of bandaging material, torn from clothing, a shelter half, a blanket, etc., or apply a folded poncho over the dressing and around the person's body to create further pressure, thus making the wound airtight. Each turn of this bandaging material must overlap the preceding one in order to provide firm, evenly distributed pressure over the entire dressing. Secure the bandages with belts, rope, or twine.

4) If the person finds it more comfortable to sit up, allow him to do so. Sitting up makes breathing less difficult, as abdominal pressure is relieved and the diaphragm muscle functions more easily. If he chooses to lie down, encourage him to lie on his injured side so that the lung on his uninjured side can receive more air. Also, the surface on which he is lying serves somewhat as a splint to the injured side and thus decreases pain.

ABDOMINAL WOUNDS

The most serious abdominal wound is one in which an object penetrates the abdominal wall and pierces internal organs or large blood vessels.

Do *not* touch or try to push protruding organs such as intestines back into the wound; apply one or more sterile dressings over them. If it is necessary to move an exposed intestine onto the abdomen in order to cover the wound adequately, then do so. Secure the dressings in place with bandages; but *do not* apply them tightly, as internal bleeding cannot be controlled by pressure and excessive pressure can cause additional injury.

Do not give or allow the person to take anything by mouth, since it will eventually pass through the injured intestines and spread contamination in the abdomen. The person's lips may be moistened to help lessen his thirst.

Leave him on his back, but turn his head to one side. Since he will most likely vomit, watch him closely to prevent him from choking.

SEVERE BURNS

Burns are damage to tissue caused by exposure to excessive heat, strong chemicals, or electricity. They are classified by cause, degree, and extent. Burns are complicated by airway blockage, carbon monoxide poisoning, lung damage, shock, and infections. Most people who die immediately in a fire die from suffocation. Those who die a few hours later usually die of shock. Those dying three to ten days after the burn usually die of infection. Other factors complicate burns but you can do little in the field to prevent them. The first job is to treat those life-threatening conditions which follow severe burns:

1) Protect the burn from further contamination, thus lessening the possibilities of infection:
2) If clothing covers the burn, cut and lift it gently away without touching the burn:
   - Do *not* try to remove pieces of cloth which have stuck to the burn or to clean the burn in any way.
   - Do *not* pull clothes over the burned area.
   - Do *not* break blisters.
   - Do *not* put ointment or any medication whatsoever on the burn.
3) Place a sterile dressing over the burned area and secure it in place with bandages. In a mass casualty situation, a clean sheet may be used in the absence of sufficient dressings.
4) Prevent shock. (See page 72 of this chapter.)
5) If the person is conscious, is not vomiting, and has no abdominal or neck wound, give him the sodium chloride-sodium bicarbonate mixture included in most first-aid kits. Dissolve 1 envelope (4.5 grams) of the mixture in 1 canteenful or quart of cool or cold water. Never use warm water, since warm salt water often causes vomiting.
   Note: If the sodium chloride-sodium bicarbonate mixture

is not available, dissolve 4 salt tablets and 2 sodium bicarbonate tablets or ½ teaspoonful of loose salt and ⅛ teaspoonful of baking soda in 1 canteenful or quart of cool or cold water. If only salt is available, use it without the soda. Otherwise, use water only.

6) Give the solution to the person slowly, having him consume the entire amount over a 1-hour period. Should he become nauseated, stop giving him the solution, to prevent vomiting and further loss of fluids; but keep the solution available for him to drink later. This solution helps restore body fluids and salts.

FRACTURES

Fractures (broken bones) can cause total disability or death of a person. On the other hand, they can often be treated so there is complete recovery. A great deal depends upon the first aid the person receives before he is moved. First aid includes immobilization of the fractured part, in addition to the application of previously discussed lifesaving measures. A basic splinting principle is to immobilize the joints above and below any fracture.

KINDS OF FRACTURES

A closed fracture is a break in the bone without a break in the overlying skin. In a closed fracture, there may be tissue damage beneath the skin. Even though an injury may be a dislocation or sprain, it should be considered as a closed fracture for purposes of applying first aid.

An open fracture is a break in the bone as well as in the overlying skin. The broken bone may have come through the skin, or debris may have gone through the flesh to the bone. An open fracture is contaminated and is subject to infection.

SIGNS AND SYMPTOMS OF A FRACTURE

A fracture is easily recognized when the bone is protruding through the skin, the part is in an unnatural position, or the chest wall is caved in. Other indications of a fracture are tenderness or pain when slight pressure is applied to the injured part, and swelling as well as discoloration of the skin at the site of the injury. Deep, sharp pain when the person attempts to move the part is also a sign of a fracture. Do not, however, encourage the person to move a part in order to identify a fracture, since movement of the part would cause further damage to surrounding tissues and promote shock. If you are not sure whether or not a bone is fractured, treat the injury as a fracture.

PURPOSE OF IMMOBILIZING A FRACTURE

A body part which contains a fracture must be immobilized to prevent the razor-sharp edges of the bone from moving and cutting tissue, muscle, blood vessels, and nerves. Furthermore, immobilization greatly reduces pain and helps to prevent or control shock. In a closed fracture, immobilization keeps bone fragments from causing an open wound, and thus prevents contamination and possibly infection. Immobilization is accomplished by splinting.

RULES FOR SPLINTING

If the fracture is an open one, first stop the bleeding; then apply a dressing and bandage as you would for any other wound. Follow these rules:

1) Apply the proven principle *"Splint them where they lie."* This means to splint the fractured part before any movement of the person is attempted and without any change in the position of the fractured part. If a bone is in an unnatural position or a joint is bent, *do not try to straighten it*. If a joint is not bent, *do not try to bend it*. If circumstances make it essential to move a person with a fracture of a lower extremity before a splint can be applied, use the uninjured leg as a splint by tying the fractured one to it; then grasp the person beneath the armpits and pull him in a straight line only. *Do not roll him or move him sideways*.

2) Apply a splint so that the joint above the fracture and the joint below the fracture are immobilized.

3) Use padding between the injured part and the splint to prevent undue pressure and further injury to tissue, blood vessels, and nerves. This is especially important at the crotch, in the armpit, and on places where the splint comes in contact with bony parts such as the elbow, wrist, knee, and ankle joint.

4) Bind the splint with bandages at several points above and below the fracture, but do not bind so tightly that it interferes with the flow of blood. No bandage should be applied across the fracture.

Tie bandages so that the knot is against the splint, and tie them with a square knot.

5) Use a sling to support a splinted arm which is bent at the elbow, a fractured elbow which is bent, a sprained arm, and an arm with a painful wound.

Splints   Splints may be improvised from such items as boards, poles, sticks, tree limbs, rolled magazines or newspapers, and cardboard. If nothing is available for a splint, the chest wall can be used to immobilize a fractured arm, and the uninjured leg can be used to immobilize, to some extent, a fractured leg.

Padding   Padding may be improvised from such items as a jacket, blanket, poncho, shelter half, or leafy vegetation.

Bandages   Bandages may be improvised from belts, rifle slings, handkerchiefs, or strips torn from such items as clothing and blankets. Narrow materials such as wire or cord should not be used to secure a splint in place.

Slings   Slings may be improvised by using the tail of a coat or shirt, belts, and pieces torn from such items as clothing and blankets. The triangular bandage is ideal for this purpose.

SPINAL COLUMN FRACTURES

It is often impossible to be sure whether or not a person has a fractured spinal column. Be suspicious of any back injury, especially if the person has fallen or his back has been sharply struck or bent. If a person has received such an injury and he lacks feeling in his legs or lacks the ability to move them, you can be reasonably sure that he has a severe back injury which should be treated as a fracture. You must remember that, if there is a fracture, bending the spinal column can cause the sharp bone fragments to bruise or cut the spinal cord and result in permanent paralysis. The spinal column must maintain a sway-backed position to remove pressure from the spinal cord.

If the injured party is not to be transported, follow these steps:

1) If the person is conscious, caution him not to move.
2) Leave him in the position in which he is found. Do not move any body part.
3) If he is lying with his face up, slip a blanket or material of similar size under the arch of his back to support the spinal column

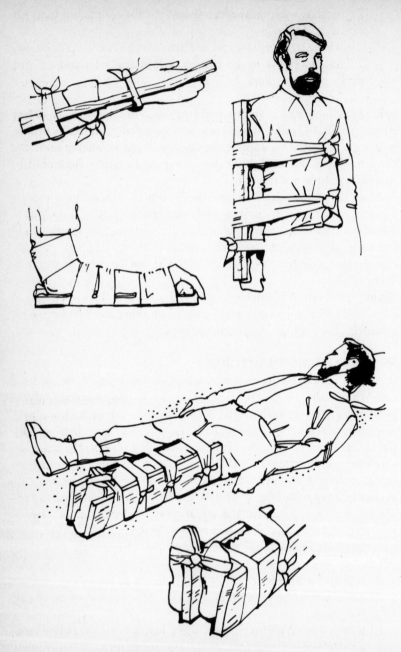

Fig. 5-10   Types of Splints

in a swaybacked position. If he is lying with his face down, do not put anything under any part of his body.

If the injured party must be transported follow these rules:

Face-up position—If the person is lying with his face up, transportation must be by litter or a firm substitute, such as a wide board or a flat door, longer than the person is tall. Tie his wrists together loosely over his waistline with a cravat or strip of cloth. Lay a folded blanket across the litter where the arch of his back is to be placed. Using a four-man team, place the person on the litter without bending his spinal column:

1) Kneeling on the knee nearer the person's feet, the second, third, and fourth men position themselves on one side of the victim, while the first man positions himself on the opposite side.
2) All men in close coordination gently lift the victim about 8 inches; then the first man slides the litter under the victim, insures that the blanket is in proper position, and returns to his original position.
3) All men in close coordination gently lower the victim onto the litter.

Face-down position—If the victim is lying with his face down, he must be transported in this same position. Using the four-man team, lift him onto a regular litter or a blanket roll litter, keeping the spinal column in a swaybacked position. If a regular litter is to be used, first place a folded blanket on the litter at the point where the chest will be placed.

NECK FRACTURES

A fractured neck is extremely dangerous. Bone fragments may bruise or cut the spinal cord just as in the case of a fractured back. If the victim is not to be transported until medical personnel arrive, follow these steps:

1) If the victim is conscious, caution him not to move. Moving may cause death.
2) Leave the victim in the position in which he is found. If the neck is in an abnormal position, immobilize it in this position.

Triangular Bandage

Belt Sling

Double Sling (separated shoulder)

Shirttail Sling

Fig. 5-11   Types of Slings

3) If he is lying with his face up, keep his head still, raise his shoulders *slightly,* and slip a roll of cloth which has the bulk of a bath towel under his neck. The roll should be thick enough to arch the neck only slightly, leaving the back of his head on the ground. Do not bend the neck or head forward. Do not raise or twist the head.

4) Immobilize the victim's head. This may be accomplished by padding heavy objects such as rocks or his boots and placing them on each side of his head. If it is necessary to use his boots, they should first be filled with stones, gravel, sand, or dirt, and tied tightly at the top. It may be necessary to stuff pieces of material in the tops of the boots to secure the contents.

If the victim must be transported the services of at least two persons are necessary, because the head and trunk must be moved in unison. The two persons must work in close coordination to avoid bending the neck in any way. The proper procedure is described as follows:

1) Place a wide board lengthwise beside the victim. It should extend at least 4 inches beyond his head and feet.

2) If the victim is lying with his face up, the first man steadies his head and neck between his hands while the second man, with one foot and one knee placed against the board to prevent it from slipping, grasps the victim at his shoulder and hip and gently slides him onto the board.

3) If the victim is lying with his face down, the first man steadies the victim's head and neck between his hands while the second man gently rolls him over onto the board.

4) The first man continues to steady the victim's head and neck while the second man raises his shoulders *slightly,* places padding under his neck, and immobilizes his head. The head may be immobilized with his boots, with stones rolled in pieces of blanket, or with other material.

5) Secure any improvised supports in position with a cravat or strip of cloth extended across the victim's forehead and under the board.

6) Lift the board onto a litter or blanket, as available, to transport him.

FIRST AID FOR COMMON EMERGENCIES

MINOR WOUNDS

Most small wounds, such as cuts, usually do not bleed very much. Some bleeding is helpful, as it helps to clean the wound. Infection from contamination is the principal danger. If you receive a minor wound, take the following first-aid measures:

1) Do not allow anything to touch the wound, except as described below.
2) Wash the surrounding skin thoroughly with soap and water. Gently clean the wound. If a disinfectant solution (tincture of benzalkonium or another acceptable solution) is available, apply it to the wound. (In no instance should solutions stronger than 1:750 be used.)
3) Place a sterile compress over the wound without allowing it to touch anything else, and secure it in place with a bandage.
4) If supplies and conditions permit, change bandages frequently.

Important: If clothing or other forms of cloth such as tent canvas are used as compresses or bandages, the cloth should always be boiled before using.

MINOR BURNS

Minor burns may be caused by exposure to dry heat, hot liquids, chemicals, electricity, or rays of the sun. If you receive a minor burn, you should immerse it in a cold stream or flush it with the coldest water available until the pain subsides (usually about 5 minutes). Minor burns are of two types, distinguished by the absence or presence of blistering or charring.

Since the skin is most likely to break when it is blistered or charred, cover it with a sterile compress to protect it from contamination and possible infection. Do not attempt to break the blisters. Secure the compress in place with a bandage.

If the burn does *not* cause the skin to blister, char, or break, it is a minor burn even though it may cover a large area of the body, as in mild sunburn. It is not necessary to cover such a burn with sterile compresses. To relieve pain, remove the burned area from the air by immersing it in cold water, or cover it with burn salve, vaseline, or a solution of baking powder (or flour) and water. If none of these materials are available, moist clay or earth will suffice.

FOREIGN BODY IN THE EYE

If a foreign particle gets into the eye, do not rub the eye. If the particle is beneath the upper eyelid, grasp the eyelashes of the upper lid and pull the lid up and away from contact with the surface of the eyeball. Hold the eyelid in this manner until tears flow freely. The tears will frequently flush out the particle.

If tears fail to flush out the particle, have someone else inspect your eyeball and lower lid. When the object is discovered, remove it with the moist corner of a clean handkerchief.

If the object is not in the lower lid, inspect the upper lid. Grasp the eyelashes with thumb and index finger and place a match stick or small twig over the lid. Pull the lid up and over the stick. Examine the inside of the lid while the injured part looks down. Gently remove the particle with the moist corner of a clean handkerchief.

If the foreign particle is glass or metal or it cannot be removed by the techniques described above, bandage both of the victim's eyes and get him to a medical treatment facility.

Note: If only one eye is bandaged, the victim will use his unaffected eye. Since eye movements are synchronized, use of the unaffected eye may result in movement of the affected one, thereby subjecting it to further injury.

If caustic or irritating material, such as battery acid, ammonia, etc., gets into the eye, immediately flush it with a large volume of water. To flush the right eye, turn the head to the right side; to flush the left eye, turn the head to the left side. This prevents the caustic or irritating material from being washed into the other eye.

FOREIGN BODY IN THE EAR, NOSE, OR THROAT

Never probe in an attempt to remove a foreign body from the ear. An insect in the ear may be removed simply by attracting it with a flashlight held to the ear. If this fails, it may be drowned or immobilized by pouring water into the ear. Foreign objects in the ear can sometimes be flushed out with water. However, if the object is something which will swell when wet, such as a seed or particle of wood, do not pour water into the ear.

Probing into the nose will generally jam a foreign object tighter. Damage to the nasal passages can also result. Try to remove the object by gently blowing the nose. If this fails, seek medical aid.

Coughing will frequently dislodge a foreign object from the throat. If this fails and the object can be reached, try to remove it with the fingers; but be careful to avoid pushing it further down the throat. There is great danger of respiratory obstruction if the object cannot be removed, so get medical aid as quickly as possible. An alternate method, the Heimlich hug, is described at the end of this section.

DROWNING

Drowning occurs when air is shut off from the airway by water or any other fluid, causing spasm of the vocal cords and blockage of the airway. Many victims who appear lifeless may recover if artificial respiration is performed promptly and efficiently. Speed is essential. Every moment of delay decreases the victim's chance of survival. It is frequently possible to start the mouth-to-mouth method of artificial respiration before the victim is brought ashore. As soon as his head is clear of the water and his mouth is within reach of your mouth, start artificial respiration. If other rescuers can help carry the victim ashore, do not make a break in the artificial respiration. Once the victim is ashore, do not waste valuable seconds to turn him in an attempt to drain water from his lungs, but continue the artificial respiration.

ELECTRIC SHOCK

Electric shock accidents frequently result from contact with a "live" wire, and occasionally occur when a person is struck by lightning. If a person has come in contact with an electric current, take the following steps:

1) Turn off the switch or power source if it is nearby, but do not waste time looking for it. Instead use a dry wooden pole, dry clothing, dry rope, or some other material which will not conduct electricity to remove the person from the wire. If a pole is not handy, simply drag the victim off the wire by means of a loop of dry rope or cloth. Do not touch the wire or the victim with your bare hands or you will also be shocked.

2) Administer artificial respiration immediately after freeing the person from the wire, since electric shock often causes breathing to cease. Also check the victim's pulse, since electric shock may also cause his heart to stop. If you do not feel a pulse immediately, administer closed-chest heart massage with an artificial respiration.

THE HEIMLICH HUG

A person whose trachea is obstructed by food cannot breathe, cannot speak, turns cyanotic, and collapses. He has only four minutes to live, unless you save him by applying the Heimlich hug:

If the victim is standing or sitting:

1) Stand behind him and wrap your arms around his waist.
2) Make a fist with one hand and place it against the victim's abdomen slightly above the navel and below the rib cage; then grasp the wrist of this hand with your other hand.
3) Press your fist forcefully into the victim's abdomen with a quick upward thrust, causing a sharp exhalation of air to blow the food out the airway.
4) Repeat several times, if necessary.

If the victim is lying on his back:

1) Facing him, kneel astride his hips.
2) With one of your hands on top of the other, place the heel of your bottom hand on the victim's abdomen, slightly above the navel and below the rib cage.
3) Press forcefully with the heel of your hand into the victim's abdomen with a quick upward thrust.
4) Repeat several times, if necessary.

If the victim is lying face down, turn him over and proceed as above.

TRANSPORTING THE WOUNDED

Transporting a wounded person by litter is safer and more comfortable for him than it is by manual means. It is also easier for you. Manual

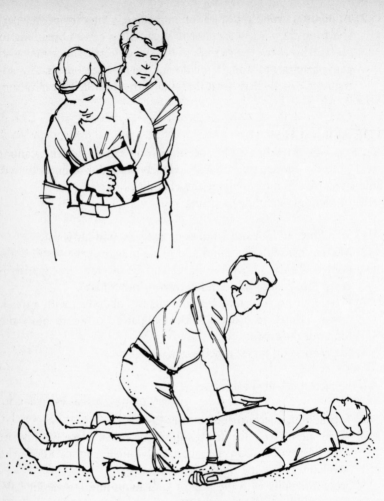

Fig. 5-12   The Heimlich Hug

transportation, however, may be the only feasible method because of the terrain. In this situation, the injured person should be transferred to a litter as soon as one can be made available or improvised.

HANDLING THE WOUNDED
Although the wounded person's life may have been saved through the application of appropriate first-aid measures, it can be lost through

careless or rough handling in transporting him. Therefore, before you attempt to move the wounded person, you must evaluate the type and extent of his injury and insure that dressings over wounds are adequately reinforced and that fractured bones are properly immobilized and supported to prevent them from cutting through muscle, blood vessels, and skin. Based upon your evaluation of the type and extent of the victim's injury and your knowledge of the various manual carries, you are to select the best possible method of manual transportation. If the wounded person is conscious, he should be told how he is to be transported. This will help allay his fear of movement and gain his cooperation.

MANUAL CARRIES

Manual carries are accomplished by one bearer or by two bearers. Two-man carries are used whenever possible. They provide more comfort to the injured person, are less likely to aggravate injuries, and are also less tiring for the bearers, thus enabling them to carry the victim farther.

Some carries may be inappropriate because of the nature of the person's injury. For example, certain carries cannot be used if the person has a fractured arm, neck, back, hip, thigh, or leg. The position in which the injured person should be placed for lifting depends upon the particular carry to be used.

Fireman's Carry   The fireman's carry is one of the easiest ways for one man to carry another. After an unconscious or disabled person has been properly positioned, he is raised from the ground in the first four steps of the carry.

1) After rolling the victim onto his abdomen, straddle him; then extend your hands under his chest and lock them together. Lift the victim to his knees as you move backward.
2) Continue to move backward, thus straightening the victim's legs and locking his knees.
3) Walk forward, bringing the victim to a standing position but tilted slightly backward to prevent his knees from buckling.
4) As you maintain constant support of the victim with your left arm, free your right arm, quickly grasp his right wrist, and raise your arm high. Instantly pass your head under his raised arm, releasing it as you pass under it. Move swiftly to face the victim

Fig. 5-13   The Fireman's Carry

Alternate Grip

Fig. 5-13   The Fireman's Carry

and secure your arms around his waist. Immediately place your right toe between his feet and spread them 6 to 8 inches apart.

5) With your left hand, grasp the victim's right wrist and raise his arm over your head.
6) Bend at the waist and knees; then pull the victim's arm over and down your left shoulder, thus bringing his body across your shoulders. At the same time, pass your right arm between his legs.
7) Place the victim's right wrist in your right hand and place your left hand on your left knee for support in raising.
8) Rise with the victim comfortably positioned. Your left hand is free for use as needed.

Supporting Carry   In the supporting carry, the injured person must be able to walk or at least hop on one leg, using the bearer as a crutch. This carry can be used to transport a person as far as he is able to walk or hop.

Arms Carry   Carrying a victim cradled in your arms is useful for moving someone a short distance and for placing him on a litter.

Saddle or Piggyback Carry   Only a conscious victim can be transported this way, as he must be able to hold onto the bearer's neck.

Packstrap Carry   In the packstrap carry, the injured person's weight rests high on the bearer's back, making it easier for the bearer to carry him a moderate distance. To eliminate the possibility of injury to the person's arms, the bearer must hold the person's arms in a palms-down position.

1) Lift victim from ground as in fireman's carry.
2) Supporting the victim with your arm around him, grasp his wrist closest to you and place his arm over your head and across your shoulder. Move in front of him while supporting his weight against your back, grasp his other wrist, and place this arm over your shoulder.
3) Bend forward and hoist him as high on your back as possible so that all his weight is resting on your back.

Belt Carry   The belt carry is the best one-man carry for a long distance. The injured person is securely supported by a belt upon the shoulders of the bearer. The hands of both the bearer and the victim are left free for carrying a weapon or equipment, climbing banks, or surmounting other obstacles. With the hands free and the victim secured in place, the bearer is also able to creep through shrubs and under low-hanging branches.

1) Link together two pistol belts to form a sling. (If pistol belts are not available for use, other items, such as one rifle sling, two cravat bandages, two litter straps, or any suitable material which will not cut or bind the victim, may be used.) Place the sling under the victim's thighs and lower back so that a loop extends from each side.
2) Lie between the victim's outstretched legs. Thrust your arms through the loops and grasp the victim's hand and trouser leg on his injured side.
3) Roll toward the victim's uninjured side onto your abdomen, bringing the victim onto your back. Adjust sling as necessary.
4) Rise to a kneeling position. The belt will hold the injured person in place.
5) Place one hand on your knee for support and rise to an upright position. The victim is now supported on your shoulders.
6) Carry the injured person with your hands free.

TWO-MAN CARRIES
One man carrying an injured person in a fireman's or pistol-belt carry position can move that person greater distances faster at greater comfort to both the victim and the bearer than two or more men carrying a victim together. However, two or more men can move an injured person a short or moderate distance faster than one man working alone. The easiest method is for each of the two men to hold one of the victim's arms around their necks after bringing the injured person to his feet. Then—either supporting the victim around the waist or, if he is taller than the bearers, lifting him and supporting him by the thighs—they can carry him to the litter or vehicle. Another method involves cradling the victim in the bearers' arms or carrying him between two men; one holding his legs, the other supporting his torso. However, walking with an injured person slung between you and another bearer is uncomfortable if you have to move any distance over difficult terrain. Swifter, surer progress can be made with the fireman's or pistol-belt carry.

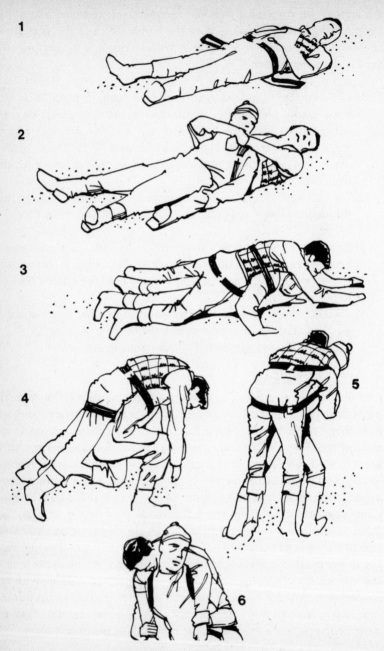

Fig. 5-14   The Belt Carry

Fig. 5-15   The Two-Man Carry

IMPROVISED LITTERS

A litter stretcher can be improvised from many different things. Most flat-surfaced objects of suitable size can be used as litters. Such objects include boards, doors, window shutters, benches, ladders, cots, and poles tied together. If possible, these objects should be padded.

Satisfactory litters can also be made by securing poles inside such items as blankets, shelter halves, tarpaulins, jackets, shirts, sacks, bags, bedticks, and mattress covers. Poles can be improvised from strong branches, rifles, tent supports, skis, and other items.

If no poles can be obtained, a large item such as a blanket can be rolled from both sides toward the center; then the rolls can be used to obtain a firm grip when carrying the injured person.

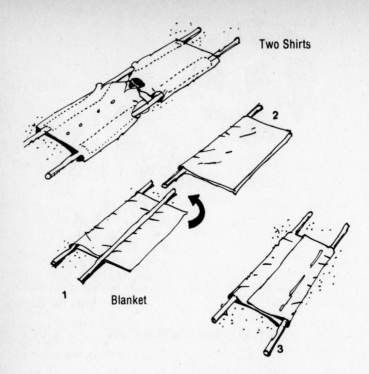

Two Shirts

2

1   **Blanket**

3

Fig. 5-16   Improvised Litters

CHAPTER SIX

Basic Survival Skills

The purpose of this chapter is to provide the reader with techniques for obtaining the basic elements of survival—food, water, and clothing—as well as information of immediate concern within the survival environment.

The techniques that will be covered are appropriate in any part of the world, though they are most applicable to the temperate zones of—for example—the United States and Europe, where extreme terrain and weather conditions are not the overriding survival factors. Information relating to the basic survival elements under specialized weather and terrain circumstances is provided in subsequent chapters.

IMMEDIATE ACTIONS

Follow these procedures:

1) Get away from any immediate danger, such as the wreckage of a plane crash and leaking fuel.
2) Check injuries and give first aid.
3) Throw up a temporary shelter. Separating yourself from the elements will enable you to think more clearly. In extreme cold, start a fire at once.
4) Rest and relax until shock and fatigue have subsided. Leave ex-

tensive planning until later, but size up the situation by following the instructions and information provided in Chapter One.

Once you have relaxed, familiarize yourself with the environment and take stock of the situation. The situation itself—such as an immediate need for food or water or the existence of severe or complex injuries—may dictate the next steps you should follow. Once these needs have been taken care of, give immediate attention to the following:

1) Make signaling preparations. Sweep the horizon with a signal mirror or other reflective device at regular intervals. At night, signal with a flashlight or make a signal fire. Spread out parachutes, life preservers, or any other brightly colored objects available to you. Arrange ground signals in *geometric patterns* (they will stand out more that way). Almost all ships and planes are equipped with emergency kits. If available, use fluorescent dye for signaling on water or snow. Hoist a signal flag at the highest point of your location.

2) Make rescue preparations. Clear all obstacles that would impede or delay rescue operations. If rescue is imminent, pack all gear that you will be taking with you. Prepare the injured for transport. Know body signals for ground-to-air communication.

3) Determine your position by the best means available. See Chapters Two and Three ("Finding Direction with a Map or Compass," "Finding Direction without a Map or Compass").

4) Make decisions to move or to stay where you are. The best course is usually to stay and await rescue, particularly if you are the victim of an air crash. There are, however, several considerations that may make it more necessary or advantageous to travel:
   • You are certain of your position and you know in what direction and how far to go to reach help.
   • You have adequate supplies and provisions for travel.
   • After waiting several days, you are convinced that the possibility of rescue is remote.
   • A member of your party is severely injured and time is a critical factor.

5) Make camp. Pick the location of your camp carefully. Try to be near a water supply. Don't make camp at the base of steep slopes

or in areas where you run the risk of avalanches, rockfalls, flood, or battering by winds.

SHELTER

The primary function of shelter is to protect the individual from the dangers and hazards peculiar to the survival environment. A well-constructed shelter can also provide comfort and psychological well-being. The longer the duration of the survival situation the more important these considerations become.

A hand-built shelter can range from a quick and simple lean-to to a fully insulated log cabin. The sophistication of the shelter you choose to build is dependent upon several factors.

Fundamental to this decision are the tools available to you and whether the shelter is temporary or semipermanent. Without at least a knife and a hatchet or axe your efforts must necessarily be limited to constructing a simple shelter, even if you anticipate a lengthy stay. Other major considerations are the time available for woodcrafting activities and one's expertise in the woodcrafting art.

There is not enough room here to discuss woodcrafting techniques in any great detail. Moreover, expert woodcrafting requires a great deal of skill. If you are not already well versed in its application, there is little chance of learning it from reading a book.

However, a quite adequate shelter can be constructed with few or no tools and a limited knowledge of woodcrafting technique. The key to building an effective and habitable shelter is to *improvise*. Improvisation, combined with creativity and basic woodcrafting skill learned through practice, can produce a sturdy, comfortable shelter.

SELECTING A SITE
Try to pick a well-drained camp site on a knob or high spot of ground, in an open place well back from swamps (but not too distant from your fresh water supply). Mosquitoes will be less bothersome, the ground will be drier, and breezes are more likely. In mountainous jungle, the nights are cold. Get out of the wind. Avoid dry riverbeds. They can be flooded in a few hours, sometimes by rains so distant from you that you are not aware that any rain has fallen.

TYPES OF SHELTER

The type of shelter built depends on the time available for preparing it and whether it is to serve as a permanent or semipermanent structure. Some simple shelters are:

The Parachute Shelter—made by draping a parachute (or any available material) over a rope or vine stretched between two trees.

The Thatch Shelter or A-Frame—made by covering an A-type framework with a good thickness of palms or other heavy leaves, pieces of bark, or mats of grass. Slant the thatch shingle-fashion from the bottom upward. This type of shelter is considered ideal, since it can be made completely waterproof.

The Lean-to—or standard timber shelter. When using a lean-to, however, it is important that you be tactically located where you can build a fire large enough to spread warmth equally throughout the shelter. The proper placing of the lean-to and fire in relation to prevailing winds is another consideration. This shelter can be improved by the use of a fire and reflector, which is built of green logs and placed on the opposite side of the fire from the opening of the lean-to. Large stones stacked behind the fire also reflect heat.

The Parateepee—a tent made from a parachute. It is easily built and especially suited for protection against damp weather and insects. It is possible to cook, eat, sleep, rest, and make signals without having to go outside. A number of good poles about 12 to 14 feet long are required for parateepee construction.

A Willow Shelter—made by tying willow trees together to form a framework which can be covered by fabric. There is no particular design for this type of shelter, but it should be large enough for one man and his equipment. Place the open end of the willow shelter at right angles to prevailing winds. Pack the edges of the cover down with earth or snow to prevent wind from blowing under it.

A Bough Shelter—created from the branches of a fallen tree. Shelters made of boughs do not reflect the heat of a fire and leak during a rain. But boughs may serve as a temporary shelter.

A Log Shelter—made by placing two poles on a large log and covering the frame with foliage. This shelter is not suitable for use as a permanent camp.

Caves—should be avoided if other shelter can be built. Caves limit escape in case of danger, increase the risk of carbon monoxide poison-

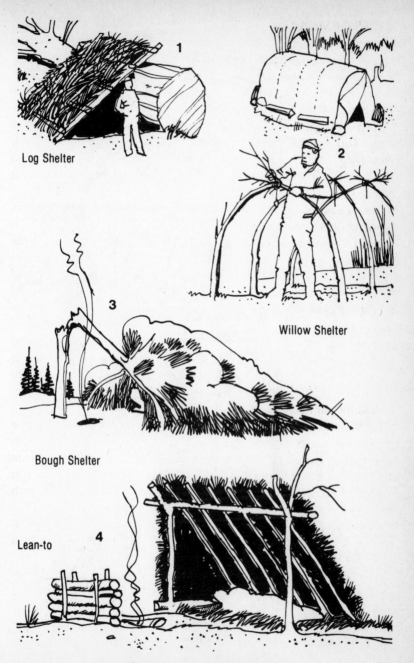

Log Shelter

Willow Shelter

Bough Shelter

Lean-to

1

2

3

4

Fig. 6-1 Types of Shelters

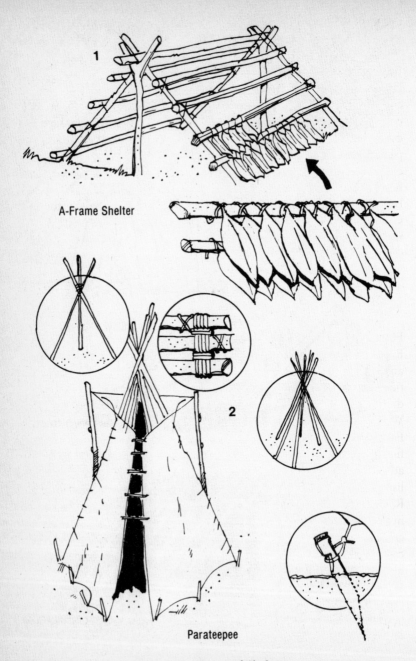

1

A-Frame Shelter

2

Parateepee

Fig. 6-1   Types of Shelters

ing from fires, and may collapse or be closed off by rockfalls or harsh weather.

BEDS

Do not sleep on the ground. When you complete the shelter, build a comfortable bed. Make it so that you will be insulated against the cold, damp ground. First warm and dry the ground by building a fire over the bed area, and then stamp the hot coals into the ground. If a parachute is available, spread it over a bed of leaves or ferns. (A parachute may also be used as a hammock.) Make sure the leaves and branches are free of insects and other small forms of life. To build a bed of boughs, insert the branches into the ground with the tips slanted in the same direction. Place them about 8 inches apart. Cover the boughs with finer branches.

WEATHER

FORECASTING WEATHER

Even with the most sophisticated equipment, predicting the weather is an imprecise and often inaccurate science. However, your ability to anticipate weather changes, particularly in areas of extreme climatic conditions, can be instrumental to your survival effort.

Wind   The direction of the wind is the easiest weather sign to read. Fashioning a flag out of a piece of cloth, or simply holding a wetted finger into the wind or throwing a few blades of grass into the air, are adequate indications of wind direction. Once wind direction is established you can predict the weather that is imminent for your location. Rapidly shifting winds indicate an unsettled atmosphere, and a change in weather condition is likely. In the continental United States, winds generally move in a west-to-east direction. Northeasterly winds indicate dryer, cooler air while winds from the southeast bring warmer, humid air and the probability of rain.

Wind-Chill Factor   The combined effect of cold air and wind on the body, called the wind-chill factor, dramatically accelerates the loss of body heat. For example, in a 2-mph wind, exposed flesh will freeze at -40°F; in a 20-mph wind, exposed flesh will freeze at 12°F. In cold climates the primary and minimal function of shelter is to provide protection from the wind.

Clouds Clouds come in a variety of shapes and patterns, and a general knowledge of clouds and the atmospheric conditions they indicate can help you predict the weather.

Cumulus, the white billowy clouds which are the most familiar, are generally a sign of good weather. However, when cumulus clouds begin to build vertically, forming massive "heads," they should be considered storm clouds. Dark anvil-shaped cumulus clouds moving in your direction indicate an approaching thunderstorm.

The light, feathery *cirrus* clouds are generally harbingers of fair weather. However, in cold climates, if cirrus clouds begin to multiply perceptibly and are accompanied by increasing winds blowing steadily from a northerly direction, this is a sign of an oncoming blizzard.

Stratus and *nimbus* clouds are low-lying solid coverings of dark clouds, and generally mean drizzle or rain.

Cumulus, cirrus, stratus, and nimbus clouds may combine into a multitude of formations and, influenced by altitude, can indicate a variety of weather conditions. The cirro-cumulus, or "mackerel" clouds, resembling the layered appearance of fish scales, are a warning that precipitation can be expected within the next 12 to 15 hours.

Other Weather Signs

1) If smoke rises from a fire in a thin vertical column, this is a fair-weather indicator. Low-rising smoke that is "flattened out" indicates stormy weather.
2) The color of the sky at morning and evening can help you predict the weather. Remember: "Red sky at night, sailor's delight. Red sky in morning, sailors take warning."
3) In the mornings, if the grass is dew-laden, this generally indicates fair weather. Dry grass indicates rain. Remember: "When the dew is on the grass, rain will never come to pass. When grass is dry at morning light, look for rain before the night."
4) Birds and insects fly lower than normal to the ground in heavy, moisture-laden air. Precipitation is likely. Insect activity increases before a storm; the activity of bees increases before fair weather.
5) A low-pressure front, often indicated by slow-moving or imperceptible winds and heavy, humid air, is a promise of bad

weather which will generally linger for several days. Low pressure can also be "smelled" and "heard." The sluggish, humid air releases wilderness odors that are less perceptible under high pressure conditions. Also, noise carries farther and sounds are sharper.

HAZARDS

For specific tropical, desert, arctic, and sea-related hazards, see the appropriate chapters.

DISEASES, INSECTS, AND HAZARDS FROM SMALLER FORMS OF LIFE
See Chapter Five ("First Aid").

POISONOUS SNAKES
The common fear of snakes is due to unfamiliarity and misinformation. Even the harmless types are usually regarded with apprehension. There is no need, however, to fear snakes—once you know something about them, their habits, how to identify the dangerous kinds, the simple precautions to take to prevent snakebite, and the first-aid measures to use in the very rare emergency of being bitten.

Most snakes are nonpoisonous. There are four types of poisonous snake found in North America: the water moccasin, the rattlesnake, the copperhead, and the coral snake.

For first aid for snakebites, see Chapter Five ("First Aid").

For identification of poisonous snakes of the world, see Appendix I.

DANGER FROM MAMMALS
Most stories about the dangers from larger animals are fiction, and only a handful of those who have encountered a survival situation have actually been harmed or killed by animals. But very few animals will refuse to fight if forced into a corner. Many animals are dangerous when wounded, or when they are protecting their young. Old exiles or hermits such as elephants, boars, or buffalos that have been cast off by the herd are often cantankerous and belligerent. Lions, tigers, and leopards that are too old to successfully hunt other animals may become man-eaters. Such animals, however, are rare.

In arctic and subarctic regions, bears are surly and dangerous. If you hunt them, do not shoot unless you are sure to kill. The polar bear rarely comes on land, but is attracted by the smell of food caches or animal carcasses. It is a tireless, clever hunter and should be treated with great caution. Bears in general are considered the most dangerous and unpredictable members of the wild animal kingdom.

Avoid wild buffalos because of their mean tempers. Approach wild pigs with caution. Elephants, tigers, and other large animals avoid man if given a chance, but they may charge when startled.

Bites from all canines (dogs, jackals, foxes) as well as from some other meat eaters may cause rabies. Bloodsucking vampire bats are not dangerous unless they are rabid or their bite becomes infected.

If you encounter a dangerous animal, follow these rules:

1) Don't panic. Don't make any sudden movements. Move out of danger gradually.
2) Do not cause the animal to feel cornered or threatened.

To avoid contact with a dangerous animal:

1) Keep a clean camp.
2) Keep all food out of sight and, if possible, locked up.
3) Do not eat or keep food in your shelter.
4) Limit nighttime activities. Most large animals hunt at night.
5) Never disturb a lair or a den, and never get caught between a mother and her offspring.

DANGER FROM PLANTS

The danger from poisonous plants in other regions of the world is no worse than in parts of the United States. As a rule, poisonous plants are not a serious hazard, but under certain conditions, they can be dangerous. The two general types of poisonous plant are those poisonous to touch and those poisonous to eat.

Plants Poisonous to Touch   Most of the plants poisonous to touch belong to either the sumac or the spurge families. The three most important poisonous plants in the United States are poison ivy, poison oak, and poison sumac (see fig. 6-2). Poison ivy is a low-growing ground shrub or clinging vine with shiny leaves arranged in groups of three. Poison oak is a shrub-like plant with oval leaves that also grow in groups of three. Poison sumac has smooth and narrow parallel leaves which grow from a woody stem. Poison ivy, oak, and sumac all have clusters of white berries. Knowledge of the appearance and effects of these plants will help you in other parts of the world, where similar plants flourish. A good field treatment for these poisonous plants is to apply wet wood ashes to the affected area of the body.

Symptoms of plant poisoning are similar in all parts of the world—reddening, itching, swelling, and blisters. The best treatment after contact with these plants is a thorough washing using, if available, a strong soap.

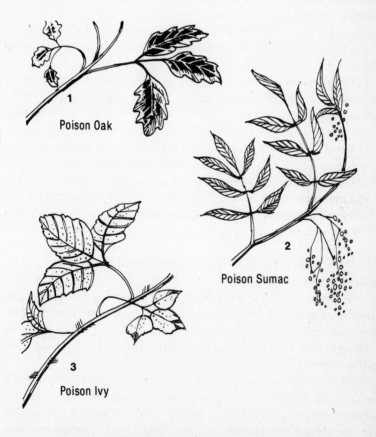

1
Poison Oak

2
Poison Sumac

3
Poison Ivy

Fig. 6-2   Poisonous Plants of North America

Plants Poisonous to Eat   The number of poisonous plants is not great in comparison to the number that are nonpoisonous and edible. A good rule is to learn the plants that are edible and eat only those you recognize (see "Edible Plants" section in this chapter).

WATER

Drinking water is essential to survival. Assuming no physical activity, a man can go without water for up to ten days in temperatures of 50°F, seven days at 90°F, and two days in temperatures of 120°F. At these limits the body becomes incapacitated by dehydration. Death will follow.

The only relief for dehydration is water, and much of the initial survival activities should be directed toward obtaining an adequate water supply.

It should be pointed out that thirst is not an accurate indication of the need for water. Oftentimes, particularly in colder climates, a man performing intensive labor will be totally unaware that he has become partially dehydrated because he feels no desire for water.

Minimal daily water requirements are determined by a number of factors, but particularly by climate and temperature conditions and the amount of daily physical activity. In a survival situation, the availability and accessibility of water are fundamental considerations.

If water is plentiful, drink at regular and frequent intervals, consuming small to medium (½-quart) quantities at one time.

THE DANGERS OF DRINKING NONPOTABLE WATER
No matter how overpowering your thirst may seem, do not drink nonpotable water. One of the worst hazards to survival is waterborne diseases. Treat all water either by boiling for at least one minute or by using water treatment tablets.

The diseases and organisms you may contract by drinking nonpotable water include:

Dysentery—Causes severe and prolonged diarrhea with bloody stools, fever, and weakness. If you suspect dysentery, eat frequently and try drinking coconut milk, boiled water, or the juice of boiled bark. Coconut milk is a laxative and should be consumed in small quantities. Eat boiled rice if it is available.

Cholera and typhoid—Even though you have been inoculated, these diseases may be contracted unless you are very careful about the water you drink.

Flukes—Blood flukes exist in stagnant, polluted water, especially in tropical areas. If swallowed, the fluke will bore into the bloodstream, live as a parasite, and cause painful, often fatal, diseases. Flukes (worm parasites) may also penetrate the unbroken skin while a person is wading or bathing in contaminated water.

Leeches—Small leeches are particularly prevalent in African streams. If swallowed, a leech can hook itself to the throat passage or inside the nose. While in this position it will suck blood, create a wound, and move to another area. Each new wound will continue to bleed, opening the door for infection. Sniff highly concentrated salt water to remove these parasites from the nose, or pick them out with improvised tweezers.

Muddy, Stagnant, and Polluted Water   If you have exhausted all other sources and are still without water, you may drink water from a muddy or stagnant pool, even though it may have an odor and be unpleasant. Caution: Before using, boil this water for at least 1 minute.

To clear muddy water:

- Let it stand 12 hours; or
- Pass it through about 3 feet of bamboo that is filled with sand. Stuff grass in one end to contain the sand; or
- Pour it into a cloth that has been filled with sand. Boil polluted water and add charcoal from the fire to remove the odors. Let the water stand for about 45 minutes before drinking.

FINDING WATER

When there is no surface water, tap through the earth's water table for ground water—rain or melted snow that has sunk into the ground. Access to this table and its supply of generally pure water depends upon the contour of the land and the type of soil.

Rocky Soil   Look for springs and seepages. Limestones have more and larger springs than any other type of rock. Because limestone is easily dissolved, caverns are readily etched in it by ground water. Look in these caverns for springs.

Because lava rock is porous, it is a good source of seeping ground water. Look for springs along the walls of valleys that cross the lava flow.

Look for seepage when a dry canyon cuts through a layer of porous sandstone.

In areas abundant in granite rock, look over the hillsides for green grass. Dig a ditch at the base of the greenest area, and wait for the water to seep in.

Loose Soil Water is usually more abundant and easier to find in loose soil than in rocks. Look for ground water along valley floors or on the slopes bordering the valley, because it is in these areas that the water table is most likely to surface. Springs and seepages may also be found above the high watermark of rivers and streams after the water has receded.

Before digging for water, look for signs that it is present. Dig in the floor of a valley under a steep slope, or dig out a green spot where a spring was during the wet season. In low forests, along the seashore, and in river plains, the water table is close to the surface. Very little digging usually yields a good supply of water.

Runoff water is found above the water table and includes streams, stagnant pools, and water in bogs. Consider this water contaminated and dangerous even if it is away from human habitation.

Along the Seashore Water can be found in the dunes above the beach or even on the beach itself. Look in hollows between sand dunes for visible water, and dig if the sand seems moist. On the beach, scoop holes in the sand at low tides about 100 yards above the high tide mark. This water may be brackish, but it is reasonably safe. Run it through a sand filter to reduce the brackish taste.

Do not drink seawater. Its salt concentration is so high that body fluids must be drawn to eliminate it. Eventually the kidneys will cease functioning.

On Mountains Dig in dry stream beds, because water is often present under the gravel. When in snowfields, put snow in a container and

Fig. 6-3   The Water Table

place it in the sun out of the wind. Improvise tools from flat rocks or sticks if no digging equipment is available.

Water from Plants If unsuccessful in your search for ground or runoff water, or if you do not have time to purify the questionable water, a water-yielding plant may be the best source. Clear, sweet sap from many plants is easily obtained. This sap is pure and chiefly water. Check the following sources in an emergency:

1) Many plants with fleshy leaves or stems store drinkable water. Try them whenever you find them.
2) The barrel cactus of the southwestern United States is a possible source of water. Use it only as a last resort and only if you have the energy to cut through the tough, outer, spine-studded rind. Cut off the top of the cactus and smash the pulp within the plant. Catch the liquid in a container. Chunks may be carried away as an emergency water source. A barrel cactus 3½ feet high will yield about 1 quart of milky juice. *This is an exception to the rule that milky or colored sap-bearing plants should not be eaten.*

Other Sources Cattails, greasewoods, willows, elderberry rushes, and salt grass grow only where ground water is near the surface. Look for these signs and dig. Places that are visibly damp, where animals have scratched, or where flies hover, indicate recent surface water. Col-

Fig. 6-4   The Barrel Cactus

lect dew on clear nights by sponging it up with a handkerchief. During a heavy dew, you should be able to collect about a pint an hour.

Deserts, Tropics, and Oceans   For specialized discussions of finding water in these areas, see the appropriate chapters.

THE WATER STILL

One method of acquiring water is through a "water still." It works in the following manner: The sun's heat raises the temperature of the air and soil under a plastic sheet until the air is saturated. Vapor condenses in tiny drops on the cooler undersurface of the plastic and slowly runs down the sloping underside of the plastic, dripping off into a bucket.

Although stills produce about half as much water from 4 P.M. to 8 A.M. as they do during the daylight hours, they do produce some water at night. After sundown, the plastic cools rapidly, while the temperature of the soil remains relatively high, so water vapor continues to condense on the undersurface of the plastic.

To construct a water still, see fig. 6-5. The basic materials for setting up your own survival "still" are:

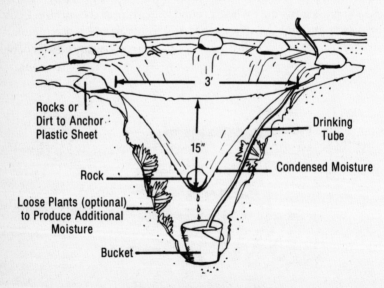

Fig. 6-5   The Water Still

1) A 6 by 6 foot sheet of clear plastic. (Heavy, clear plastic, roughened in production, is preferable because water drops cling best to it. It is possible to roughen the surface of thinner plastics with fine sand.)
2) Smooth, fist-sized rock.
3) A bucket, a jar, or a cone of foil, plastic, or canvas to catch water.
4) Flexible plastic tubing, about 5 feet. (You can manage without the plastic tubing, but it allows you to drink water without removing the bucket from the hole and interrupting the solar cycle.)

Do not expect to begin drinking water immediately. The least you should have in twenty-four hours is a pint; however, a quart or more may be obtained. The "still" may also become a possible source of food. The water bucket under the plastic attracts snakes and small animals, which crawl down the top surface of the plastic and then cannot climb back out.

FIREMAKING

Fire is needed for warmth, keeping dry, signaling, cooking, and purifying water by boiling. Survival time is increased or decreased according to your ability to build a fire when and where needed.

If matches are available, a fire can be built under any weather conditions. When operating in remote areas, always carry a supply of matches in a waterproof case *on your person*. Matches can be waterproofed by coating with nail polish or liquid paraffin.

FUEL, TINDER, AND LOCATION
Small fires are easier to build and control than large ones. A series of small fires built in a circle around you in cold weather gives more heat than one big fire.

Locate the fire carefully to avoid setting a woods on fire. If the fire must be built on wet ground or snow, first built a platform of logs or stones. Protect the fire from the wind with a windbreak or reflector. This will focus the heat in the desired direction.

Use standing dead trees and dry, dead branches for fuel. The inside of fallen tree trunks will supply dry wood in wet weather. In treeless areas, rely on grasses, dried animal dung, animal fats, and sometimes even coal, oil shale, or peat, which may be exposed on the ground. If near the wreckage of an aircraft, use a mixture of gasoline and oil as fuel. Be careful how you ignite and feed this fire. Almost any plant can be used for firewood; however, do not burn the wood of any contact-poisoning plant, such as poison ivy or poison oak. Their poisonous agents are released when the plant is burned.

Use kindling that burns readily to start the fire, such as small strips of dry wood, pine knots, bark, twigs, palm leaves, pine needles, dead upright grass, ground lichens, ferns, plant and bird down, and the dry, spongy threads of the giant puffball (which, incidentally, are edible). Cut dry wood into shavings before attempting to set it afire. One of the best and most commonly found kindling materials is punk, the completely rotted portions of dead logs or trees. Dry punk can be found even in wet weather by knocking away the soggy outer portions with a knife, stick, or even your hands. Even when wet, the resinous pitch in pine knots or dried stumps ignites readily. Loose bark of the living birch tree also contains a resinous oil which burns rapidly. Arrange this kindling in a "wigwam" or "log cabin pile," so sufficient oxygen can circulate to cause the fire to take hold most readily.

Bank the fire properly. Use green logs or the butt of a decayed, punky log to keep the fire burning slowly. Keep the embers out of the wind. Cover them with ashes, and put a thick layer of soil over them. It takes less work to keep the fire going than to build another one.

On polar ice, or in areas where other fuels are unavailable, blubber or other animal fat is a source of fuel. In the desert, animal dung may be the only available fuel.

FIRE WITHOUT MATCHES
Prepare some extremely dry tinder before attempting to start a fire without matches. Once prepared, shelter this tinder from the wind and dampness. Some excellent tinders are punk, lint from cloth, rope or twine, dead palm frond, finely shredded dry bark, dry powdered wood, the inner lining of bird nests, wooly materials from plants, and wood dust produced by insects, (which is often found under the bark of dead trees). To save tinder for future use, store it in a waterproof container.

Sun and Glass   A camera lens, a convex lens from a binocular, or a lens from a telescopic sight or flashlight may be used to concentrate the rays of the sun on the tinder.

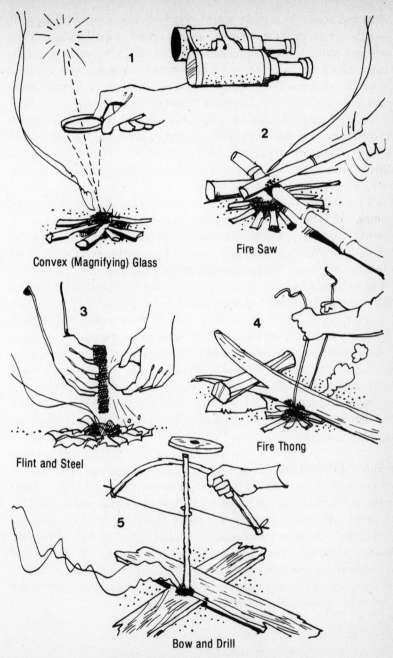

1 Convex (Magnifying) Glass

2 Fire Saw

3 Flint and Steel

4 Fire Thong

5 Bow and Drill

Fig. 6-6   Fire Without Matches

Flint and Steel   This is the best method of igniting bone-dry tinder if you do not have matches. Use the flint fastened to the bottom of a waterproof match case. A hard piece of stone will serve as a substitute. Hold the flint as near the tinder as possible and strike it with a knife blade or other small piece of steel. Strike downward so that the sparks will hit in the center of the tinder. When the tinder begins to smolder, fan or blow it gently into a flame. Gradually add fuel to the tinder, or transfer the burning tinder to the fuel pile. If you do not get a spark with the first rock, try another.

Wood Friction   Since the use of friction is a difficult method of starting a fire, use it only as a last resort.

Bow and drill—Make a strong bow strung loosely with a shoelace, string, or thong. Wrap the line once around a dry, soft shaft of wood, and use the bow to spin the shaft in a small block at one end and a slab of bone-dry hardwood at the other. This procedure forms a black powdered dust on the hardwood, which eventually catches a spark. When smoke begins to rise, there should be enough spark to start a fire. Lift the hand-held block and bow, and add tinder.

Fire thong—Use a strip of dry rattan, preferably about 2 feet long, and a dry stick or small limb. Elevate this stick off the ground. Split the end of the elevated stick and hold it open with a small wedge made of rock or wood. Place a small wad of tinder in the split, leaving enough room to insert the thong behind it. Secure the stick with your foot, and work the thong back and forth until the tinder begins to smoulder.

Fire saw—The fire saw consists of two pieces of wood which are sawed vigorously against each other. This method of starting fires is commonly used in the jungle. Use split bamboo or other soft wood as a rub stick and a dry sheath, such as that of the coconut flower, as the wood base. A good tinder is the fluffy brown covering of the apiang palm or the dry material found at the base of coconut palm leaves.

Ammunition and powder—Prepare a sheltered pile of kindling and wood. Place the powder from several cartridges at the base of the pile. Take two rocks and sprinkle a little powder on one rock. Then grind the two rocks together immediately above the powder at the base of the pile. This will ignite the powder on the rock and, in turn, the larger amount of powder and kindling wood.

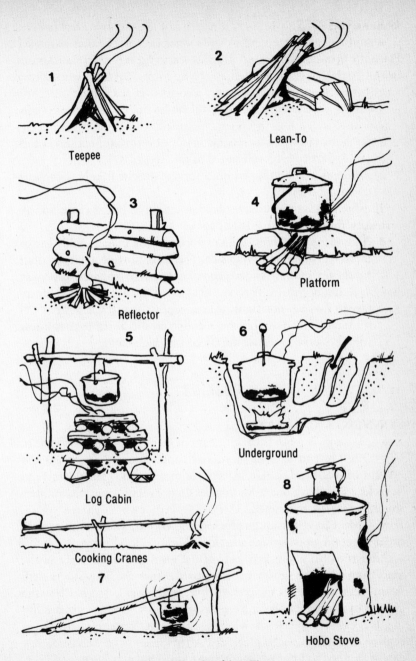

1 Teepee

2 Lean-To

3 Reflector

4 Platform

5 Log Cabin

6 Underground

Cooking Cranes

7

8 Hobo Stove

Fig. 6-7   Cooking Fires

COOKING FIRES

A small fire and some type of stove are best for cooking purposes. Place the firewood crisscross and allow it to burn down to a uniform bed of coals. Make a simple fireplace by using two logs, stones, or a narrow trench on which to support a vessel over the fire.

There are several types of "survival stoves":

1) A "hobo stove," which is made out of a tin can, conserves fuel and is particularly well suited to the Arctic.
2) A simple crane propped on a forked stick will hold a cooking container over a fire.
3) A fire that is to be used for baking should be built in a pit and allowed to burn into a bed of coals.
4) An underground fireplace, developed by the Indians, adds one or more vents on the upwind side. The vents provide a built-in draft for the fire burning under a cooking utensil in much the same way as a chimney stove. This type of cooking fire has a distinct advantage in survival situations, where security is essential, since it will substantially reduce the smoke and flame incidental to cooking. It will also serve to reduce the effects of a high wind.

COOKING

SKINNING AND CLEANING

Fish As soon as a fish is caught, cut out its gills, and skin or scale it. Gut the fish by cutting open its stomach and removing all entrails. Do not cut off the head. There is valuable meat in the "shoulders" and "cheeks." Small fish under four inches do not require gutting, but they should be scaled or skinned.

Fowl Most fowl should be plucked and cooked with the skin on in order to retain moisture and provide additional food value.

After the bird is plucked, cut off the head and make a slit in the anus from which the guts can be removed. Wash the body cavity with fresh, clean water. Save the gizzard, liver, and heart for stew. Clean the gizzard by cutting it open and removing its seeds, grit, and gizzard lining. It is easier to pluck a fowl after scalding it. Waterfowl are an exception; they are easier to pluck dry. After some fowl are cooked, they can be skinned to improve flavor, but food value may be lost.

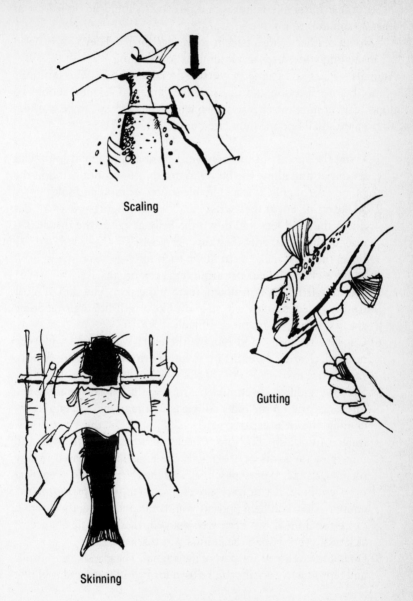

Scaling

Gutting

Skinning

Fig. 6-8   Dressing Fish

Scavenger birds like vultures and buzzards should be boiled for at least 20 minutes to kill their parasites.

Save all feathers (except from scavenger birds). They can be used for insulating your shoes or clothing or for bedding.

Animals   Fleas and parasites will leave a cooled body. Wait until this occurs before cleaning and dressing the carcass. Cleaning should be done near running water, if possible, where the carcass can be washed. To prepare small and medium-sized animals:

1) Hang the carcass head downward from a convenient limb. Cut its throat and allow the blood to drain into a container. Boil the blood thoroughly. It is a valuable source of food and salt.
2) Make a ring cut at the "wrist" and "ankle" joints and a "Y" cut down the hind legs and down the belly as far as the throat. Do not cut the meat, only the skin.
3) From the chest make a cut down each foreleg.
4) Make a clean circular cut around the sex organs.
5) Working from the butt down, remove the skin. The skin of most freshly killed animals will strip off like a well-fitted glove. Some species, however, are more difficult.
6) Cut into the belly, and remove the entrails from the windpipe upward, clearing the entire mass with a firm circular cut to remove the sex organs.
7) Save the kidneys, liver, and heart. Use the fat surrounding the intestines and on the hide. All parts of a mammal are edible, including the meaty parts of the skull such as the brain, eyes, tongue, and fleshy portions. Check the heart, kidneys, liver, and intestines for spots or worms. If the animal is diseased in any manner, danger is present while handling the meat and preparing it for cooking. If you have gloves, use them while preparing the animal. They will help prevent you from contracting the disease. Once the animal has been well cooked, there is little chance of sickness, even though the animal was diseased.
8) Do not throw away any part of the animal. The glands and entrails and reproductive organs can be used for bait in traps and fishlines.

TANNING

Save the skin. It is light when dried and is good insulation as a bed cover or article of clothing. The skin may be cured by removing all excess flesh and stretching the hide on a frame. Tannic acid can be obtained by stripping the inner bark from oak trees and soaking it in water. The stronger the solution, the more effective it will be. The hide should be alternately soaked in this solution, then suspended in a shady place to dry. The greater the number of applications, the better the hide will be cured. Tannic acid is also found in chestnut, mimosa, and hemlock trees, and in tea.

Larger animals   To prepare, follow the steps outlined above, except that greater care (and sturdier ropes) will be required to hang the heavier animal's carcass from a tree. If this is impossible, repeat the above procedures but clean the animal on the ground.

Rodents   Wood or desert rats and mice are palatable meat, particularly if cooked in a stew. These rodents should be skinned, gutted, and boiled. Rats and mice should be boiled about 10 minutes. Either may be cooked with dandelion leaves. Always include the livers.

Rabbits   Rabbits are tasty but add few fats to a diet. They are easy to trap and kill. To skin, make an incision behind the head or bite out a piece of skin to allow insertion of your fingers. Peel back the hide. To clean the rabbit, make an incision down the belly, spread open, and swing strongly downward. Most of the intestines will fly out. What remains can be scraped and washed away. (Save the heart and liver, if unspotted.)

Other edible animals   All mammals are edible. Dogs, cats, hedgehogs, porcupines, and badgers should be skinned and gutted before cooking. Prepare them as a stew with a quantity of edible leaves.

Reptiles   Snakes and lizards are edible. Remove the head and skin before eating. Lizards are found almost everywhere, especially in tropical and subtropical regions. Broil or fry the meat.

HOW TO COOK

Cooking makes most foods more tasty and digestible. It also destroys bacteria, some toxins, and harmful plant and animal products.

Boiling   When meat is tough, boiling is the best way to prepare it for later frying, roasting, or baking. Boiling is probably the best method of cooking because it conserves the natural juices of the food. The "stock" that is obtained from boiling is excellent nourishment containing, among other things, much-needed salt and fat. Boiling is difficult at high altitudes and is impractical at altitudes in excess of 12,000 feet.

Vessels for boiling—Water can be boiled in vessels made of waterproof cloth or canvas, bark or leaves, but such containers burn above the waterline unless the vessel is kept moist or the fire kept low. Half a green coconut or a section of bamboo cut well above or just below a joint can be used as a container for boiling. *Such containers will not burn until after the water boils.* Bark vessels can be made from birch bark or the thin inner bark of many species of trees. The bark should be free of holes or cracks, and can be made supple by gentle roasting over a fire.

Banana leaves also make good containers. Secure the sides with thorns or slivers of wood. Water can be boiled in a scooped out hole, in clay pots, or in hollow logs by dropping heated stones into them. This was the method used by American Indians before Europeans introduced metal containers.

Roasting or Broiling   This is a quick way to prepare wild plant food and tender meat. Roast meat by putting it on a stick and holding it near embers. A crane is easily improvised from green branches. Roasting hardens the outside of the meat and helps retain the juices.

Baking   Baking is cooking in an oven with steady, moderate heat. The oven may be a pit under the fire, a closed vessel, or a leaf or clay wrapping. To bake in a pit, first fill it with hot coals. Drop the covered vessel containing water and food in the pit. Place a layer of coals over it and cover with a thin layer of dirt. If possible, line the pit with stones so that it holds more heat. Pit cooking protects food from flies and other pests and reveals no flame at night.

Steaming   Steaming can be done without a container and is suitable for foods that require little cooking, like shellfish. Place the food in a pit filled with heated stones over which leaves have been placed. Put more leaves over the food. Then force a thick stick through the leaves down to the food pocket. Pack a layer of dirt on top of the leaves and around the stick. Remove the stick and pour water through the hole. This is a slow, but effective, way to cook.

Parching   Parching may be a desirable method of preparing some foods, especially grains and nuts. To parch, place the food in a metal container and heat slowly until it is thoroughly scorched. In the absence of a suitable container, a heated, flat stone may be used.

Utensils   Anything that holds food or water may be used as a container—coconut, turtle or sea shells, leaves, bamboo, or a section of bark.

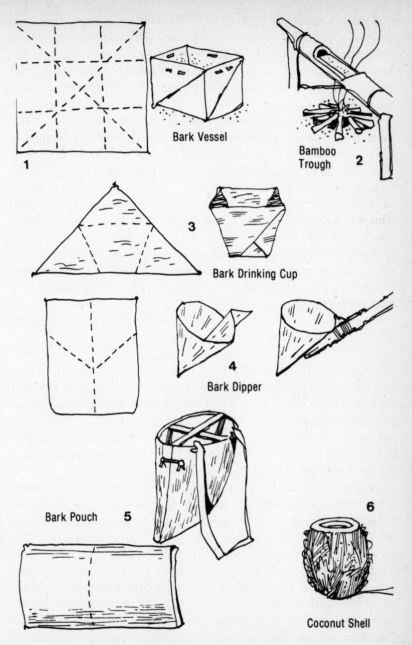

Bark Vessel

1

Bamboo Trough

2

3

Bark Drinking Cup

Bark Dipper

4

Bark Pouch   **5**

6

Coconut Shell

Fig. 6-9   Wilderness Vessels and Utensils

COOKING PLANT FOOD

Soaking, parboiling, cooking, or "leaching" are methods of improving taste. Circumstances and the nature of the food dictate the method. Acorns can be made palatable by being "leached." (Leaching is done by crushing food and pouring boiling water through it while it is held in a strainer of some sort.)

Pot herbs—Boil leaves, stems, and buds until tender. If the food is bitter, several changes of water will help to eliminate the bitterness.

Roots and tubers—These can be boiled, but are more easily baked or roasted. Some roots and tubers *must* be boiled to remove harmful substances such as oxalic acid crystals.

Nuts—Most nuts can be eaten raw, but some, such as acorns, are better crushed than parched. Chestnuts are tasty roasted, steamed, or baked.

Grains and seeds—Grains and seeds are more tasty when parched, but can be eaten raw. Grains and seeds may be ground into meal or flour.

Sap—You can dehydrate to a syrup any sap containing sugar. Boil away the water.

Fruit—Bake or roast tough, heavy-skinned fruit, and boil juicy fruit. Many fruits, however, are palatable raw.

COOKING ANIMAL FOOD

Boil animals larger than a domestic cat before roasting or broiling them. Cook the meat as fast as possible when broiling, because it toughens over a slow fire. When cooking larger animals, cut them into small pieces. If the meat is exceptionally tough, stew it with vegetables. When baking or broiling any meat, use fat if possible. When baking, put the fat on top so that it melts and runs over the meat.

Small game—Small birds and mammals can be cooked whole. However, remove entrails before cooking. Wrap a big bird in clay and bake it. The clay removes the feathers when it is broken from the cooked carcass. Boiling is the best method of cooking cleaned, small game, because there is less waste. Flavor the bird by stuffing it with coconut, berries, grains, roots (onions), and greens. Save and eat these additions.

Fish—Fish may be roasted on an improvised grill of green sticks or baked in leaves and clay, or they may be cooked over direct heat by using a crane. All freshwater fish and other freshwater foods should be thoroughly cooked, because they may contain disease-producing organisms.

Reptiles and amphibians—Frogs, small snakes, and lizards can be roasted on a stick. Large snakes and eels are better if boiled first. Boil turtles until the shell is loose. Remove. Cut up the meat and mix it with tubers and greens to form a soup. Salamanders, roasted on a stick, are edible. Skin all frogs and gut snakes before cooking. The skin of a snake is not toxic, but its removal improves the taste of the meat.

Crustacea—Many crabs, crayfish, shrimp, prawns, and other crustacea require cooking in order to kill disease-producing organisms. Since crustacea spoil rapidly, they should be cooked immediately after capture. For best results, boil them alive.

Mollusks—Shellfish can be steamed, boiled, or baked in the shell. Shellfish make an excellent stew with greens or tubers.

Insects—Grasshoppers, locusts, large grubs, termites, ants, and other insects are easy to catch, and provide nourishment. They are best fried or roasted.

Eggs—Edible at all stages of embryo development, bird and turtle eggs are among the safest of foods. Hard boiled eggs can be carried for days as reserve food.

SEASONING
Salt can be obtained by boiling seawater. The ashes of burned nipa palm boughs, hickory, and of some other plants contain salt that can be dissolved in water. When the water has been evaporated, the salt has a black tint. The citric acid in limes and lemons can be used to pickle seaweeds, fish, and other meat. Dilute two parts fruit juice with one part salt water. Allow the fish or meat to soak for half a day or longer.

BAKING BREAD
Bread may be made with flour and water. If possible, use seawater for the salt. After kneading the dough well, place it in a sand-lined hole. Then place sand on top of the dough and cover with glowing coals. By experimentation, you should be able to balance the dough and fire temperatures to prevent sand from clinging to the cooked bread. Another method of baking bread is to twist it around a green stick from which the bark has been removed and place it over a fire. The stick should be bitten first to determine if the sap is so sour or bitter that it will affect the taste of the bread. Bread may also be made by spreading dough into thin sheets on a hot rock. A little leaven (dough allowed to sour) added to the bread dough improves the loaf.

PRESERVING FOOD

Freezing   In cold climates, preserve excess food by freezing.

Drying   Plants and meat can be dried by wind, sun, air, or fire, or any combination of these four. The object is to remove the water.

Smoking   Cutting the meat "with the grain" into ¼-inch strips and drying it in the wind or in smoke will produce "jerky." Put the strips of meat on a wooden grate and dry until the meat is brittle. Use willow, alders, cottonwood, birch, and dwarf birch for firewood because pitch woods such as pine and fir will make the meat unpalatable. A parachute-teepee makes a good smoke house when the flaps at the top are closed. Hang the meat high and build a slow smouldering fire under it. A quicker way of smoking meat is by the following method—dig a hole in the ground about 1 meter deep and ½ meter wide. Make a small fire at the bottom of the hole (after starting the fire, use green wood for smoke). Place an improvised wooden grate about ¾ meter up from the bottom. Use poles, boughs, leaves, or any available material to cover the pit. After one night of heavy smoking, the meat should be in a condition to remain edible for five to seven days. If it is possible to smoke the meat for two nights, it will remain edible for two to four weeks or longer. When properly smoked, the meat should look like a dark, brittle, curled stick, but it is very tasty and nutritious.

Preserving Fish, Bird, and Plant Foods   The methods of preserving fish and birds are much the same as for other meats. To prepare fish for smoking, cut off the heads and split the fish from their backs to their bellies. Then spread the fish flat and skewer them in that position. Thin willow branches with bark removed make good skewers. Fish may also be dried in the sun. Hang them from branches or spread them on hot rocks or on the sides of your raft. When the meat dries, splash it with seawater to salt the outside. Do not keep seafood unless it is well dried and salted.

Plantains, bananas, breadfruit, leaves, berries, and other wild fruits can be dried by air, sun, wind, or fire, with or without smoke. Cut fruit into thin slices and place them in the sun or next to a fire.

STORING FOOD

A cache, or any place where food and supplies can be protected or hidden, should be used for storing fish and meat. To build a simple food cache, string a rope between two trees. Throw a second rope over the first, tie one end of the rope to the food supply or carcass, and hoist it

Fig. 6-10   Wilderness Caches

a safe distance from the ground. Anchor the other end of the rope to a stake or a tree.

HUNTING

WEAPONS

A spear is the simplest hunting weapon, but if you have any elastic material, fashion a slingshot from a light but sturdy forked branch. Use large pebbles for ammunition. Such weapons are remarkably accurate and an effective way to collect small game and birds.

If you have time and available material, try fashioning a bow and arrows. This is far more efficient and versatile for hunting most animals than using a spear.

FINDING GAME

The secret to successful hunting is seeing the quarry before it sees you. Hunt in the early morning or at dusk, and watch for signs such as tracks, trails, trampled underbrush, and droppings that tell of the presence of game. When approaching a ridge, lake, or clearing, slow down and peer first at distant, then closer, ground. In general, apply the military principles of movement and concealment.

Hunting animals and birds is not an easy job for even the most experienced woodsman; therefore, as a beginner, "stand hunt." Find a place where animals pass—a trail, watering hole, or feeding ground. Hide nearby, always downwind so the animals cannot detect your scent. Wait for game to come within range of your weapon. Remain absolutely motionless.

When stalking an animal, do so downwind, moving slowly and noiselessly only when it is feeding or looking the other way. *Freeze* when it looks your way.

Animals depend upon their keen senses of sight, hearing, and smell to warn them of danger. Birds can see and hear exceptionally well, but lack a sense of smell. During nesting periods they are more accessible. Because of this, you can catch them more easily in the spring and early summer. They nest in trees, branches, cliffs, or marshes, and by watching for birds moving back and forth on a regular flight path, you can locate their nests.

SHOOTING GAME

If you have a weapon and see a chance to use it, whistle sharply to encourage the quarry to stop, giving you a chance for a standing shot. On large game, aim for the chest, neck, or head. In the event you wound an animal and it runs, slowly and carefully follow the blood trail. If wounded severely, the quarry will lie down soon if not followed too fast, and will usually weaken and be unable to rise. Approach cautiously and finish it off.

After killing a large animal such as a deer, gut and bleed it immediately. Cut the musk glands from between the hind legs and at the joints of the hind legs. Be careful not to cut the bladder or stomach while removing internal organs.

TRAPPING

If you expect to trap with any kind of success, you must decide what kind of animal to trap, how the animal will react, and the type of bait to use.

Rodents and rabbits are easy to trap. These small mammals have regular habits and confine themselves to limited areas of activity. Locate a hole or run, then bait and set one of the traps illustrated on pages 137 and 138.

TRAPPING HINTS

1) To catch a mammal that lives in a hollow tree, try inserting a short forked stick in the hole and twisting, so that any loose skin will wrap around the fork. Keep the stick taut while pulling the animal out.

2) Use smoke to drive animals out of their dens. Snare or club the quarry as it emerges.

3) Bait a fish hook with a minnow and place it near water to catch gulls, crows, and other scavengers.

4) Set snares or traps at night in runways containing fresh tracks or droppings. Place snares in areas previously used for butchering animals. Use animal entrails for bait. After setting a trap in a runway, erect barriers on either side of it. These barriers should be made of dead branches, sticks, and dry leaves shaped to form

a funnel leading the animal into the trap. After erecting the barriers, sprinkle animal blood or bladder contents in the area. This will help neutralize your scent. Rain will accomplish the same purpose better.

A BASIC SNARE
The most basic snare is set perpendicular to a hole or trail and attached to a heavy branch or stone. As the animal moves into the snare opening, the slip knot secures the loop around its neck and chest, and the animal's sudden lunging tightens it more. Use light, flexible wire if possible: It is less easily observed (darken if not already tea-stained or rusty), slips closed more readily, and is more difficult for an animal to bite through. This snare can be attached to a log or "drag" which slows down the animal, allowing it to be captured.

OTHER TYPES OF SNARES
Spring snare—This snare is particularly useful on game trails. Fasten the loop to a log, tree, or forked stake, and set it near a bush or limb as illustrated on page 137.

Baited spring snare—Fasten a slip noose to the end of a bent sapling. Open the noose wide enough to fit over the animal's head but not wide enough for its body to slip through. Secure the trigger so that it holds the sapling. Make it sufficiently loose so that a slight jerk in the noose will free the trigger.

Spring and spear trap—Trap jungle mammals using a bamboo spring and spear snare. As the quarry strikes the cord or wire that is secured to the trigger mechanism, the trigger is released and the spear is driven by the force of the bamboo spring.

Deadfall—Build a simple deadfall with a rock or heavy log and tilt it at a steep angle on a figure-4 trigger. Tie the bait on the trigger. When the game disturbs the bait, the weight will fall (see fig. 6-11).

FISHING

It is difficult to state the best time to fish, because different species feed at different times, both day and night. As a general rule, look for fish to feed just before dawn and just after dusk; just before a storm as the

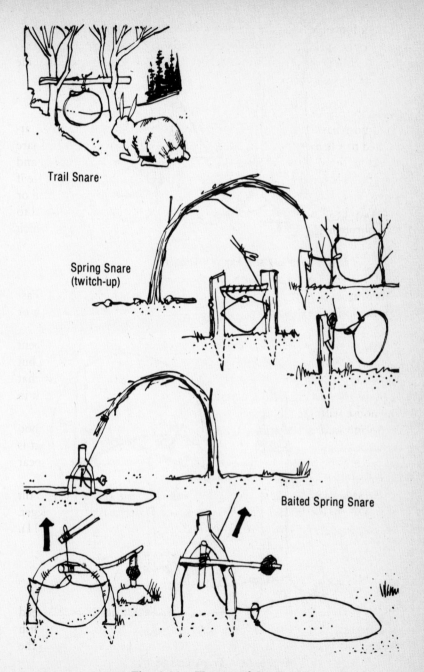

Trail Snare

Spring Snare
(twitch-up)

Baited Spring Snare

Fig. 6-11 Traps and Snares

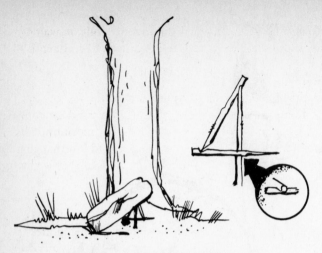

Simple Deadfall Using Figure 4 Trigger

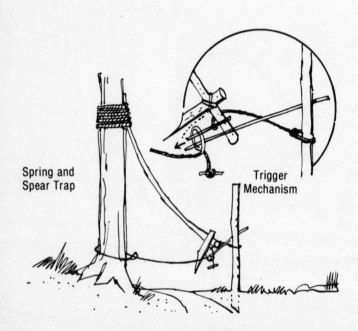

Spring and
Spear Trap

Trigger
Mechanism

Fig. 6-11   Traps and Snares

front is moving in; and at night when the moon is full or waning. Jumping minnows and dimpled water are good signs of feeding fish.

WHERE TO FISH

The place selected to start depends on the type of water and the time of day. In fast running streams in the heat of the day, try deep pools that lie below the riffles. Toward evening or in the early morning, drift your bait near submerged logs, undercut banks, and overhanging bushes. On lakes in the heat of the summer, fish deep. In the evening or early morning in summer, fish the shallows.

BAIT

As a general rule, fish bite bait taken from local waters. Look along the water's edge for aquatic insects and minnows, and on the bank for worms and terrestrial insects. If you catch a fish, inspect its stomach to see what it has been eating; try to duplicate this food. Use its intestines and eyes for bait if other sources are unproductive. When using worms, cover the point and barb. With minnows, try to use the small fish alive by hooking through the back (above the backbone), tail, or lips. If using dead bait, do not bury the hook so completely it cannot pull out to catch the fish.

Make artificial lures from bits of brightly colored cloth, feathers, or bright metal fashioned to duplicate injured minnows.

MAKING HOOKS

If you have no hooks, improvise them out of insignia, pins, bone, or hardwood. By twisting bark or cloth fibers, a sturdy line can be fashioned. Using tree or vine fiber, knot the ends of two strands and secure them to a solid base. Hold a strand in each hand and twist clockwise, crossing one above the other counterclockwise. Add fiber as necessary to increase the length of the line. If parachute suspension lines are available, use these for heavy fish. Nails can be fashioned into hooks. There are times when the most sophisticated equipment and suitable baits do not catch fish. Do not be discouraged; try again later in the day or try another method tomorrow.

TROT LINES

Trot lines provide a practical method for catching fish if you remain for a period of time near a lake or stream. Tie several hooks along a line with a suitable weight or sinker at the end. Bait the hooks and fasten the line to a low-hanging branch that will bend but not break when a fish is hooked. Keep this line in the water as long as you are in the area, checking it periodically to remove fish and rebait the hooks.

An excellent hook for a trot line is the gorge or skewer hook. This is nothing more than a sliver of wood or bone to which the line is tied midway. Sink the gorge into a chunk of bait, so the gorge lies flush with the line and can be easily swallowed. After the fish swallows the bait and you yank on the line, the gorge will swing crosswise and lodge in the fish's stomach.

JIGGING

This method requires an 8- to 10-foot limber cane or similar type pole, a hook, a piece of brilliant metal shaped like a commercial fishing lure, a 2- to 3-inch strip of white flesh, pork rind, or fish intestine, and a piece of line about 10 inches long. Attach the hook just below the lure on the end of the short line, and tie the line to the end of the pole. Working near weed beds, dabble the lure just below the surface of the water. Occasionally slap the water with the tip of the pole to attract large fish to the area. This method is more effective at night.

FISHING BY HAND

This method is effective in small streams with undercut banks or in shallow ponds left by receding flood waters. (This method is *not* recommended where poisonous water snakes or electric fishes are found.) Place your hands in the water and allow them to reach water temperature. Reach under the bank slowly, keeping your hands close to the bottom if possible. Move your fingers slightly until you contact a fish. Then work your hand gently along its belly until you reach its gills. Grasp the fish firmly just behind the gills and be careful of the dorsal and pectoral spines of catfish.

In fast-moving streams, particularly in salmon runs in the northern United States, fish can be swatted out of the water with the hand. Bears catch fish effectively in this manner.

MUDDYING

Small isolated pools caused by the receding waters of flooded streams are often filled with small fish. Stir up the mud in the bottom of these puddles by shuffling through them or using a stick. The fish will often

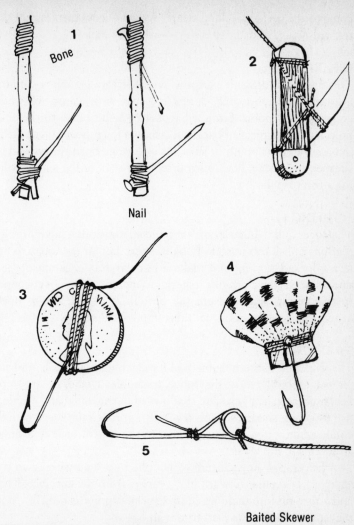

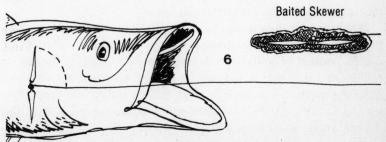

Fig. 6-12   Improvised Fish Hooks

come to the surface seeking clearer water. Throw them out of the water with your hands or stun them with your stick.

SPEARING

This method is difficult except when the stream is shallow and the fish are large and numerous, during the spawning season, or when fish congregate in pools. Strap a bayonet or knife blade to the end of a pole; sharpen a piece of bamboo; lash two long thorns on a stick; fashion a hone spear point; or split a stick, wedge open the two sides, and sharpen their ends. Position yourself on a rock or log and wait quietly for a fish to swim by.

NETTING

The edges and tributaries of lakes and streams often have sizable populations of fish too small to hook or spear, but large enough to net. Select a forked sapling and make a circular frame. Stitch or tie your undershirt or the cloth-like material found at the base of coconut trees to this frame, making sure the bottom is closed. Scoop upstream around rocks or in pools with this improvised net.

TRAPPING

This is a time-consuming method for catching both fresh- and saltwater fish, especially those that move in schools. In lakes or large streams, fish approach the banks and shallows in the morning and evening. Sea fish traveling in large schools regularly approach the shore with the incoming tide, often moving parallel to the beach, or hide around obstructions in the water.

A fish trap is an enclosure with a blind opening where two rock or stake walls extend outward like a funnel from the entrance. The time and effort put into building a trap depends upon the need for food and the length of time you plan to stay in one spot.

If near the sea, pick a trap location at high tide and build it at low tide. On rocky shores, use natural rock pools. On coral islands, use natural pools in or on the reefs by blocking the openings as the tide recedes. On sandy shores, use sandbars and the sloughs they enclose. Build the trap as a low stone or stake wall extending into deeper water and forming an angle with the shore. Drive the fish toward this shallow angle, where some will be stranded.

SHOOTING

If you have a weapon and sufficient ammunition, try shooting fish. Due to the distortion of parallax, aim slightly under fish in water less than 3 feet deep. A hand grenade exploded in a school of fish will supply food for days.

EDIBLE PLANTS

There are at least 300,000 different kinds of wild plants in the world. A large number of them are potentially edible. Very few are deadly when eaten in small quantities (see edibility guidelines). Complete descriptions of all the wild food plants are beyond the scope of this manual; therefore, the information and illustrations included are limited to a sampling of those plants which are most abundant and most easily recognized. Within this particular section you will find plants that are most commonly found in the temperate regions of the world. Information and illustrations of plants which grow in more extreme as well as temperate climates will be found in the chapters on specific climates.

EDIBILITY GUIDELINES

When in doubt about which plants are poisonous and which are not poisonous, observe rodents, monkeys, bears, and various other vegetable-eating animals. Usually the food these animals eat is safe for humans. Birds are not reliable, as they often eat berries that are poisonous to humans. Use these rules as a general guide:

1) Taste or chew a small piece of any plant you do not recognize. If it is bitter or disagreeable, do not eat it.
2) When in doubt, cook all plant food. Many food poisons are removed by cooking.
3) Avoid eating plants with milky juice and do not let milky juice contact your skin. This rule does not apply to wild figs, breadfruit, papaya, and barrel-cactus.
4) Avoid ergot poisoning by discarding all grasses, cereals, and grains which have black spurs in place of normal seed grains.
5) Although most berries are edible, many are poisonous. Stick to berries you recognize.

6) Avoid eating mushrooms and other fungi. Only a few types are poisonous, but mushrooms come in such a variety of shapes, colors, and sizes that only an expert can be totally confident in determining those that are edible.

If you eat a plant you suspect is poisonous, induce vomiting.

EDIBLE PARTS OF PLANTS

Plants, whether water or land types, whether in temperate, desert, arctic or tropical regions, furnish the following edible parts:

1) Roots and other underground parts: tubers, rootstalks, and bulbs
2) Shoots and stems
3) Leaves
4) Nuts
5) Seeds and grains
6) Fruit
7) Bark

Roots and Other Underground Parts: Tubers   All tubers are found below the ground and must be dug. Cook them by boiling or roasting. Following are some examples of tubers:

Solomon's seal—Tubers of Solomon's seal grow on small plants and are found in North America, Europe, northern Asia, and Jamaica. Boiled or roasted, they taste much like parsnips.

Water chestnut—The water chestnut is a native of Asia, but it has spread to both tropical and temperate areas of the world, including North America, Africa, and Australia. It is found as a free-floating plant on rivers, lakes, and ponds. The plant covers large areas wherever it grows and has two kinds of leaves—the submerged leaf, which is long, root-like, and feathery; and the floating leaves, which form a rosette on the surface of the water. The nuts borne beneath the water are an inch or two broad, with strong spines that give them the appearance of a horned steer. The seed within the horny structure may be roasted or boiled.

Nut grass—Nut grass is widespread in many parts of the world. Look for it in moist sandy places along the margins of streams, ponds, and ditches. It grows in both tropical and temperate climates. Nut

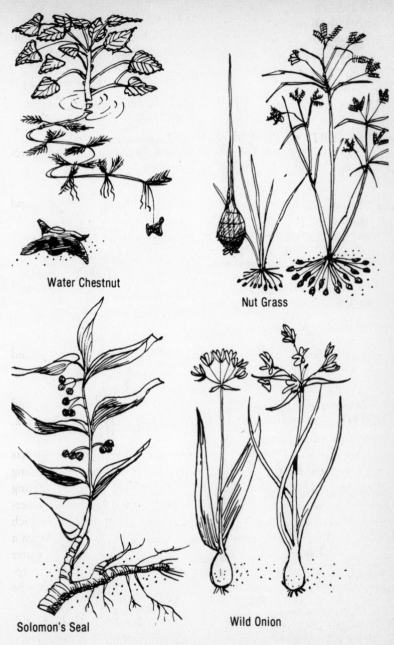

Water Chestnut

Nut Grass

Solomon's Seal

Wild Onion

Fig. 6-13   Edible Roots and Other Underground Parts:
Tubers and Bulbs

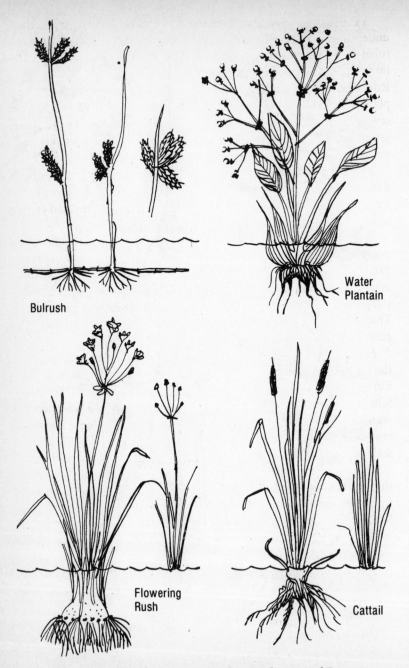

Bulrush

Water Plantain

Flowering Rush

Cattail

Fig. 6-13   Edible Roots and Other Underground Parts:
Tubers and Bulbs

grass differs from true grass in that it has a three-angle stem and thick underground tubers that grow one-half to one inch in diameter. These tubers are sweet and nutty. Boil, peel, and grind them into flour. This flour can be used as a coffee substitute.

Roots and Other Underground Parts: Roots and Rootstalks These plant parts are storage devices rich in starch. Edible roots are often several feet long and are not swollen like tubers. Rootstalks are underground stems, and some are several inches thick and relatively short and pointed. Following are examples of edible roots and rootstalks:

Bulrush—This familiar tall plant is found in North America, Africa, Australia, the East Indies, and Malaya. It is usually present in wet swamp areas. The roots and white stem base may be eaten cooked or raw.

Water plantain—This white-flowered plant is found most frequently around freshwater lakes, ponds, and streams, where it is often partly submerged in a few inches of water. It is usually abundant in marshy areas throughout the north temperate zone, and has long-stalked, smooth, heart-shaped leaves with three to nine parallel ribs. Thick, bulb-like rootstalks which grow below the ground lose their acrid taste after being dried. Cook them like potatoes.

Flowering rush—The flowering rush grows along river banks, on the margins of lakes and ponds, and in marshy meadows over much of Europe and temperate Asia. It grows in Russia and much of temperate Siberia. The mature plant, usually found growing in a few inches of water, reaches a height of three or more feet and has loose clusters of rose-colored and green flowers. The thick, fleshy underground rootstalk should be peeled and boiled like potatoes.

Cattail—The cattail is found along lakes, ponds, and rivers throughout the world, except in the tundra and forested regions of the far north. It grows to a height of six to fifteen feet, with erect, tape-like, pale green leaves one-quarter to one inch broad. Its edible rootstalk grows up to one inch thick. To prepare these rootstalks, peel off the outer covering and grate the white inner portion. Eat them boiled or raw. The yellow pollen from the flowers can be mixed with water and steamed as bread. In addition, the young growing shoots are excellent when boiled like asparagus.

Roots and Other Underground Parts: Bulbs All bulbs are high in starch content and, with the exception of the wild onion, are more palatable if they are cooked.

Wild Onion—This is the most common edible bulb and is a close relative of the cultivated onion. It is found throughout the north temperate zones of North America, Europe, and Asia. The plant grows from a bulb buried three to ten inches below the ground. The leaves vary from narrow to several inches wide. The plant grows a flower that may be white, blue, or a shade of red. No matter what variety of onion is found, it can be detected by its characteristic "onion" odor. All bulbs are edible.

The wild potato is a tuber which is found throughout the world, but especially in the tropics. For a description of this plant see Chapter Seven ("Survival in the Tropics").

Shoots and Stems   Edible shoots are similar in appearance to asparagus. Although some can be eaten uncooked, most shoots are better if they are parboiled for 10 minutes, the water drained off, and reboiled until they are sufficiently tender for eating.

Edible ferns—Ferns are abundant in moist areas of all climates, especially in forested areas, gullies, along streams, and on the edge of woods. They may be mistaken for flowering plants, but by careful observation, you should be able to distinguish them from all other green plants. The undersurface of the leaf is usually covered with masses of brown dots which are covered with yellow, brown, or black dust. These dots are filled with spores and their presence makes ferns easily distinguishable from plants with flowers.

On all ferns, select young stalks (fiddleheads) not more than 6 to 8 inches high. Break them off as low as they remain tender; then close your hand over the stalk and draw it through to remove the wool. Wash and boil in salted water, or steam until tender.

Bracken—This is one of the most widely distributed ferns. It grows throughout the world, except in the Arctic, in open, dry woods, recently burned clearings, and pastures. It is a coarse fern with solitary or scattered young stalks, often one-half-inch thick at the base, nearly cylindrical, and covered with rusty felt; the uncoiling frond is distinctly three-forked with a purplish spot at each angle. This spot secretes a sweet juice. Old fronds are conspicuously three-forked, and the rootstalk is about one-quarter-inch thick, creeping, branching, and woody.

* * *

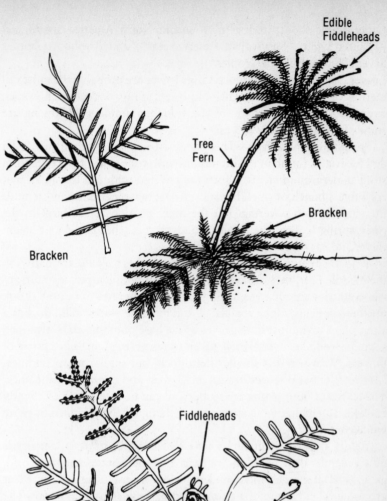

Edible
Fiddleheads

Tree
Fern

Bracken

Bracken

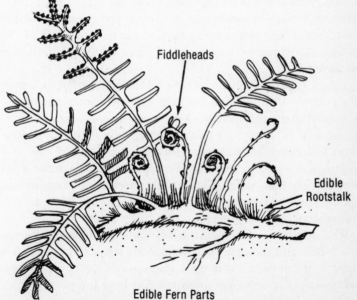

Fiddleheads

Edible
Rootstalk

Edible Fern Parts

Fig. 6-14   Edible Shoots and Stems

Other edible shoots and stems found in North America are *Mescal* (Chapter Eight, "Survival in Desert Areas") and *Bamboo* (Chapter Seven, "Survival in the Tropics").

Leaves Plants which produce edible leaves are probably the most numerous of all plant foods. They can be eaten raw or cooked; however, overcooking destroys many of the valuable vitamins. Following are some plants with edible leaves:

Spreading Wood Fern—This plant, especially abundant in Alaska and Siberia, is found in the mountains and woodlands. It sprouts from stout underground stems, which are covered with old leafstalks that resemble a bunch of small bananas. Roast these leafstalks and remove the shiny brown covering. Eat the inner portion of the fern. In the early spring, collect the young fronds or fiddleheads, boil or steam them, and eat them like asparagus.

Wild Dock and Wild Sorrel—Although these plants are native to the Middle East, they are often abundant in both temperate and tropical countries and in areas having high and low rates of rainfall. Look for them in fields, along roadsides, and in waste places. Wild dock is a stout plant with most of its leaves at the base of its six- to twelve-inch stem. It produces a very small, green to purplish, plume-like cluster of flowers. Wild sorrel is smaller than dock, but similar in appearance. Many of its basal leaves are arrow-shaped and contain a sour juice. The leaves of both plants are tender and can be eaten fresh or slightly cooked. To eliminate the strong taste, change the water once or twice while cooking.

Wild Chicory—Originally a native of Europe and Asia, chicory is now generally distributed throughout the United States and the world, as a weed along roadsides and in fields. Its leaves are clustered at ground level at the top of a strong, underground, carrot-like root. The leaves look much like dandelion leaves, but are thicker and rougher. The stems rise two to four feet and are covered in summer with numerous bright blue heads of flowers (also resembling a dandelion's, except for color). The tender young leaves can be eaten as a salad without cooking. Grind the roots as a coffee substitute.

Wild Rhubarb—This plant grows from southeastern Europe to Asia Minor and through the mountainous regions of central Asia to China, and can be found in open places, along the borders of woods and streams, and on mountain slopes. The large leaves grow from the

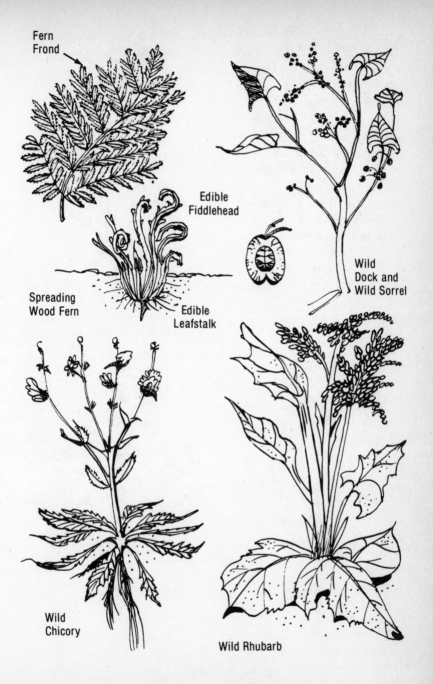

Fern
Frond

Edible
Fiddlehead

Spreading
Wood Fern

Edible
Leafstalk

Wild
Dock and
Wild Sorrel

Wild
Chicory

Wild Rhubarb

Fig. 6-15   Edible Leaves

151

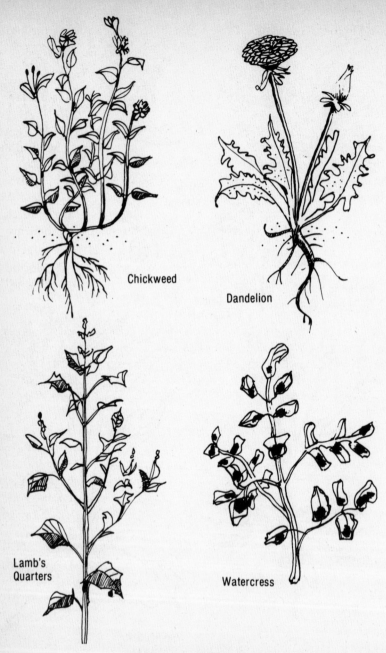

Fig. 6-15   Edible Leaves

base of long stout stalks. These stalks flower and rise above the large leaves, and may be boiled and eaten as a vegetable.

Other plants with edible leaves are dandelion, watercress, lamb's quarters, and chickweed.

Other edible leaves indigenous to North America are *Water Lettuce, Horseradish Tree,* and *Lotus Lily* (Chapter Seven, "Survival in the Tropics"), *Arctic Willow* (Chapter Nine, "Survival in Cold Climates") and *Prickly Pear* (Chapter Eight, "Survival in Desert Areas").

Nuts Nuts are among the most nutritious of all plant foods, and they contain valuable protein. Plants bearing edible nuts grow in all climatic zones and continents of the world except the Arctic. Some nuts of the temperate zones are walnuts, filberts or hazelnuts, almonds, hickory nuts, acorns, beechnuts, and pine nuts. Tropical-zone nuts include coconuts, Brazil nuts, cashew nuts, and macadamia nuts. Following are some edible nuts:

English Walnut—In the wild state, this nut is found from southeastern Europe across Asia to China. It is abundant in the Himalayas, and grows on a tree that sometimes reaches sixty feet in height. The leaves of the tree are divided, which is a characteristic of all walnut species. The walnut itself is enclosed by a thick outer husk, which must be removed to reach the hard inner shell of the nut. The nut kernel ripens in autumn.

Hazelnut (Filbert)—Hazelnuts are found over wide areas of the United States, especially in the eastern half of the country. They also grow in Europe and in eastern Asia from the Himalayas to China and Japan. Growing mostly on bushes six to twelve feet tall, hazelnuts exist in dense thickets along stream banks and open places. The nut is enveloped by a bristly, long-necked husk; it ripens in the fall. It can be eaten either dried or fresh.

Chestnut—Wild chestnuts are highly useful as a survival food. They grow in central and southern Europe, and from central Asia to China and Japan. The European chestnut is the most common variety: it grows along the edge of meadows and is a forest tree some sixty feet in height. The ripe or unripe nut can be prepared either by roasting it in embers or by boiling the kernel that lies within the shell. If the nut is boiled, mash it like potatoes before eating it.

Acorns (English Oak)—There are many varieties of oak, but the English oak is typical of those found in the north temperate zone. It often grows sixty feet tall, and the leaves are deeply lobed. The acorns grow out of a cut, and are not edible raw because of the bitter tannin contained in the kernel. Boil the acorns for 2 hours, pour out the water, and soak the nut in cold water. Change the water occasionally, and after three or four days, grind the acorns into paste. Make the paste into mush by mixing it with water and cooking it. You can make flour out of this paste by spreading and drying it.

Beechnut—Beechnut trees grow wild in moist areas of the eastern United States, Europe, Asia, and North Africa. They are common throughout southeastern Europe and across temperate Asia, but do not grow in tropical or subarctic areas. The beechnut is a large tree—sometimes reaching eighty feet in height—with smooth, light-gray bark and dark green foliage. Mature beechnuts fall out of their husk-like seed pods, and the nut can be broken with your fingernail. Roast and pulverize the kernel; then boil the powder for a satisfactory coffee substitute.

Swiss Stone Pine—Swiss stone pine is distributed widely in Europe and northern Siberia. The needles grow typically in bunches, and the edible seeds or nuts grow in woody cones which hang either separately or in clusters near the tips of the branches. The nuts grow at the base of the cone scales and, when mature, will fall out of the ripe cone. Eat these raw or roasted.

Although it grows wild in the tropics, another nut, the coconut, can be found in tropical regions of North America. For a description and illustration see Chapter Seven ("Survival in the Tropics).

Seeds and Grains The seeds of many plants,. such as buckwheat, ragweed, amaranth, goosefoot, and the beans and peas from bean-like plants, contain oils rich in protein. The grains of all cereals and many other grasses are also rich in plant protein. They may be ground between stones, mixed with water, and cooked to make porridge, or parched. Grains like corn can also be preserved for future use when parched.

Other plants with edible seeds and grains indigenous to North America are *Lotus Lily, Bamboo,* and *Rice.* For descriptions and illustrations see Chapter Seven ("Survival in the Tropics").

Fruit Edible fruit is plentiful in nature and can be classified as dessert or vegetable. Dessert fruits include the familiar blueberry and crow-

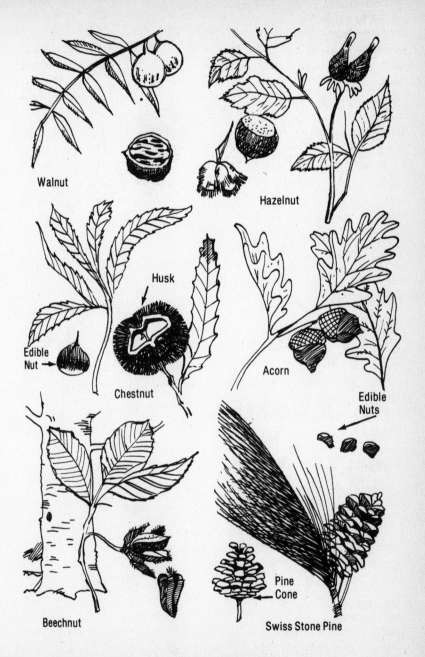

Walnut

Hazelnut

Husk

Edible
Nut

Chestnut

Acorn

Edible
Nuts

Beechnut

Pine
Cone

Swiss Stone Pine

Fig. 6-16   Edible Nuts

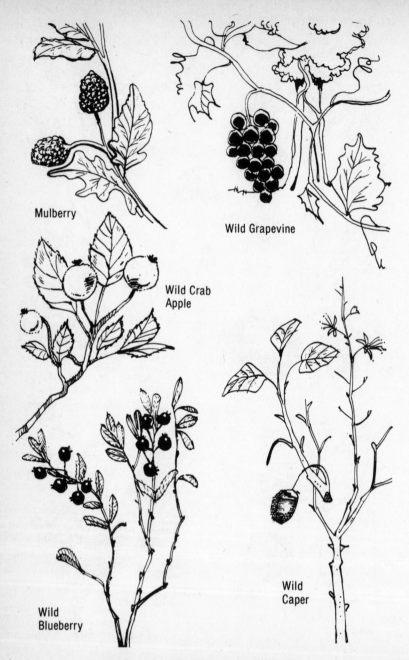

Mulberry

Wild Grapevine

Wild Crab Apple

Wild Blueberry

Wild Caper

Fig. 6-17   Edible Fruits and Berries

berry of the North, and the cherry, raspberry, plum, and apple of the temperate zone. Vegetable fruits include the common tomato, cucumber, pepper, eggplant, and okra.

Some wild fruits and berries of the United States (but common also in other areas) are:

Wild huckleberries, blueberries, and whortleberries—Large patches of wild huckleberries thrive on the tundra in Europe, Asia, and America in late summer. Farther south throughout the Northern Hemisphere these berries and their close relatives, the blueberry and whortleberry, are common. When they appear in the tundra of the north, these wild berries grow on low bushes. Their relatives to the south are borne on taller shrubs which may reach six feet in height. They are red, blue, or black when ripe.

Mulberry—Mulberry trees grow in North and South America, Europe, Asia, and Africa. In the wild state they are found in forested areas, along roadsides, and in abandoned fields, and often grow twenty to sixty feet tall. The fruit looks like the blackberry and is one to two inches long. Each berry is about as thick as your finger and varies in color from red to black.

Wild grapevine—This parasite plant is found throughout the eastern and southwestern United States, Mexico, Mediterranean areas, Asia, the East Indies, Australia, and Africa. Its leaves are deeply lobed and are similar to those of cultivated grapes. The fruit hangs in hunches and is rich in natural, energy-giving sugar. Water can also be extracted from the grapevine.

Wild crab apple—This fruit is common in the United States, temperate Asia, and Europe. Look for it in open woodlands, on the edge of woods, or in fields. The apple looks like its tame relative, and can be easily recognized wherever it may be found. This fruit can be cut into thin slices and dried for a food reserve.

Wild caper—This plant grows either as a spring shrub or small tree about twenty feet tall, in North Africa, Arabia, India, and Indonesia. It is leafless, with spine-covered branches, flowers, and fruit that grows near the tips of the branches. Eat the fruit as well as the flower buds.

Another fruit, the *wild fig*, can sometimes be found in the deserts of North America. For a description, see Chapter Eight ("Survival in Desert Areas").

Bark The inner bark of a tree—the layer next to the wood—may he eaten cooked or raw. You can make flour from the inner bark of cottonwood, aspen, birch, willow, and pine trees by pulverizing it. Avoid the outer bark, because of the presence of large amounts of tannin.

Pine bark is rich in vitamin C. Scrape away the outer bark and strip the inner bark from the trunk. Eat it fresh, dried, or cooked, or pulverize it into flour.

CLOTHING

The primary functions of clothing in a survival environment are to help the body maintain its normal temperature and to protect the body against weather, injuries, insects, and other small forms of life. If you find yourself lost or stranded, you will have few clothing options, and will probably have to make do with the clothes you are wearing at the time.

Clothing is particularly important in cold weather areas, the tropics, and the desert. Clothing-related information is provided in the chapters dealing with these environments. However, there are several general rules regarding the care and use of clothing that should be followed:

1) Keep clothes clean. Wash clothes regularly. Sleep in clothing; but if you have more than one layer, allow clothing you are not wearing to air out at night.
2) In cool climates, do not overdress when performing heavy labor. Your body heats up rapidly when performing physical activity. Cooling perspiration can cause chills and fever.
3) When moving through underbrush, tuck pants legs into socks or bind clothing at ankles and wrists. Button all buttons.
4) Keep socks and shoes dry. Warm them over a fire and air them out at night. Improper care of footwear will cause blisters, chafing, and immersion foot, which can lead to immobilization.

CHAPTER SEVEN

Survival in the Tropics

TERRAIN

There is no standard jungle. A "primary" jungle is easily recognized by its abundance of giant trees. The tops of these trees form a dense canopy more than one hundred feet from the ground. Under this canopy, there is little light or underbrush. This type of jungle is relatively easy to traverse.

Primary jungle growth has been cleared in many areas of the world to allow for cultivation. This land, when cleared and left idle, is reclaimed by jungle growth; it then becomes a sea of dense underbrush and creepers. This is "secondary" jungle, and is much harder to traverse than primary jungle.

Well over half the land in the tropics is cultivated in some way or another, primarily in connection with rubber, tea, and coconut plantations. If in a plantation area, look for the people who tend the crop—they may be able to offer assistance.

Dry scrub country is more open than the wet jungle, but is difficult to travel through because of its lack of topographic features, people, and trails. It can be traversed, however, with a compass, common sense, and confidence.

IMMEDIATE CONSIDERATIONS

The odds of being rescued or spotted under a dense canopy of jungle vegetation are far less than in other parts of the world. You may wish to start walking.

If you are the victim of an air crash, the most important items to take with you from the site of the crash are a machete, or another sharp metal instrument to cut through jungle growth, a compass, a first-aid kit, and a parachute or other thin material to use for mosquito netting and shelter.

TRAVEL

Travel is best accomplished without panic. If you are alone in the jungle, depending on the circumstances, the first move is to relax and think the problem out. You should:

1) Pinpoint your position as accurately as possible to determine a general line of travel to safety. If a compass is not available, use the sun in connection with a watch as an aid to direction.
2) Take stock of water supplies and rations.
3) Move in one direction, but not necessarily in a straight line. Avoid obstacles; do not fight them. In hostile territory, take advantage of natural cover and concealment.
4) There is a technique for moving through jungle; blundering only leads to bruises and scratches. Turn the shoulders, shift the hips, bend the body, and shorten or lengthen, slow or quicken your pace as required.

SHELTER

The shelter information discussed in Chapter Six ("Basic Survival Skills") is applicable to most tropical situations. The A-frame type of shelter works particularly well; use a good thickness of palm leaves or the broad leaves of young banana trees. Build a hot fire on a flat stone or on a platform of small stones. When the stones are well heated, place a leaf on them and allow it to turn dark and glossy. At this stage, the leaf is more water repellent and durable, and can be used as a shingle. After the shelter is finished, dig a small drainage ditch leading downhill; it will keep the floor dry.

Do not sleep on the ground; make yourself a bed of bamboo or small branches covered with palm leaves. A parachute hammock may serve the purpose. You can make a crude cover from tree branches or ferns; the bark from a dead tree is better than nothing.

ENVIRONMENTAL HAZARDS

Tropical environments present ideal conditions for growth of vegetation and animals. If you know what to look for, tropical environments offer an abundance of food sources.

But the same environmental conditions increase the danger of biological hazards. Living things tend to grow larger and to act more aggressively in tropical environments than in other parts of the world.

POISONOUS PLANTS

Certain tropical plants are poisonous and should be avoided: They are:

White mangrove or *blind-your-eye*—This white-leaved plant with white berries is found in mangrove swamps, estuaries, and near the coast. Sap causes blistering on contact. *It will blind you if it contacts your eyes.*

Cowhage or *cowitch*—This three-leaved plant with purple drooping flowers and fuzzy seed pods is found in thickets and brush country, but never in true forests. The hairs of the flowers and pods cause irritation. *Blindness results if they contact the eyes.*

Nettle trees—This plant is widespread, especially in or near ponds. It has a rough or "tooth-fringed" leaf that is poisonous to touch, causing a burning sensation.

Thorn apple or *jimson weed*—This plant is also found in temperate zones, along roads or in cultivated fields (particularly with soybeans). It has a purplish-white, trumpet-like flower, ragged leaf edges, and a spiked seed pod. All parts of this plant are poisonous, especially the seeds.

Pangi—This viny plant with heart-shaped leaves is found mainly in the Malayan jungle. Its seeds contain prussic acid, and are dangerous when eaten raw, but edible when roasted.

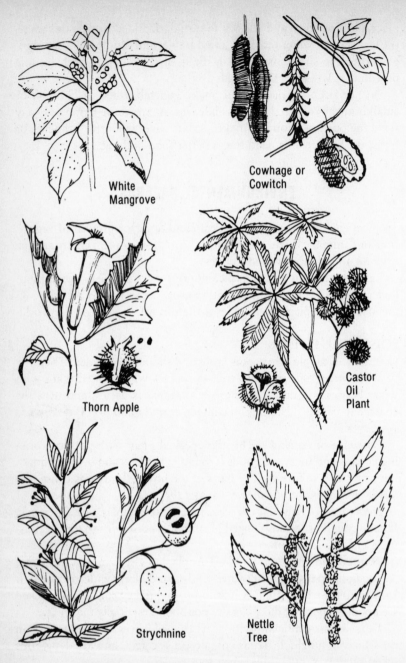

White Mangrove

Cowhage or Cowitch

Thorn Apple

Castor Oil Plant

Strychnine

Nettle Tree

Fig. 7-1 Poisonous Plants of the Tropics

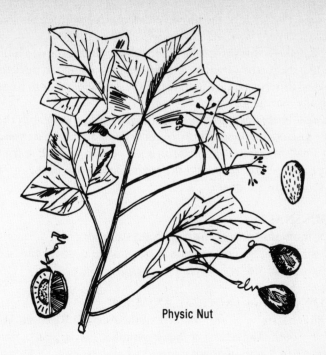

Physic Nut

Pangi

Fig. 7-1   Poisonous Plants of the Tropics

Physic nut—The seeds of the physic plant, a shrub with maple-like leaves, act as a violent laxative.

Castor oil plant—This shrub-like plant, whose radiated leaves look something like the top of a miniature palm tree, is common in thickets and open sites. Its seeds mature in burr-like clusters and are both toxic and powerfully diarrhetic.

Strychnine—These dogwood-like shrubs grow wild throughout the tropics. The luscious-looking white or yellow fruit (about the size and shape of a small orange) is abundant in southeastern Asia. The fruit has an exceedingly bitter pulp, and the seeds contain one of the most potent poisons known to man.

POISONOUS SNAKES
For identification of snakes of the tropics see Appendix I ("Poisonous Snakes of the World"). For treatment of poisonous snakebite see Chapter Five ("First Aid").

OTHER DANGEROUS TROPICAL ANIMALS
Piranha   Piranha are small fish that live in the Amazon River and its tributaries in South America. The black piranha, the largest of the species, grows to a length of about one and a half feet. Piranha are attracted by even the most minute amount of blood in the water. These flesh-eating creatures are extremely dangerous. For safety purposes assume that all tropical South American streams are piranha-infested, though they prefer clear backwater eddies to swift muddy rivers. If crossing a piranha infested stream is absolutely necessary, throw the bleeding carcass of an animal into the stream and then cross at a safe distance *upstream*.

Electric Eels   These cylindrical, hose-like creatures live in most tropical waters, though they are more common to the rivers of South America, and can be found near banks and in shallow pools. Electric eels are sluggish and nonaggressive, but the muscular bodies of large eels can produce an electric shock strong enough to knock over a horse. Electric eels can grow to a length of eight feet and a thickness of one and a half feet.

Crocodiles and Alligators   These amphibious reptiles are found in widely separated areas of the world. Alligators are found only in the southern United States and along the Yangtze River in China; crocodiles are found in coastal swamps, inlets, and tidal rivers of the South

Pacific, and in some areas of Africa and Madagascar. The American crocodile, found along coastal regions of Mexico, the West Indies, Central America, Colombia, and Venezuela, will usually avoid man. The crocodile is considered more treacherous and vicious than the alligator, but generally is not dangerous when left alone.

HEALTH HAZARDS

Do not expect to remain vigorous in jungle areas unless you maintain your health. Even under ideal conditions, this is difficult, but the chances are increased by some common sense rules.

1) Do not hurry. Never try to beat the jungle by speed—it is not possible.
2) Avoid climbing high terrain except for taking bearings. A long detour over flat ground is preferable.
3) Take care of your feet by changing and washing your socks often. Also, protect your footwear from cracking and rotting by working grease or animal fat into the leather.
4) Should you develop a fever, make no attempt to travel. Wait until the fever abates. Drink plenty of water.
5) Ticks, leeches, mosquitoes, insects, and other pests constitute a real danger to your health and safety. Combat them with insect repellent or by avoiding areas where they are prevalent.
6) Avoid infections. In the heat and dampness of the tropics, wounds quickly become infected. Protect a wound or sore with a clean dressing. Sterilize whatever bandage you improvise if you do not have regular first-aid equipment.
7) Prevent heat exhaustion, heat cramps, or heat stroke by replacing the water you lose through perspiration. Drink plenty of potable water. If you feel the effects of heat, rest in the shade.

Diseases common in tropical areas include:
Malaria, Dengue Fever, Yellow Fever and Encephalitis—All are caused by bites from disease-carrying mosquitoes. Symptoms are severe chills and high fever. If you suspect you have contracted one of these diseases, rest and drink liquids.
Dysentery—Caused by polluted food or drinking water.

Sandfly Fever—This has symptoms similar to malaria. Drink plenty of water or other liquids; rest until fever abates.

Typhus—There are several types of typhus found in tropical areas, among which are the flea-borne and louse-borne varieties. The general symptoms are severe headaches, weakness, fever, and generalized body aches. The victims usually have a dusky complexion and may or may not develop a pink mottled or splotchy rash. Some untreated forms of typhus have mortality rates of up to 40 percent. Strict attention to personal hygiene, avoidance of contact with lice- or flea-ridden rodents, and avoidance of mite-infested grassy areas is essential. Louse-borne typhus infection of vaccinated adults is mild and may go unrecognized. Keep your inoculations current.

Exhaustion—The combination of heat and humidity in the tropical environment drains the body of energy faster than in other parts of the world. Pace your activities and get plenty of rest.

Prevent heat exhaustion, heat cramps, or heat stroke by replacing the water and salt lost through perspiration. Drink plenty of potable water; if you have salt, mix two tablets to a canteen (quart) of water. If you feel the effects of heat, relax in the shade and drink ½ canteen of this salted water every 15 minutes. Continue this treatment until you feel better.

Immersion Foot—Immersion foot took more soldiers out of combat action in Vietnam than booby traps and land mines combined. It is similar to trench foot, except in the manner in which it is caused. It results from immersion of the feet in water or constant wetness of the feet for a prolonged period, usually in excess of twelve hours.

There are two types of immersion foot. Type one is confined to the sole of the foot and is called "warm water immersion foot." It occurs where there are many creeks, streams, canals, and swamps to cross, with dry ground between them. After about three days, the thick outer layer of the skin on the soles of the feet becomes white and wrinkled. Some of the creases in the soles of the feet become very tender on walking. During the next two or three days, the pain becomes severe and the feet swell slightly. When the boot is removed, it may be impossible to put it on again because of the pain and swelling. The pain is greatest on the heels and balls of the feet. The victim feels as if he is walking on pieces of rope in the boot. The only treatment is rest with boots and socks off. See that the skin is dried and stays dry. In a day or so the wrinkling, whiteness, and sogginess disappear. The pain leaves, although the soles of the feet remain tender on walking for a few days. In three to six days, the thick skin on the soles begins to peel.

Type two is called "paddy foot." This condition involves the tops of the feet and the legs. It is common where one has to wade through muddy rice paddies, swamps, creeks, streams, and canals, and the exposure to water is almost constant. This disease is most prevalent when the temperature of the water or mud remains about 85°F or higher.

It involves the tops of the feet, the ankles, and the legs up to the boot tops. In two or three days, the skin turns red, a cellulitis appears, and much swelling occurs. Because of the swelling, there is much pain and tenderness, and the skin is stretched and hard. As a result, it is easily bruised and scraped. Large, deeper, raw spots or abrasions of the skin may be caused by the rubbing of the boot against the soggy skin. Fifty percent of the victims of "paddy foot" develop tender, swollen lymph nodes in the groin. Mild to moderate fever (100 to 102°F) may be present.

For treatment, get to a dry area, remove hoots and socks, and rest with the feet elevated. Within six hours the edema becomes soft and pitted. Dents show after finger pressure. Pain, swelling, and fever subside after a few days of rest.

To arrest in its early stages, dry out the wet skin of the feet and legs for 10 hours.

WATER

Finding water in jungle country is usually not difficult. Use these hints:

1) The water from clear, swift-flowing streams containing boulders is an ideal source for drinking and bathing. However, before drinking any water, make it potable by boiling or by chemical means.
2) Water that is almost clear can be obtained from muddy streams or lakes by digging a hole on the land 1 to 6 feet from the bank. Allow the water to seep in and the mud to settle.
3) Water may be obtained from vines and plants. Not all vines yield palatable water, but try any vine found. Use the following method for tapping a vine. It will work on any species:

- Cut a deep notch in the vine as high up as you can reach.
- Cut the vine off close to the ground and let the water drip into your mouth or a container.
- When the water ceases to drip, cut another section off the top. Repeat this until the supply of fluid is exhausted.

Coconuts, particularly when green, supply milk which is both pleasant and nourishing—*in small quantities*. This juice is a violent laxative. A sugary sap can be obtained by cutting the flower spikes. Coconuts are available throughout the year. A drinkable sugary sap can also be obtained from the buri, nipa, sugar, and other palm trees.

PLANTS THAT CATCH AND HOLD WATER

Bamboo stems often have water in the hollow joints. Shake the stems of old, yellowish bamboo. If a gurgling sound is heard, cut a notch at the base of each joint and catch the water in a container.

In the American tropics, the overlapping, thickly growing leaves of the pineapple-like bromeliads may hold a considerable amount of rainwater. Strain the water through cloth to eliminate most of the dirt and water insects.

Other water-yielding plants include the traveler's tree of Madagascar, the umbrella tree of western tropical Africa, and the baobab tree of northern Australia and Africa.

FOOD

There is an abundance of food in the jungle, but some may be poisonous. Any food eaten by a monkey is generally safe for human consumption. In many inhabited areas of the tropics, cultivated fruits and vegetables and other foods are fertilized with human waste and are a source of disease. Never eat such fruits raw unless you have peeled them or cut off the outer surface with a knife. Cook all vegetables before eating them.

EDIBLE TROPICAL PLANTS

The tree-covered tropics offer the stranded survivor a large assortment of survival foods, but most people are quite unfamiliar with most

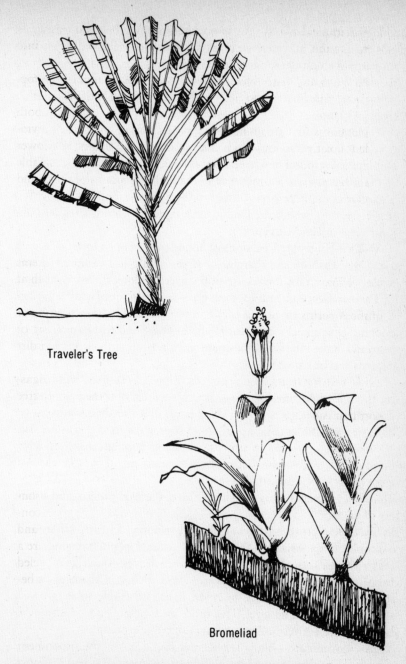

Traveler's Tree

Bromeliad

Fig. 7-2   Plants That Catch and Hold Water

kinds of tropical plants. We know the coconut, banana, pineapple, and citrus fruits in American markets, but there are literally hundreds more quite unknown in this country. Several kinds of widely dispersed tropical fruits and vegetables are illustrated in the manual, with supplementary information on how to detect other kinds of wild, edible tropical plants.

Poisonous plants are found in the tropics, but in no greater proportion to the nonpoisonous kinds than in the United States. Follow the edibility rules found in Chapter Six ("Basic Survival Skills").

Plant life above the timberline in the high mountains of the tropics is similar in many respects to that in the far north and the Arctic. If it is necessary to live off the land in such regions, refer to Chapter Nine ("Survival in Cold Climates").

Tropical food plants occur most abundantly in open forest clearings, along the seashore and margins of streams, and in swamps. The wet, dense, primary rain forests are poor places to look for survival food.

The best place to find food plants is an abandoned native garden. Cultivated forms of plants persist long after fields have been abandoned. These places may occur along the shore and riverbanks, or may be found in the interior of the country. Nearly all of the fruits found in gardens can be eaten.

Look first for fruits, nuts, or seeds. They can be used immediately for food. The tender end buds or starchy centers of some palm trunks, young bamboo shoots, roots, or grasses, and the shoots and flower buds of the wild banana, are all good sources of food. Ferns are usually abundant in the moist tropics, and make good greens. Even when no food is available, the tender twigs of many plants may be chewed; most kinds have some food value.

Tubers Tropical tubers include the taro, the wild potato, and a variety of yams.

The taro—grows in moist, forested regions of nearly all tropical countries. This large, smooth-skinned ground plant has long, wide (heart-shaped), single-pointed, light green leaves which grow singly from the main trunk. The flower is four inches in diameter, tulip-shaped, and yellow-orange in color. It has an edible tuber growing slightly below ground level. This tuber must be boiled to destroy irritating crystals. After boiling, eat the tuber like a potato.

The wild potato—like all tubers, is found below the ground and must be dug, then cooked by boiling or roasting. The plant is small

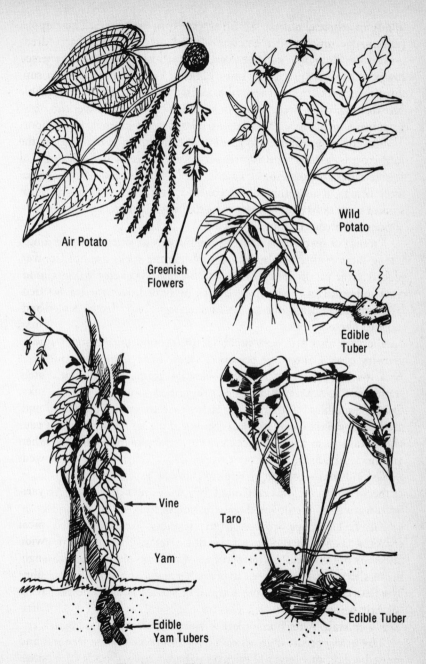

Air Potato

Greenish Flowers

Wild Potato

Edible Tuber

Vine

Yam

Edible Yam Tubers

Taro

Edible Tuber

Fig. 7-3 Edible Tubers and Yams

and found throughout the world, especially in the tropics. This type of potato is poisonous when eaten uncooked.

Yams—are edible, both the vines, above ground, and the tubers, below ground. There are at least seven hundred kinds of tropical yam vines, distributed in the tropical and subtropical parts of the world. Don't confuse them with the sweet potato or so-called yam sold in American markets; these are not true yams, but are related to the morning glory.

Yams occur in abandoned gardens of the natives, in clearings in the jungle areas, and in forested areas if not too dense. Cook all kinds. A few varieties are poisonous if eaten fresh. All kinds may safely be eaten after being cut into thin slices, covered with wood ashes, and then soaked in streams or salt water for 3 to 4 days. This gets rid of the poisonous properties of some wild kinds.

The native method of cooking nonpoisonous yams is to dig a pit, put in large rocks, and build a fire. When the rocks are hot, food is placed in the pit on green leaves, and the hole is covered with palm or other large leaves. Earth may also be mounded over the leaves. In a half hour or so, the yams are well done. Yams may also be boiled and mashed like potatoes.

The yam also produces tubers above ground on the stems of the growing vine. Called "air potatoes," these are common in southeast Asia. But unless you can clearly identify nonpoisonous types, they should not be eaten until soaked as described above.

Other Vegetables Other edible plants that are easily recognized and grow abundantly in the tropical regions of the world are the Ti plant, the tapioca (also called the cassava or manioc plant), the wild tulip, and the wild gourd.

The Ti plant—is found in tropical climates, especially on the islands of the South Pacific. It is cultivated over wide areas of tropical Asia. In both the wild and cultivated state, it ranges from six to fifteen feet in height. It has large, coarse, shiny, leathery leaves arranged in a crowded fashion at the tips of the thick stems. The leaves are green and sometimes reddish. This plant grows a large plume-like cluster of flowers that usually droops. It bears berries that are red when ripe. The fleshy rootstalk is edible and full of starch, and should be baked for best results.

The tapioca—or manioc plant is found in all tropical climates, especially in wet areas. It grows to a height of three to nine feet and has jointed stems and finger-like leaves. There are two kinds of manioc

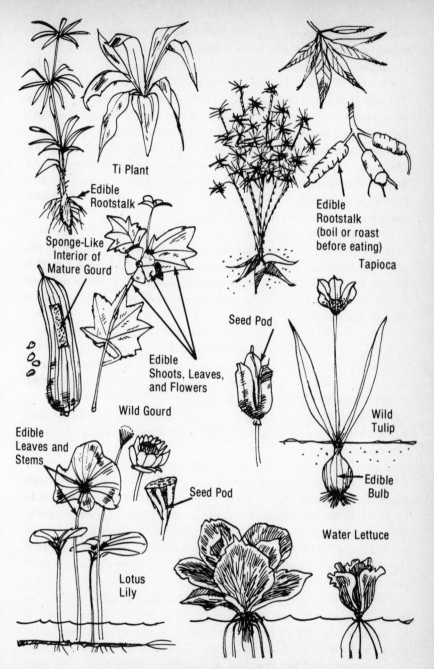

Ti Plant

Edible
Rootstalk

Edible
Rootstalk
(boil or roast
before eating)

Tapioca

Sponge-Like
Interior of
Mature Gourd

Seed Pod

Edible
Shoots, Leaves,
and Flowers

Wild Gourd

Wild
Tulip

Edible
Bulb

Edible
Leaves and
Stems

Seed Pod

Water Lettuce

Lotus
Lily

Fig. 7-4   Other Edible Tropical Plants

that have edible rootstalks—bitter and sweet. The bitter manioc is the common variety in many areas, and is poisonous unless cooked. If a rootstalk of bitter manioc is found, grind the root into a pulp and cook it for at least ½ hour. Flatten the wet pulp into cakes and bake. Another method of cooking this bitter variety is to cook the roots in large pieces for 1 hour, then peel and grate them. Press the pulp and knead it with water to remove the milky juice. Steam it, then pour it into a plastic mass. Roll the paste into small balls and flatten them into thin cakes. Dry these in the sun, and eat them baked or roasted. Sweet manioc rootstalks are not bitter and can be eaten raw, roasted as a vegetable, or made into flour. You can use this flour to make dumplings or the cakes described above.

The wild tulip—is found in Asia Minor and central Asia. The bulb of the plant can be cooked and eaten as a substitute for potatoes. The plant bears flowers for a short time in the spring, and these resemble the common garden tulip except that they are smaller. When red, yellow, or orange flowers are absent, a seed pod can be found as an identifying characteristic.

The wild gourd or luffa sponge—is a member of the squash family and grows similarly to watermelon, cantaloupe, and cucumber. It is widely cultivated in tropical areas, and it might be found in a wild state in old gardens or clearings. The vine has leaves three to eight inches across, and the fruit is cylindrical, smooth, and seedy. Boil and eat the fruit when it is half ripe; eat the tender shoots, flowers, and young leaves after cooking them. The seeds can be roasted and eaten like peanuts.

Water lettuce—grows throughout the Old World tropics in both Africa and Asia, and in the New World tropics from Florida to South America. It is found only in very wet places, usually as a floating water plant. Look for it in still lakes, ponds, and backwaters, and for the little plantlets growing from the margins of the leaves. These are rosette-shaped, and they often cover large areas in the regions in which they are found. The plant's leaves look much like lettuce and are very tender. Boil the leaves before eating.

The lotus lily—grows in fresh water, lakes, ponds, and slow streams from the Nile basin through Asia to China and Japan, and southward to India. It also grows in the Philippines, Indonesia, northern Australia. and the eastern United States. The leaves of the lotus lily are shield-shaped, one to three feet across. They stand five to six feet above the surface of the water, and grow either pink, white, or yellow flowers four to six inches in diameter. Eat the young stems and leaves after cooking, but remove the rough outer layer of the young stems before cooking or eating. The seeds are also edible when ripe. Remove the bitter embryo from the seeds, then boil or roast them. Also edible are the rootstalks, which become fifty feet long with tuberous enlargements. Boil these and eat them like potatoes.

Trees, Shoots, and Stalks   These include the multi-purposed bamboo, the baobab and the horseradish tree, and many varieties of palm.

Bamboo—This plant grows in the moist areas of warm temperate and tropical zones. It is found in clearings, around abandoned gardens, in the forest, and along rivers and streams. Bamboo resembles corn and sugar cane plants. The mature stems are very hard and woody, whereas the young shoots are tender and succulent. Cut these young shoots as you would asparagus, and eat the soft tip ends after boiling. Freshly cut shoots are bitter, but a second change of water eliminates the bitterness. Remove the tough protective sheath around the root before eating. Also edible is the seed grain of the flowering bamboo. Pulverize this, add water, and press it into cakes; or boil it like rice.

Other uses of bamboo: The mature woody stems can be used in the construction of shelters, rafts, and cooking utensils.

Baobab—This tree is found in open bush country throughout tropical Africa. It can be spotted by its enormous girth and swollen trunk, and by the relatively low stature of the tree. A mature tree sixty feet high may have a trunk thirty feet in diameter. It produces large white flowers about three inches across that hang loosely from the tree. The tree also bears a mealy, pulpy fruit with numerous seeds. These are edible, and the leaves can be used as a soup vegetable.

Horseradish Tree—This tropical plant is native to India but is widespread in other tropical countries throughout southern Asia, Africa, and America. Look in abandoned fields and gardens and on the edges of forests for a rather low tree, from fifteen to forty-five feet high. The leaves have a fern-like appearance and can be eaten old or young, fresh or cooked, depending on their state of hardness. At the ends of the branches are flowers and long, pendulous fruit that resemble giant beans. Cut the long, young seed pods into short lengths and cook them like string beans. Young seed pods can be chewed when they are fresh. The roots of this plant are pungent and can be ground for seasoning, much as you do true horseradish.

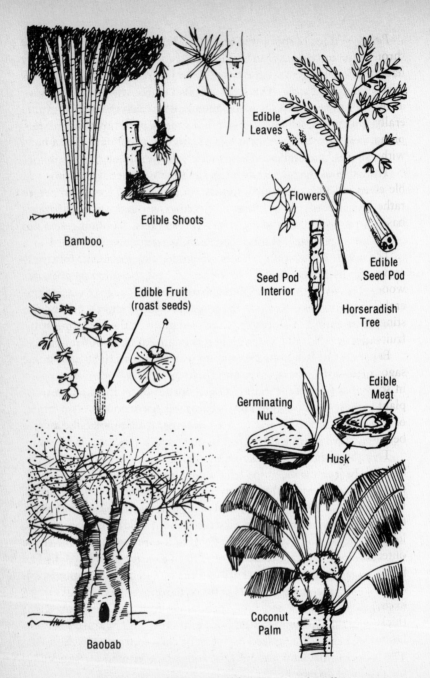

Edible Shoots

Bamboo

Edible Leaves

Flowers

Seed Pod Interior

Edible Seed Pod

Horseradish Tree

Edible Fruit (roast seeds)

Germinating Nut

Edible Meat

Husk

Baobab

Coconut Palm

Fig. 7-5 Food From Tropical Trees and Stalks

Palms—At least 1,500 different kinds of palms are distributed throughout the tropical world. They grow in almost every conceivable habitat—seashore, swamp, desert, grassland, and jungle. Palms vary in size from a few feet to one hundred feet tall. Some are climbers, such as the rattan palms. The palms assume many different forms, but generally they are easy to recognize. The leaves are of two main types: pinnate (like feathers), such as the date palm; or palmate (like a hand with webbed fingers), such as the fan or cabbage palm.

The cabbage (terminal bud) or growing point of most palms is edible either cooked or raw. It is located on the tip of the trunk, often rather deeply buried, but enclosed by the crown of leaves or sheathing base of the leaf stem. Some, but not all, cabbages are bitter.

The sap of many palms is drinkable and nourishing.

The nuts of palms are generally produced in clusters below the leafy crown. Nuts of all New World palms are edible, although many are woody and therefore unpalatable. None are poisonous. Nuts of several Old World palms—fishtail and sugar palms—contain microscopic stinging crystals which cause immediate intense pain if eaten. But the fruits of most Old World palms are edible, if not too woody.

Enormous quantities of edible starch are stored in the trunks of the sago, sugar, fishtail, and giant buri palms. The palms occur principally in southeast Asia and the neighboring islands of Indonesia. Another plant, the cycad, found throughout the same area, produces quantities of starch from its thick trunk. The palm-like cycad looks like a cross between a tree fern and a palm.

The pith of the sago palm is used for food in the Southwest Pacific and in southeast Asia. It grows wild in almost every swamp and in most streams and lakes. It is often planted or cultivated by natives on higher ground. Sago palms grow up to twenty-five feet high and about two feet thick. Their feather-like fronds have a thick midrib bearing long spines. Cut the tree down before flowers appear; then remove the outer bark, revealing the inner pith. Mash or knead it in a trough made from the base of a sago stem. Let the starch water run into another sago container, where it will precipitate into a fine flour. Pour off excess water. Cook as you would oatmeal, boiling in water until it is thick. Dip out spoonfuls onto leaves and allow them to cool. These gelatinous cakes may be eaten at once or kept for several days. You may also make pancakes of sago, baking them on stone or pottery. Slices of the pith may be baked.

The coconut palm is widely cultivated and grows wild throughout much of the moist tropics, especially on the east coast of Africa, tropical America, Asia, and the South Pacific islands. It grows mostly near the seashore, but sometimes occurs some distance inland. It does not abound along desert coasts, especially the west coast of continental areas.

The cabbage or growing heart of the coconut palm is an excellent vegetable, cooked or raw. This delicacy has been called "Millionaire's Salad."

All or part of the husk of the young nut may be sweet; if so, chew it like cane. Drink the milk from the nut. You may get over two pints of cold fluid from one young nut, especially at the jelly stage, when the flesh is soft. A ripe nut will gurgle when shaken near your ear. But do not drink from very young or old nuts.

Grate or chop up the meat or flesh as it firms up; this makes it easier to digest.

Fallen nuts germinate where they lie. In these, both milk and meat are used up, but the cavity is filled with a spongy mass called the bread. Eat this raw, or toasted in a shell over the fire. It tastes good and is very sustaining. Eat the sprouts like celery.

There are many other survival uses for the coconut palm. Coconut oil is a good preventive for sunburn as well as an aid in keeping off chiggers and other insects. It can also be used for cooking. In addition, coconut oil is a good preventive against salt-water sores and bloating. Before going fishing on the reef, smear your legs and feet with oil, to keep your skin in good condition even when you stand in salt water for many hours.

You can get coconut oil easily by exposing the meat of the coconut to the sun. The oil will run more quickly if you grate or pound the meat before placing it in the sun. You can also get oil by heating the coconut meat over a slow fire. If you have any kind of cooking pot or a section cut from a bamboo tree, you can boil coconut meat in water. When the mixture cools, the oil will rise to the top.

Fruits, Nuts, and Berries Fruits, nuts, and berries grow abundantly throughout all tropical regions. Raspberries, blackberries, and mulberries are sometimes found at high elevations in the tropics. They look sufficiently like the forms you are familiar with at home to be recognized. Some of them may be too seedy to be palatable, but they won't hurt you.

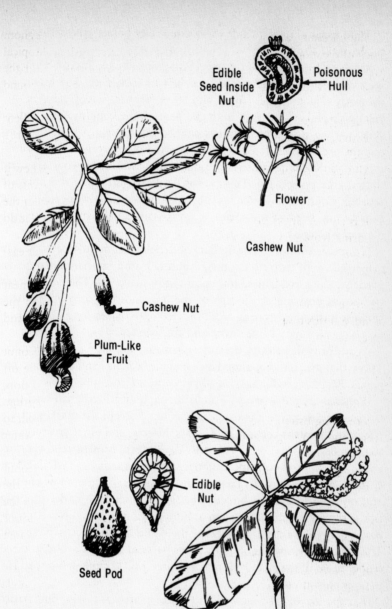

Edible Seed Inside Nut

Poisonous Hull

Flower

Cashew Nut

Cashew Nut

Plum-Like Fruit

Edible Nut

Seed Pod

Tropical Almond

Fig. 7-6   Edible Nuts

179

Wild tropical nuts include the coconut (see palms), the cashew, and the tropical almond.

Cashew Nut—This nut grows in all tropical climates, on a spreading evergreen tree that reaches a height of forty feet. The leaves are normally eight inches long and four inches wide; flowers are yellowish-pink. The fruit is thick, pear shaped, pulpy, and red or yellow when ripe, with a kidney-shaped nut growing at the tip. This nut encloses one seed and is edible roasted. The green hull surrounding the nut contains an irritant poison that will blister your eyes and tongue like poison ivy. This poison is destroyed when the nuts are roasted. Caution, however, must be taken when roasting or boiling the cashew nut, because the steam or smoke can cause temporary or permanent blindness.

Tropical Almond—The Indian or tropical almond tree is widely dispersed in all tropical countries, and is found in abandoned fields, gardens, along roadsides, and upon sandy seacoasts. The edible seeds or kernels growing at the tips of the branches are surrounded by a spongy, husk-like covering from one to three inches long. These kernels have an almond-like flavor and consistency.

Fruits provide perhaps the most plentiful food source in the tropics. Those that are found in abundance include bananas and plantains, papayas, Bael fruit, wild figs, breadfruit, and the roseapple.

Bananas and Plantains—Found throughout all tropical and subtropical regions; ripe bananas, such as one finds in the market, rarely occur on the plant because birds, bats, insects, and other creatures get to them first. Plantains are generally dark green, brown, yellow, or orange, and seem like unripe bananas. Green bananas are edible when cooked. Boil, fry, or roast them. Plantains never soften even when ripe, and must be roasted or boiled. The flower buds and tender growing tips at the upper end of the stem of both kinds are also edible. Ripe bananas may be preserved if you slice them and dry the pieces in the sun. The tender growing shoots, soft inner parts of the thick root, and the tender heart of the stem base may be eaten raw or boiled. No wild banana is poisonous.

Banana leaves are tough. Use them for plates, as a wrapping paper substitute, and for roofing materials.

Papaya—This tree grows in all tropical countries, especially in moist areas. It is found around clearings and former habitations, and also in open sunny places in uninhabited jungle areas. The papaya tree

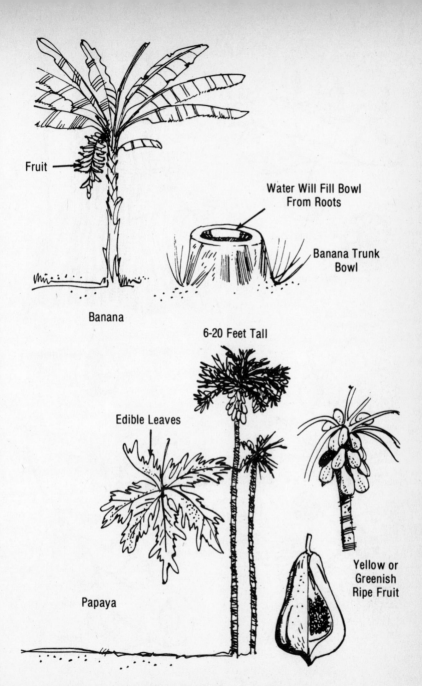

Fruit

Water Will Fill Bowl
From Roots

Banana Trunk
Bowl

Banana

6-20 Feet Tall

Edible Leaves

Papaya

Yellow or
Greenish
Ripe Fruit

Fig. 7.7   Tropical Fruits

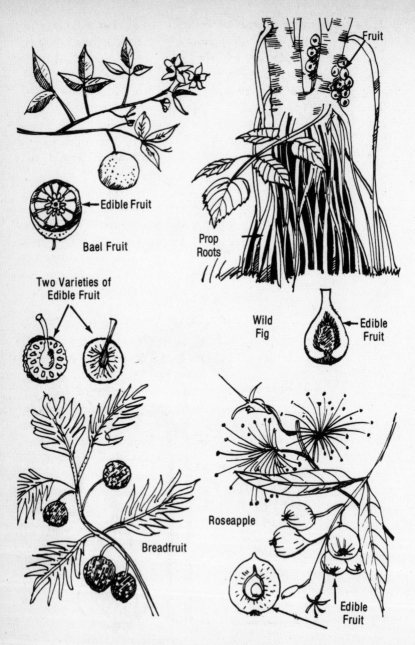

Edible Fruit

Bael Fruit

Two Varieties of
Edible Fruit

Fruit

Prop
Roots

Wild
Fig

Edible
Fruit

Breadfruit

Roseapple

Edible
Fruit

Fig. 7.7   Tropical Fruits

is six to twenty feet tall, with a soft hollow trunk that will break under your weight if you try to climb it. This trunk is rough and the leaves are crowded at the top. The yellow or greenish fruit grows among and below the leaves, directly from the trunk, and is squash-shaped. It is high in vitamin C, and can be eaten raw or cooked. The milky sap of the unripe fruit is a good meat tenderizer if rubbed into the meat. Avoid getting this juice into the eyes—it will cause intense pain and temporary or even permanent blindness. The young papaya leaves, flowers, and stems are also edible. Cook them carefully and change the water at least twice.

Bael Fruit—This fruit grows on small, citrus-type trees and is related to oranges, lemons, and grapefruit. It is found wild in the region of India bordering the Himalaya Mountains, in central and southern India, and in Burma. The tree is eight to fifteen feet tall with a dense and spiny growth, while the fruit is two to four inches in diameter, gray or yellowish, and full of seeds. Eat the fruit when it is just turning ripe, or mix the juice with water for a tart but refreshing drink. Like other citrus fruits, this is rich in Vitamin C.

Wild Fig—Most of the 800 varieties of wild fig grow in tropical and subtropical areas having abundant rainfall; however, a few desert kinds exist in America. The trees are evergreen, with large, leathery leaves. Look in abandoned gardens, along roadways and trails, and in fields for a tree with long aerial roots growing from its trunk and branches. After identifying the tree, look for the fruit, which grows out directly from the branches and resembles a pear. Many varieties are hard and woody and covered with irritating hairs; these are worthless as survival food. The edible type is soft when ripe, almost hairless, and green, red, or black in color.

Breadfruit—The breadfruit is a common tropical tree. It grows up to forty feet tall, with leathery leaves one to three feet long. The fruit is delicious when ripe, and it can be eaten raw, boiled, or grilled over the embers of a fire. To eat it raw, remove the skin first; then pick off the lumps of flesh to separate the seeds, and discard the hard outer covering. To cook, cut in small pieces and boil for 10 minutes. For grilling, scrape the fruit and remove the stalk.

Roseapple—This tree is native to the Indo-Malayan region, but has been planted widely in most other tropical countries. This tree (ten to thirty feet high) also appears in a semi-wild state in thickets, waste places, and secondary forests. It has tapering leaves about eight inches long and greenish-white flowers up to three inches across. The fruit is two inches in diameter, greenish or yellow, and has a rose-like odor. It is excellent fresh or cooked with honey or palm sap.

Seeds and Grains   Rice grows wild throughout the world and is found in the tropics in wet, low-lying areas. Millet, a cousin to rice, is found through much of the Old World (Europe, Asia, Africa, and the Middle East), widely throughout India, and in the warmer parts of South America.

The following four types of seeds and grains are commonly found in tropical environments:

Rice—Rice normally grows in wet areas as a cultivated plant. It is found in tropical, warm, and temperate countries throughout the world; however, wild rice exists in Asia, Africa, and parts of the United States. It is a coarse grass growing to a height of three to four feet, with rough, hard leaf blades one half to two inches wide. The rice grains grow inside a hairy, straw-colored covering out of which the mature grains shatter when ripe. Roast these rice grains, and beat them into a fine flour. Combine the flour with palm oil to make cakes. Wrap these in large green leaves and carry them for future use. Rice may also be prepared by boiling.

Goa Bean—This plant grows in tropical Africa, Asia, the East Indies, the Philippines, and Formosa. The bean is edible, common in the tropics, and found in clearings and around abandoned gardens. It is a climbing plant, covering trees and shrubs, it has a bean nine inches long and leaves six inches long, and it produces bright blue flowers. The mature pods are four-angled with jagged wings. Eat the young pods like string beans; prepare the mature seeds by parching or roasting them over hot coals. Eat the roots raw and the young leaves raw or steamed.

Pearl Millet—Grown widely in India and parts of southeast Asia, Arabia, Egypt, and the warmer parts of Africa and South America, this millet may be found in abandoned fields. The millet grain is pulverized and may be cooked as porridge, pressed into cakes, or used to thicken a sauce or soup. The pearl millet is very high in food value.

Italian Millet—The common millet is found in Korea and north China, but it is widely grown elsewhere in Asia and Africa, especially where the cultivation of rice is not possible. Italian millet is a form of one of our common barnyard grasses. The small yellowish grain is

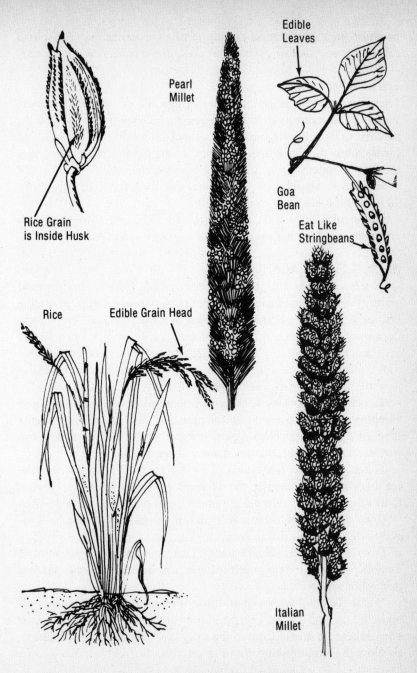

Rice Grain
is Inside Husk

Pearl
Millet

Edible
Leaves

Goa
Bean

Eat Like
Stringbeans

Rice

Edible Grain Head

Italian
Millet

Fig. 7-8   Edible Seeds and Grain

produced in abundance on the seed-head. The grains, pulverized and eaten as a porridge or pressed in cakes, are very high in food value.

FISH
There are very few poisonous fish in tropical fresh waters, but some species are dangerous to handle. These include spiny fish like catfish, toothy fish like piranha, and certain shocking fish like electric eels and catfish. Only the shocking fish cannot be safely converted to food. (See the "Environmental Hazards" section of this chapter.)

Eat only small portions of any fish. If no ill effects occur after about 20 minutes, it is safe to continue eating.

Fish spoil quickly in the tropics and should be eaten soon after they are caught. *Do not eat the entrails or eggs of tropical fish.*

ALONG TROPICAL SHORES
A variety of edible and dangerous marine life exists in and around tropical seawaters and tributaries. For information on tropical marine life, see Chapter Ten ("Sea and Coastal Survival").

Poisoning Fish General fishing information is provided in Chapter Six. However, in the tropics, there are various plants and other materials which natives use for poisoning fish. The active poison in these is harmful only to cold-blooded animals. Fish poisons include:

The derris plant—This woody vine with purple flowers and a seed pod grows in Southeast Asia. Powder the roots and throw them into a stretch of water that has been blocked with a stake "fence" both up and downstream. In a short time, distressed fish will begin rising to the surface.

The Barringtonia tree—This plant (see fig. 7-9) is found near the sea in Malaya, Indonesia, the Philippines, and parts of Polynesia. Crush the seeds and throw them into a pond or other enclosed water.

Coral and seashells—Lime will kill fish. Burn coral and seashells together to obtain this fish poison.

Frogs, Newts, and Salamanders—These small amphibious animals inhabit areas surrounding fresh water in warm and temperate climates throughout the world.

"Fish" for frogs with a small piece of colorful cloth tied to a hook on light line, and a pole. Creep carefully along the shore until you see one. Dangle the lure in front of the frog. It will throw out its tongue to swallow the lure, thinking it's an insect.

Hunt frogs at night with a light when they can be located by their croaking. Club them or snag the larger ones on a hook and line. Eat the entire body after skinning.

Newts and salamanders are found under rotting logs or under rocks in areas where frogs are abundant. All are edible. However, do not eat toads. They have adapted to an existence away from the safety of water by evolving various toxins in their skins. Some of those safe to eat still taste terrible.

Mollusks These include such freshwater invertebrates as snails, clams, and mussels. Most members of this group are edible; however, be sure that the mollusk is fresh and that you boil it. If eaten raw, you may be inviting parasites into your body.

Crustaceans Fresh- and saltwater crabs, crayfish, lobsters, shrimp, and prawns are included in this class. Most of them are edible, but they spoil rapidly and some harbor harmful parasites. Look for them in moss beds and under rocks, or net them from tidal pools. Freshwater shrimp are abundant in tropical streams, especially where the water is sluggish. Here they cling to branches or vegetation. Cook the freshwater forms; eat the salt-water varieties raw, if desired.

Insects Grubs, grasshoppers, termites, and most other insects have food value and are palatable if properly prepared. Use them to provide stock for soup or to add protein to stews.

Reptiles Snakes, lizards, alligators, and turtles are all possible food sources. Freshwater snakes, both poisonous and nonpoisonous, frequent lakes and streams where the water is sluggish and the banks are littered with driftwood and overhanging branches. Although poisonous snakes are edible, use extreme caution when searching for them.

There are only two poisonous lizards in the world: the gila monster and the beaded lizard, found in the arid areas of the American southwest, Mexico, and Central America. They are dangerous, but sluggish and easily avoided, and should not be taken for food unless you are desperate. All other lizards are edible, and many are found in the tropics. The simplest way to catch them is with a noose made from a light wire, string, or fiber. Slowly ease the noose over the lizard's head and pull tight. They will usually sit still while this is being done.

Small alligators and crocodiles are also suitable survival fare. Alligators and crocodiles between one foot and four feet in length are on their own, and manageable if caught on hook and line or speared at

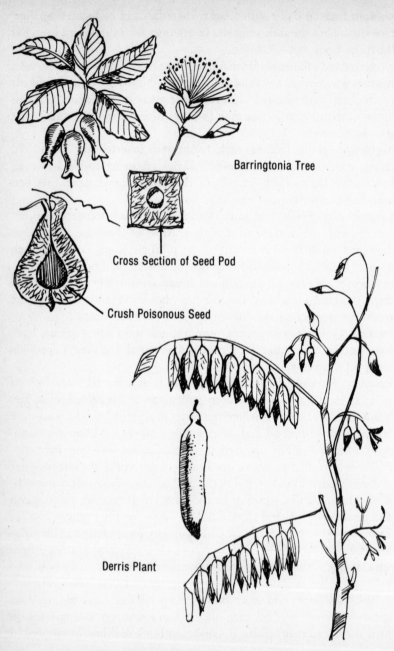

Barringtonia Tree

Cross Section of Seed Pod

Crush Poisonous Seed

Derris Plant

Fig. 7-9   Plants Used to Poison Fish

night by flashlight. A hatchet blow between the eyes will kill these reptiles instantly. Large alligators and reptiles should be heated over a fire before attempting to skin them, as the heat will help loosen the heavier plates covering their backs. After skinning, cut away all the firm white meat and boil or fry.

Freshwater turtles and land tortoises are edible and are found in all but the coldest regions of the world. Club or catch the aquatic turtles on a line. Be careful with the larger snapping ones. They can be safely handled by lifting them by the tail, but beware of their savage bite. In the spring, if you find an aquatic turtle on land, try to locate her nest if she has already spawned. The eggs are nutritious, and—although sometimes gritty in texture—quite flavorful. If the turtle has not yet spawned, she will still be carrying the eggs within her. Save them for food.

FIREMAKING

Wood is plentiful—even if it is wet outside, the heart of dead wood will be dry enough to burn. You can also find dry wood hanging in the network of vines or lying on bushes.

In palm country, you can get good tinder by using the fibers at the bases of palm leaves. The insides of dry termite nests make good kindling.

Green leaves thrown on a fire make a smudge that will help keep off mosquitoes.

Keep spare wood dry by stowing it under your shelter. Dry out wet kindling and fuel near your fire for future use.

CLOTHING

Keep your body covered to prevent malaria-carrying mosquitoes and other pests from biting you, to protect your skin against infection caused by scratches from thorns or sharp grasses, and to prevent sunburn in open country.

Follow these specific suggestions:

1) Wear long pants and shirts with sleeves rolled down. Bind pants legs snugly around boot tops or tuck your pants in the tops of

your socks and tie them securely, or improvise puttees or boots of canvas or parachute cloth to keep out ticks and leeches.

2) Loosely worn clothes will keep you cooler.

3) Wear a mosquito headnet or tie an undershirt or T-shirt around your head. Wear it especially at dawn and dusk.

4) In open country or in high grass country, wear a neckcloth or improvised head covering for protection from sunburn and dust. Move carefully through high grass; some sharp-edged grasses can cut your clothing to shreds.

5) If you lose your shoes or they wear out, you can improvise a practical pair of sandals by using a piece of bark for the soles and a piece of canvas for the uppers and heel straps.

6) Dry your clothing before nightfall to avoid discomfort from cold.

7) Wash clothing, especially socks, daily. Dirty clothes not only rot but may lead to skin disease.

8) Clothes which have been removed should be hung up. If laid on the ground they may collect ants, scorpions, or snakes. Always check footgear and clothing for such "guests" before putting it on.

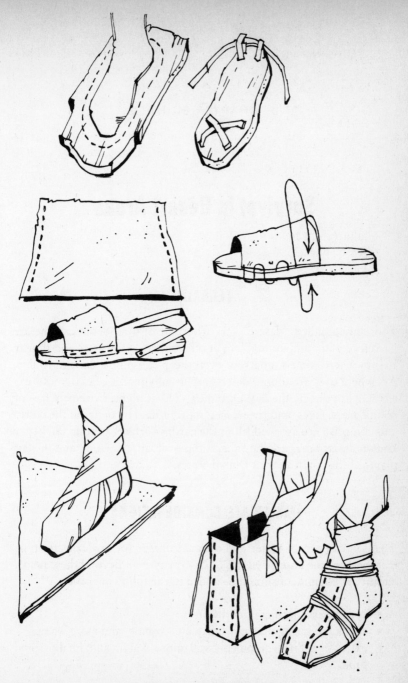

Fig. 7-10   Improvised Boots

CHAPTER EIGHT

Survival in Desert Areas

TERRAIN

Those areas called "desert" vary from salt to sand deserts. Some are barren of plant and animal life; in others there are grasses and thorny bushes where camels, goats, or even sheep can nibble enough to live. Anywhere they are found, deserts are usually places of extremes—extremely hot during the day, extremely cold at night, extremely free of plants, trees, lakes, and rivers. Deserts are found throughout the world and comprise nearly one-fifth of the earth's surface. Among the better known desert areas are the Sahara, the Arabian, the Gobi, and the flat plains of the southwestern United States.

IMMEDIATE CONSIDERATIONS

A gallon canteen of water and a signal mirror (or any reflector-type material) are the bare essentials of desert survival. Beyond these items, additional equipment should be added in the following order:

- A compass, flashlight, and water;
- shade producing material, adequate clothing, and more water;
- extra signaling equipment, still more water, and finally some food.

TRAVEL

When you decide to travel, follow these guidelines:

1) Travel only in the evening, the night, or the early morning.
2) Head for the coast, a known route of travel, a water source, or an inhabited area. Along a coast, perspiration can be conserved by wetting your clothes in the sea.
3) Follow the easiest route possible, by avoiding loose sand and rough terrain and by following trails. In sand dune areas, follow the hard floor valleys between dunes, or travel on dune ridges.
4) Avoid following stream beds to reach the sea, except in coastal desert areas or those areas with large rivers flowing across them. In most deserts, stream beds and valleys lead to enclosed basins or temporary lakes.
5) Check maps for accuracy if possible. Maps of desert regions are often inaccurate, for the terrain is always shifting.
6) Do not try to travel when visibility is bad. Take shelter during a sandstorm. Mark directions with a deep scratched arrow on the ground, a row of stones, or anything else available. Lie on your side with your back to the wind and sleep through the storm. Cover your face with a cloth. Do not worry about being buried by the sand; even in sand dune areas it takes years for sand to cover a dead camel. If possible, seek some shelter on the lee of a hill.
7) Multiply estimations of distances by three, since the absence of features often makes an under-estimate likely.
8) Mirages may often appear during the summer when you are facing the sun, although it is difficult to generalize under what conditions they will occur and what forms they will take.

SHELTER

Shelter from sun and heat and occasional sandstorms is necessary to survive in desert areas. Since materials are not generally available for building a shelter, use these hints:

1) Get some protection from the sun by covering the body with sand. Burrowing in the sand also reduces water loss. Some desert survivors report that the pressure of the sand offers valuable physical relief to tired muscles.

2) If you have a parachute or other suitable cloth, dig out a depression and cover it. In rocky desert areas, or where desert shrubs, thorn shrubs, or tufted grass hummocks grow, drape a parachute or blanket over the rocks or shrubs.

3) Make use of both natural and manmade desert features for shade or shelter—a tree, rock, cairn, or cave. The wall of a dry stream bed may provide shelter, but, after a cloudburst, your home may become suddenly flooded. Wadi-banks—along dried riverbeds, valleys, and ravines—are particularly good places to look for caves.

4) Utilize native shelter when practicable. Survivors reported during World War II that even desert tombs were used for protection against the elements.

ENVIRONMENTAL HAZARDS

WATER SCARCITY

The importance of water cannot be overemphasized. It is essential, regardless of how adequate your fond supply may be. In hot deserts, a minimum of 1 gallon per day is needed. If perspiration is controlled and travel is accomplished during the cool desert night, you can move about 20 miles on that gallon. During the heat of the day, you might travel 10 miles. Follow these guidelines for conserving water:

1) Keep fully clothed. Clothing helps control perspiration by not letting the perspiration evaporate so fast that you miss some of its cooling effect. You may feel cooler without a shirt, but you perspire more and sunburn is probable.

2) Do not hurry. You will survive longer on less water if perspiration is kept down.

3) Do not use water for washing unless you have a sure and lasting supply.

4) Do not gulp water; drink in small sips. Use water only to moisten the lips if the supply is critical.

5) Keep small pebbles in your mouth or chew grass as a means of relieving thirst. Prevent water loss by breathing through your nose. Do not talk.
6) Use salt only with water and only if there is an ample supply of water. Salt causes increased thirst.

Locating Water   A minimum of 4 quarts of water per day may be difficult to find unless a well or oasis is nearby. Since wells are the source of most water in the desert, the best way to locate them is to travel along a native or well-worn animal trail. There are other ways of locating water in the desert. Use these guides:

1) Along sandy beaches or desert lakes, dig a hole in the first depression behind the first sand dune. Rain water from local showers collects there. Stop digging when you find damp sand and allow the water to seep in. Deeper digging may produce salt water.
2) Scoop out a shallow well wherever damp sand is found.
3) Dry stream beds often have water just below the surface. It sinks at the lowest point on the outside of a bend in the channel as the stream dries tip. Dig along these bends for water.
4) Desert natives often know of lingering surface pools in low places. They cover them in various ways, so look under likely brush heaps or in sheltered nooks, especially in semiarid and brush country.
5) Dew might be a source of water, particularly in some regions. Cool stones or any exposed metal surface will serve as a dew condenser. Wipe off the dew with a piece of cloth and wring it out. Dew evaporates soon after sunrise and should be collected before then. During a heavy dew, you should be able to collect about a pint an hour.
6) Look for cisterns or natural tanks that may be located behind rocks, in gullies or side canyons, and under cliff edges. Often the ground near them is solid rock or hard-packed soil. In the absence of such markers, search for the water source by observing animal droppings.
7) Watch for flights of birds, particularly at sunset and dawn. Birds circle water holes in true desert areas. The sand grouse of Asia, crested larks, and zebra birds visit water holes at least once a day; parrots and pigeons must live within reach of water.

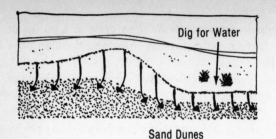

Dig for Water

Sand Dunes

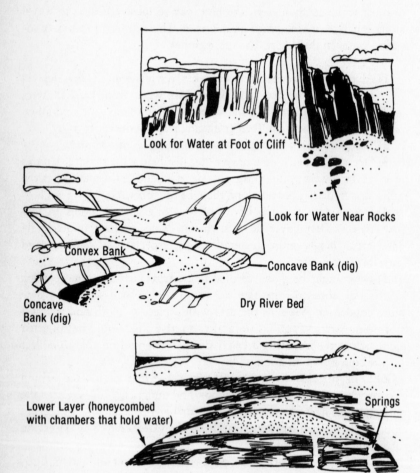

Look for Water at Foot of Cliff

Look for Water Near Rocks

Convex Bank

Concave Bank (dig)

Concave Bank (dig)

Dry River Bed

Lower Layer (honeycombed with chambers that hold water)

Springs

Porous Lava

Fig. 8-1   Hidden Desert Water Sources

8) In the Gobi desert, do not depend on plants as a source of water. The wild desert gourd may be considered a water source on the Sahara. The large barrel cactus of the American desert also contains considerable moisture which can be squeezed out of the pulp. For further information about the barrel cactus see "Finding Water" section of Chapter Six ("Basic Survival Skills").

9) Some desert plants have their roots near the ground surface. The Australian "water tree," desert oak, and blood wood are some examples. Pry these roots out of the ground and cut them into 24- to 36-inch lengths. Remove the bark and suck out the water.

10) Other water-yielding plants include the traveler's tree of Madagascar, the umbrella tree of tropical West Africa, and the baobab tree of northern Australia and Africa.

Disregard most romantic stories of poisoned wells. These tales generally originate because of bad-tasting water that contains salt, alkali, or magnesium. Desert waters, by nature of their location, are generally better filtered and more pure than water found in most cities. However, treat all water. (Boil or use chlorine tablets.) This is especially important in native villages and around civilization.

SANDSTORMS

Sandstorms are not a serious hazard if you use common sense. Do not travel in a dust- or sandstorm. Lie down with your back to the wind and cover your eyes. Mark the direction in which you were traveling with stones, a line of deep holes, or any other means available: Sandstorms can alter the landscape and obscure directional landmarks. Do not worry about getting "buried alive" by a sandstorm. Sandstorms do not pose the same threat as blizzards.

LIZARDS

No lizards found anywhere in the world are poisonous except the gila monster and the beaded lizard, which are found only in the American southwest, Central America, and Mexico. Because of the sluggishness of these lizards, they constitute little danger. Both are found only in desert areas.

HEALTH HAZARDS

DEHYDRATION

In desert heat, thirst alone is not a strong enough sensation to indicate the amount of water needed. If only enough water is consumed to satisfy thirst, it is still possible to suffer dehydration. Drink plenty of water whenever it is available, particularly at mealtime. If you drink only at mealtimes, you tend to dehydrate between meals, and while you feel restored to normal after eating and drinking, you will feel tired because of the loss of energy due to dehydration. Rationing yourself to 1 or 2 quarts of water a day is inviting disaster (at high temperatures), as small amounts of water do not prevent dehydration. Ration perspiration, not water.

Efficiency lost by dehydration is restored quickly by drinking water. No permanent harm is caused by dehydration up to 10 percent of body weight. At 150 pounds, 15 pounds can be lost through perspiration, provided you drink enough water later to gain it back. Cold water will cause stomach distress if swallowed too rapidly. You can survive a 25 percent body weight reduction through dehydration if air temperature is 85°F or cooler. At temperatures in the nineties, and up, 15 percent body weight loss through dehydration becomes dangerous.

The symptoms of dehydration are thirst and general discomfort at first, followed by an inclination to slow down any movement, and a loss of appetite. As more water is lost, you become sleepy, your temperature rises, and by the time you lose 5 percent of body weight, you begin to feel nauseated. By the time 6 to 10 percent of your body weight is lost, symptoms increase in this order: dizziness, headache, difficulty in breathing, tingling in your arms and legs, dry mouth, body turning bluish, speech indistinct, and being unable to walk.

There is no substitute for water in preventing dehydration and keeping your body operating at normal efficiency. Alcohol, salt water, gasoline, blood, or urine only increase dehydration. In an emergency, it is possible to drink brackish water (water with about half as much salt as seawater) and obtain a net gain of moisture for the body. Any liquid containing a higher percentage of waste can only harm the body's cooling system.

EXPOSURE TO THE SUN

Exposure to the desert sun can be dangerous. It can cause three types of heat collapse:

Heat Cramps—The first warning of heat collapse usually is cramps in leg and belly muscles. Keep the patient resting; give him salt dissolved in water.

Heat Exhaustion—The patient is first flushed, then pale, sweats heavily; has moist, cool skin; and may become delirious or unconscious. Treat the patient by placing him in the shade, flat on his back. Give him salt dissolved in water—two tablets to a canteen.

Heat Stroke—Heat stroke may come on suddenly. The face is red, skin hot and dry. All sweating stops. There is severe headache; pulse is fast and strong. Unconsciousness may result.

Treat the patient by cooling him off. Loosen his clothing; lay him down flat, but off the ground, in the shade. Cool by saturating his clothes with water, and by fanning. Do not give stimulants.

SUN GLARE

Though sand is not as white as snow, the concentration of ultraviolet light is greater in warm regions of the world, and the danger of sun glare can be equal to that of snow blindness. Use the same protective measures against sun glare as you would against snow blindness (see Chapter Nine). To protect the eyes against solar retinitis (direct glare from the sun), do not look at the sun and keep the eyes shaded with the brim of a hat or a "turban," with cloth extended to cover the sides of the face.

FOOD

In general, food is difficult to find in the desert. However, food is secondary to water, and you may do without it for several days without any ill effects. Ration food from the beginning. Eat nothing during the first twenty-four hours, and do not eat unless you have water.

ANIMALS

Animals are rare in the desert. Rats and lizards may be your only diet. Ungulates are sometimes found in open desert country, but they are difficult to approach. The most common desert animals are small ro-

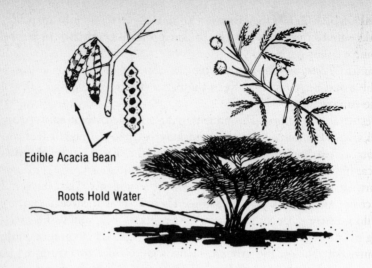

Edible Acacia Bean

Roots Hold Water

Fig. 8-2   Dual Purpose Acacia

dents (rabbits, prairie dogs, rats), snakes, and lizards, which are usually found near brush or water. Handle all reptiles with care, for some desert species are poisonous. Look for land snails on rocks and bushes.

Some birds are found on the desert. Try kissing the back of the hand with a sucking sound to attract them. Sand grouse, bustards, pelicans, gulls, and even ducks have been seen over some desert lakes. Use a baited deadfall or a hook and gorge to catch them.

The lake or water hole where pelicans and gulls are found contains fish. That's why the birds are there. Furthermore, human settlements are located wherever fish-producing waters can be found in otherwise arid latitudes.

EDIBLE PLANTS

Where there is water, there are usually plants. Some desert plants look dry and unappetizing, but others are succulent and edible. Try all soft parts above the ground—flowers, fruits, seeds, young shoots, and bark. During certain seasons, some grass seeds or bean bushes may be found. These beans grow on acacia trees that are often thorny and similar to mesquite or catclaw of the southwestern United States. All grasses are edible, but the ones found in the Sahara or Gobi are neither palatable nor nutritious. Dates may be available in the African deserts, southwestern Asia, and some parts of India and China. Try any plant found. The following are descriptions of some of the more common edible desert plants.

Mescal   This plant exists in Europe, Africa, Asia, Mexico, and the West Indies. It is a typical desert plant, but also grows in moist tropical areas. The mescal, when fully grown, has thick, tough leaves with stout, sharp tips borne in a rosette. In the center is a stalk that rises like a candle to produce a flowering head. This stalk or shoot is the edible part. Select plants having flowers not fully developed; roast the shoot. It contains fibrous, molasses-colored layers that taste sweet.

Wild Desert Gourd   Also a member of the squash family, this creeping plant grows abundantly in the Sahara Desert, Arabia, and on the southeastern coast of India. It produces a vine eight to ten feet long that runs over the ground and a gourd that grows to about the size of an orange. The seeds are edible roasted or boiled. The flowers also can be eaten, and the water-filled stem shoots may be chewed.

Prickly Pear   This plant is native to America, but grows in many desert and seacoast areas of the world, except the Arctic. It is found in the southwestern United States, Mexico, South America and along the shores of the Mediterranean. It has a thickened stem about an inch in diameter, which is full of water. The outside is covered with clusters of very sharp spines spaced at intervals, and the plant grows yellow or red flowers. This plant can be mistaken for other kinds of thick, fleshy cactus-like plants, especially in Africa. The spurges of Africa look like cacti, but contain a milky, poisonous juice. The prickly pear never produces a milky juice. The egg-shaped fruit growing at the top of the cactus is edible. Slice off the top of the fruit, peel back the outer layer, and eat the entire contents. Also edible are the prickly pear pads. Cut away the spines and slice the pad lengthwise into strips like string beans. Eat them raw or boiled.

Wild Pistachio Nut   About seven types of wild pistachio nuts grow in desert or semi-desert areas surrounding the Mediterranean, in Asia Minor, and in Afghanistan. Some plants are evergreen while others lose their leaves during the dry season. The leaves alternate on the stem and have either three large leaves or a number of leaflets. The nuts are hard and dry when mature. Eat them after parching over coals.

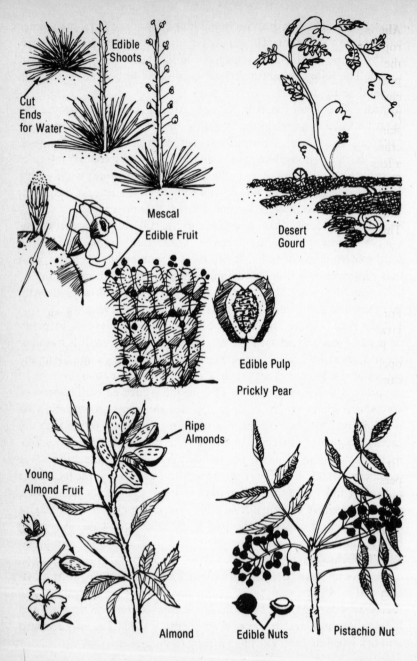

Edible Shoots

Cut Ends for Water

Mescal

Edible Fruit

Desert Gourd

Edible Pulp

Prickly Pear

Ripe Almonds

Young Almond Fruit

Almond

Edible Nuts

Pistachio Nut

Fig. 8-3   Edible Desert Plants

Almond Wild almonds grow in the semi-desert areas of southern Europe, the eastern Mediterranean area, Iran, Arabia, China, Madeira, the Azores, and the Canary Islands. The almond tree resembles a peach tree, and sometimes grows to forty feet tall. The fruit, found in clusters all over the tree, looks somewhat like a gnarled, unripened peach, with its stone (the almond) covered with a thick, dry, wooly skin. To extract the almond nut, split the fruit down the side, and crush open the hard stone. Gather and shell them in large quantities as a food reserve.

General Caution with Respect to Desert Plants: Avoid all desert plants with milky juice. They will cause much irritation to exposed skin surfaces. A white ooze running from a broken stem is a warning: This milky juice is poisonous if ingested.

FIREMAKING

For general information on firemaking, see Chapter Six ("Basic Survival Skills").

Palm leaves and similar fuel are found in or near an oasis. On the open desert, however, use any bit of dead vegetation found. Dried camel dung can be used when there is no wood available.

CLOTHING

To protect yourself against direct sunlight, excessive evaporation of perspiration, and the many annoying desert insects, follow these guidelines:

1) Keep your body and head well covered during the day. Wear long pants and a long-sleeved shirt.
2) Wear a cloth neckpiece to protect the back of your neck from the sun.
3) If sunglasses are not available, make "slit goggles" from a strip of fabric tied around or over the head.
4) If some clothing must be left behind to lighten your load, keep enough for protection against cold desert nights.
5) Wear clothing loosely.

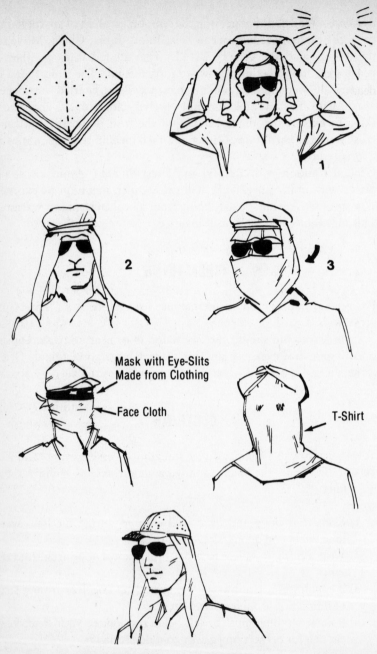

Mask with Eye-Slits
Made from Clothing

Face Cloth

T-Shirt

Fig 8-4   Protective Desert Headgear

6) Open clothing only when well shaded. Reflected sunlight can cause sunburn.

Protection of your feet may mean the difference between life and death. The following hints are helpful:

1) Keep sand and insects out of your shoes and socks, even if frequent stops are necessary to clean them out.
2) If you do not have boots, make some spiral puttees out of any available cloth. To do this, cut two strips, each 3 or 4 inches wide and about 4 feet long. Wrap them spiral-fashion upward around the top of your shoes. This will keep out most sand.
3) Remove your shoes and socks while resting in the shade. Use caution when doing this because your feet may swell, making it difficult to get the shoes back on.
4) Do not try to walk barefooted. Hot sand will blister your feet. Also, a barefoot hike across a salt flat or mire will result in alkali burns.
5) Improvise clogs to protect your feet around camp. Nail a strap to pieces of wood and attach them to your feet. Protect the tops of your feet from the sun.
6) If there are vehicles available which can be scavenged, improvise a pair of sandals out of the sidewall of an old tire. It is better, however, to reinforce the soles of your shoes with heavy cloth, if it is only the worn condition of the soles that is causing you trouble.

CHAPTER NINE

Survival in Cold Climates

TERRAIN

Landscape varies very widely in subarctic and arctic lands, and includes practically every gradation between mountain peaks and glaciers and the flattest of plains. Summer surface conditions in both the Arctic and Subarctic also include practically every gradation between the extremes of the hardest and roughest surfaces and the softest and wettest surfaces. In winter, frozen lakes, rivers, and swamps become the highways of the north.

In the Arctic, summer temperatures above 65°F are common except on glaciers and frozen seas. Temperatures in winter sometimes reach -70°F, and range up to a maximum of 32°F. An even more violent zone than the Arctic is the Subarctic. Summers are short with temperatures sometimes reaching 100°F. Winters are the coldest in the Northern Hemisphere, ranging to extremes of -60°F to -80°F in North America, and even lower in Siberia. In winter, the wind, when accompanied by low temperatures, chills man quickly. Wind-chill is the combined cooling effect of air, temperature, and wind on a heated body, rather than the temperature as recorded by a thermometer. Many areas of the Far North receive less precipitation in the form of rain or snow than the dry southwestern United States. The average annual precipitation in the Subarctic, except near seacoasts, is the equivalent of ten inches of rainfall, while in the Arctic it is generally five inches or less.

The odds of surviving in these areas of extremes are better than you think. The proper attitude—a will to survive—and a few elementary precautions will increase your chances. Learn to work with nature, not against it.

IMMEDIATE CONSIDERATIONS

Protection from the cold is an immediate and constant problem. Therefore, a fire should be started and a shelter constructed as soon as possible.

TRAVEL

If you must move, the secret of successful travel in cold weather areas is adequate protective clothing, sufficient food, rest, and a steady pace. Neither food and rest nor a steady pace is enough to permit survival without adequate protective clothing in the extreme cold and wind of the Arctic. Unless properly equipped, a better course of action in the Arctic would be to seek shelter immediately, build a fire, and "hole up" to conserve heat and energy. When weather and health conditions permit, make every effort to contact friendly inhabitants. If a hostile local population forces you to move or practice security measures, survival techniques must be varied accordingly. Evaluate climatic and physical hazards and hostile attitudes, and decide which presents the most immediate threat. When stranded in friendly territory, remain close to disabled aircraft or vehicles, and prepare to signal search-and-rescue aircraft when they arrive in your area.

Your direction should be determined by your location and the terrain. In mountainous or wooded areas, it is advisable to follow rivers downstream toward populated areas. Siberia, where rivers flow northward, is an exception. Populous areas lie south in Siberia and European Russia.

When traveling cross-country, try to follow the contour of the land; however, note that valley floors are frequently colder than slopes and ridges, especially at night. Head for a coast, a major river, or a known point of habitation.

*   *   *

During the arctic winter, there are four basic requirements that must be met to travel successfully:

Determining direction—Know your exact departure location and the location of your objective. Constellations as well as arctic "visual aids" can be used to determine direction. For instance, snowdrifts are usually on the lee or downward side of protruding objects like rocks, trees, clumps of willows, or high banks. By determining the cardinal points of the compass and from them the direction of the drifts, the angle at which you cross them will serve as a check point in maintaining a course. The snow on the south side of the ridges tends to be more granular than on the north. Other aids to determining direction are willows, alders, and poplars, which tend to lean toward the south, and coniferous trees, which are more bushy on the south side. Use these aids as a means of *very rough* estimation.

Physical stamina—Survival is synonymous with "take your time." Without proper equipment and in poor weather, there are few people who possess sufficient stamina to travel successfully in the Arctic.

Clothing—Sufficient clothing is necessary to remain dry and must be appropriate for the season and terrain.

Food, fuel, and shelter—These necessities must be available in sufficient quantities to sustain you, or you must have the equipment necessary to obtain them. More food is required when traveling than when inactive. Therefore, if food is limited and little game is present in the area to be traveled, make certain that travel is the only solution.

Obstacles to summer travel are dense vegetation, rough terrain, insects, soft ground, swamps and lakes, and unfordable rivers. Winter obstacles are soft snow, dangerous river ice, severe weather conditions, scarcity of native food, and "overflows" (stretches of water covered only by thin ice or snow). When traveling in the Arctic you should:

1) Avoid traveling during a blizzard.
2) Take care when crossing thin ice. Distribute your weight by lying flat and crawling.
3) Cross streams when the water level is lowest. Normal freezing and thawing action may cause a stream level to vary as much as

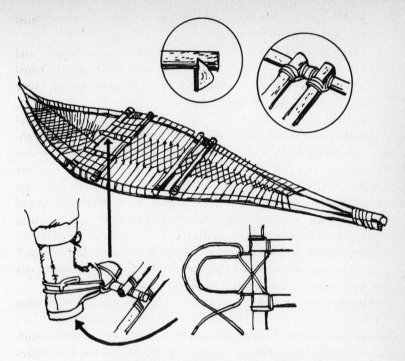

Use Parachute Suspension Lines, Wire, or Cord

Fig. 9-1   Improvised Snowshoes

two to two and a half meters per day. This may occur at any time during the day, depending on the distance from a glacier, the temperature, and the terrain. This variation in stream level should also be considered when selecting a campsite near a stream.

4) Take into consideration the clear arctic air, which makes distance estimation difficult. Under-estimates of distances are more frequent than over-estimates.

5) Avoid travel in "whiteout" conditions, when lack of contrast makes it impossible to judge the nature of the terrain.

6) Always cross a snow bridge at right angles to the obstacle it crosses. Find the strongest part of the bridge by poking ahead

with a pole or ice-axe. Distribute your weight by wearing snow-shoes or skis or by crawling.

7) Make camp early to have plenty of time to build a shelter.
8) Consider rivers—frozen or unfrozen—as avenues of travel. When rivers are frozen, they frequently are clear of loose snow, and the ice makes for easier travel.

The ability to travel successfully over snow-covered terrain is directly related to the following factors:

1) The ability to use, and the availability of, over-snow equipment. If you possess some previous training in cross-country skiing and equipment is available, travel on skis is recommended. In most snow conditions and over most types of terrain, skis provide the speediest and most energy-saving mode of travel. Use of snow-shoes requires hardly any previous training, but your speed will be much slower and travel more exhausting.
2) In deep, loose snow, skiing is exhausting, and if you have a choice of equipment, snowshoes are recommended. A light crust on the surface of the snow, however, prevents skis from sinking and provides for speedy and easy skiing. A crust hard enough to support a man makes travel on foot feasible, but even then, if equipment is available and you possess the necessary proficiency, travel on skis is recommended.
3) Improvise equipment for travel if snow is loose and deep. Make snowshoes of willow or other green wood, using a wood separator and thong, wire, cord, or suspension lines. If wreckage of an aircraft is available, make snowshoes out of seat bottoms, inspection plates, and other parts of salvage.

SHELTER

Protection is necessary to survive in winter cold. During the summer, however, shelter may be needed only as protection against insects and the sun. Suitable natural shelter may be available in caves, rock overhangs, crevices, bushy clumps, or natural terraces. Material in Chapter Six ("Basic Survival Skills") on building shelters is suitable for constructing arctic and subarctic summer shelters.

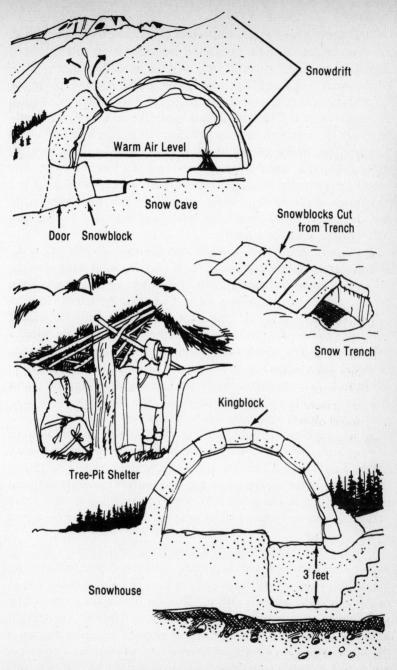

Snowdrift

Warm Air Level

Snow Cave

Door   Snowblock

Snowblocks Cut
from Trench

Snow Trench

Kingblock

Tree-Pit Shelter

Snowhouse

3 feet

Fig. 9-2   Arctic Shelters

Ideal sites for shelter differ in winter and summer. The choice during winter depends upon protection from the wind and cold, and nearness to fuel and water. In mountainous areas, the danger of avalanches, rock falls, and floods must be considered. A site should not be selected under large trees, because frozen branches, commonly known as "widow makers," tend to fall in a spear-like manner. A site should be chosen during the summer months which is relatively free of insects and near food and water. As protection against insects, it is better to select a site on a breezy ridge or in a place that receives an onshore breeze. Sites in forests and near rapid streams are desirable. Since you may be in a situation where concealment is the most important factor, the site should afford good observation and have one or two concealed routes of escape from it.

The type of shelter built depends upon the materials and time available. Regardless of the type, however, the arctic shelter must serve the principal purpose of holding the heat of a fire, or that of the body, around you so that you remain warm. Body heat is retained longer in still air. For this reason, build the shelter small, snug and windproof. It must also provide adequate ventilation to prevent asphyxiation. Make a hole at the top of the shelter to allow carbon monoxide gases and smoke to escape. Leave a small crack near the bottom to let fresh air enter.

On pack ice or snow-covered barren land, dig in, or build up the ice and snow. Building up is sometimes easier than digging in.

Of several kinds of improvised shelters, perhaps the simplest is provided by a hard-packed snowdrift hollowed out to accommodate one or more men. Even a hole in the snow provides temporary emergency shelter. This type of shelter is sometimes difficult to prepare because of the hardness of the packed snow, and frequently is impossible without proper tools. Seek out drifts near trees, as snow will be less firmly packed around and under low-hanging branches that have been covered by the drift.

A house built of snow blocks is a useful semipermanent refuge for two or more survivors. The construction of a snowhouse, however, requires considerable experience and practice. The placement of blocks in this type of structure is critical, since the blocks are supported by three impinging corners—the bottom corners and the top. The support of three corners, aided by the downward slope of the inclined plane, is the only "mystery" in snowhouse construction. Crevices between blocks are stuffed with triangular pieces of snow and finished off with soft snow gently rubbed in with a mittened hand. The snow functions as a binder and becomes stronger than the original snow blocks. A drawback in constructing this type shelter is the need for tools—knife, saw, or axe. It has been proven by Eskimos that with a knife you survive—without it you need a miracle.

ENVIRONMENTAL HAZARDS

BLIZZARDS
Blizzards and gale-force winds are common in the arctic region, and often combine to form giant snowdrifts that can bury a man in a very short time. Do not attempt to travel in blizzard conditions. Pay careful attention to weather conditions at all times. In other regions of the world, weather conditions can cause great inconvenience; in the arctic regions, inattention to weather conditions can kill.

ROCKFALLS
Rockfalls are caused by the thawing out of snow and ice that binds loose rocks together.

AVALANCHES
Any snow-covered slope of an angle greater than 20° presents the danger of an avalanche. After a snowfall, avoid all steep slopes. If caught in an avalanche, try to keep your head or some part of your body above the surface. An avalanche is like a moving "snow river" and a swimming stroke will help keep you on the surface. Move about in a horizontal position. The danger from an avalanche is suffocation. If completely covered by snow, try to create an air pocket around your head. If you sense you are about to be covered by snow, place your hands on top of your head, which creates room for maneuvering.

QUICKSAND
Glacial streams from melting snow create sandbars that are saturated with water. Avoid these areas. If walking on wet sand, test the firmness of the ground before proceeding. If you start to sink throw yourself flat and spread-eagle. Use smooth and slow swimming strokes or an "alligator crawl" to reach firmer ground.

FLOES, SLUSH, AND MELTING ICE

Arctic and subarctic springs present the hazard of melting ice and breakups. Attention, concentration, slow movement, and common sense will help you avoid this hazard.

If you fall through the ice, spread your arms immediately. It is difficult to climb back on the ice, but not impossible. Using your legs and arms for leverage, attempt to "roll out" of the water. If the ice continues to break, edge your way toward shore or firmer ice.

ICEBERGS

Icebergs, which are constantly in the process of melting, melt faster at the bottom or below the water's surface. Icebergs become top-heavy and can topple over. Avoid pinnacled icebergs. For shelter at sea seek out low, flat-topped icebergs.

WHITEOUT

Whiteout is caused by overcast skies against snow-covered ground, making it difficult to judge distance and the nature of the terrain. Under whiteout conditions, distances are more often under-estimated than over-estimated. Avoid traveling during these periods.

MAGNETIC COMPASS

Magnetic compasses respond sluggishly in the polar regions and are much less reliable in determining direction. If using a compass, don't rely on one reading. Take several readings and average the results.

POISONOUS PLANTS

Most plants in polar regions are edible. The water hemlock is, in most cases, the only seriously poisonous plant, but buttercups and some mushrooms should be avoided. *The water hemlock is one of the world's most poisonous plants.* It can be distinguished by where it grows (always in wet ground) and by the following characteristics—a hollow, partitioned bulb at the base of the hollow stem, spindle-shaped roots, and a strong, disagreeable odor which is especially noticeable in the root and bulb. It is especially abundant in marshes near southern beaches and around marshy lakes in interior river valleys. It is never found on hillsides or dry ground.

All berries in the polar region are edible with the notable exception of the baneberry, which is poisonous.

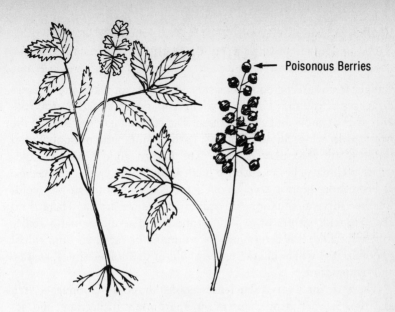

Poisonous Berries

Baneberry

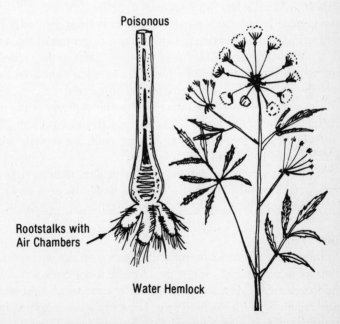

Poisonous

Rootstalks with
Air Chambers

Water Hemlock

Fig. 9-3   Poisonous Plants of the North

HEALTH HAZARDS

Danger from insects, poisonous snakes, plants, animals, and diseases decreases as you move north or south from the equator. Physical hazards such as snow and cold increase. The chief danger to health in the Arctic is freezing. Snow blindness, carbon-monoxide poisoning, and sunburn are secondary dangers. The key to good health in cold-weather climates lies in effective prevention, not in cures or remedies.

Protection against cold is one's first consideration in any cold-weather survival situation; it requires immediate action. There is no absolute temperature or exposure time that determines man's ability to survive cold; it is determined by a number of variables—individual tolerance, the wind-chill factor; wet cold or dry cold—as well as time and temperature.

There are three survival defenses against the cold—clothing, shelter, and fire. See pertinent chapters for appropriate protections and actions.

COLD WATER AND WET COLD

Submersion in icy water rapidly drains heat from the body. The only protection against freezing in cold water is to get out of the water—as soon as possible and in any way possible. Even in the coldest water, you will have a minimum of 30 minutes to reach a shore or a raft, before the body has lost sufficient heat to prove fatal.

Wet cold, from perspiration or wet clothing, dramatically increases the loss of body heat. If you begin to perspire, loosen clothing to allow the skin to dry. If wet clothing is very cold, ice crystals will form, which can be beaten off with a branch.

In all cold-weather situations, pay particular attention to protecting the extremities—the hands, the feet, the head, the ears, and the nose. Half your body heat can be lost through these areas of the body.

FROSTBITE

Prolonged exposure to extreme cold causes frostbite, or the freezing of tissue in localized areas. It is caused by a lack of circulation of blood in the frozen area. Constriction of vessels by extreme cold prevents circulation of blood in the involved area. The result is tissue anoxia and death of the tissue. Symptoms of frostbite include coldness in the affected area, followed by numbness. There is no particular pain to frostbite, and it can occur without your knowing it. The skin at first is red, then pale or waxy white. The injured part has no feeling while it is frozen. In severe frostbite, edema and hemorrhage may occur when thawed.

For treatment of frostbite, follow these rules:

1) *Carefully* remove wet or tight clothing from frostbitten area. *Do not* forcibly remove frozen shoes or clothing.
2) Warm the frostbitten area with another part of the body or someone else's body. Place frostbitten hands against your chest, between your thighs, or under the armpits.
3) If possible, thaw the frozen area in water warmed to slightly above body temperature.
4) Do not smoke, as nicotine may further constrict blood vessels.
5) *Do not apply snow or ice.*
6) *Do not exercise or massage the frozen area.*
7) Frostbite may cause blistering and peeling just as in sunburn. Do not break or open blisters.
8) Check exposed skin often. To neglect frostbite is to invite gangrene.

TRENCH FOOT
Also called immersion foot, trench foot is caused by prolonged exposure to cold and wetness and by diminished circulation. Trench foot is worsened by keeping the feet still or by wearing tight-fitting boots. Symptoms include uncomfortable coldness of the feet, clumsiness in walking, tingling and aching, and a redness and swelling of the feet.

Trench foot can be prevented by avoiding prolonged inactivity of the feet and by keeping them warm and dry. Treat trench foot as you would frostbite.

HYPOTHERMIA
This results when the body is losing more heat than it can generate. The symptoms are uncontrollable shivering, speech and thought difficulty, and skin that has turned blue and puffy.

Take action *immediately;* hypothermia can be fatal. Run, jump around, move limbs to generate body heat. Drink any hot liquid available. Get to a warm shelter or fire as soon as possible.

Insufficient rest and improper diet greatly contribute to the risk of freezing to death. Guard against fatigue.

SNOW BLINDNESS

Snow blindness is caused by brilliant reflections or glare from the snow. It can occur even on foggy or cloudy days. The first warning of snow blindness comes when variations in the level of the ground can no longer be detected; this is followed by a burning sensation of the eyes. Later the eyes hurt when exposed to even weak light. Prevention is the best cure, but if stricken, complete darkness is the best medicine. Wear sunglasses at all times. If none are available, use a piece of wood, leather, or other material, with narrow eye slits cut in it. Glare is reduced if the nose and cheeks are blackened with soot.

SUNBURN

Arctic sunburn is possible on both cloudy and sunny days, and it should be considered a dangerous possibility.

Animal tallow rubbed on the skin helps to prevent sunburn. A stubby beard also protects against sunburn. If sunburned, keep the affected part moist with animal oils, and stay out of the sun.

CARBON-MONOXIDE POISONING

The danger of suffocation by carbon monoxide is a great hazard in the Arctic. To one subjected to extreme cold, the desire to get warm and stay warm often overrules common sense. Depend on your clothing to keep you warm—not a fire. In temporary shelters, use fires and heaters only for cooking. Any type fuel burning for as little as half an hour in a poorly ventilated shelter can produce a dangerous amount of odorless carbon-monoxide fumes. Ventilation can be provided by leaving the top of the shelter open, providing another opening (for fresh air) close to the ground (door flap partially open), or by building a draft tunnel. The tunnel is buried in the floor and has an opening under the stove. The draft of the stove draws fresh air from the outside of the tent into the tunnel. If you are in a shelter and begin to feel drowsy, get into fresh air. Move slowly and breathe evenly. Above all, remove the source of the fumes. If several men are sleeping in a closed, heated shelter, one man should stay awake to watch for indications of carbon monoxide. A *yellow flame* means carbon monoxide is being formed.

If a person is overcome by carbon-monoxide poisoning, move him to fresh air and begin resuscitation. It is safe to administer mouth-to-mouth respiration to a carbon-monoxide victim.

BLEEDING

Bleeding is affected by cold weather: The blood runs thinner and takes longer to clot. Also, circulation of blood creates warmth throughout the body, and therefore loss of blood becomes critical.

Wounds should be bandaged only tightly enough to check the bleeding, and loosened when bleeding has been controlled. If possible, keep the body and the limbs comfortably warm. If bleeding continues, elevate the bleeding area and apply pressured dressing.

As a last resort (for severe bleeding from an arm or leg) or when blood is spurting from the wound, apply a tourniquet immediately. Once applied, the tourniquet must be left on, despite the probable loss of a limb due to freezing, since no replacement for lost blood will be available. *It is better to lose a limb than to lose a life.*

HYGIENE

In the Arctic, just as in other areas, good care of the body is essential. Try to keep clean. If body washing is not possible, at least try to keep the face, hands, armpits, crotch, and feet clean. Every night before going to sleep, remove the boots, dry the feet, and rub and massage them. Make provisions for drying the boots by holding them over a campfire. Do not sleep in wet socks. Put them inside the shirt next to the body to dry. If you have no fire and your shoes are wet when you go to bed, stuff them with dry grass or moss in order to speed drying.

Do not be afraid to expose the body when disposing of body wastes. The areas exposed will not stay exposed long enough to hurt you. Bury the garbage and body wastes at a distance from your shelter and water supply.

WATER

Thirst is a problem in cold regions during the winter. In order to conserve fuel for other purposes, the survivor often deprives himself of drinking water which might have been obtained by melting ice and snow. The time and energy required to chop and gather ice for water also tends to limit the supply. A survivor may become dangerously dehydrated in cold arctic regions just as easily as in hot desert areas.

Water can be obtained by cutting a hole in the ice or by melting ice. Approximately 50 percent more fuel and time are required to obtain a given amount of water from snow than from ice.

It is safe within limits to eat snow, but observe these precautions:

1) Allow snow to thaw sufficiently to be molded into a long "stick" or "ball." Do not eat snow in its natural state—it will cause dehydration instead of relieving thirst.
2) Do not eat crushed ice, as it may cause injury to your lips and tongue.
3) If you are hot, cold, or tired, eating snow will tend to chill your body.
4) There are usually many ponds, lakes, and streams from which to obtain water during the summer. Depressions on icebergs and floes contain fresh water during the warmer months, as do some protected coves and inlets where water from melting snow has accumulated. But all water, regardless of its source, should be boiled or treated with chemicals, if practicable. Pond water, although brownish in tint, is usually drinkable. The milky water of a glacial stream can be drunk after sediment is strained out or allowed to settle. Old sea ice, recognized by its bluish color and rounded corners, is drinkable. New sea ice is too salty.

Any surface that absorbs the sun's heat can be used to melt ice and snow—a flat rock, dark tarpaulin, or signal panel. Arrange the surface so that the water drains into a hollow or container.

FOOD

The chances of finding different types of food in the Arctic depend on the time of year and the place. Arctic shores normally are scraped clean of all animals and plants by winter ice; but even north of the timberline, where mice, fish, and grubs are not readily available, enough food can be found to keep you alive. Meat should never be fried, as this method of cooking eliminates the fat necessary for good health in cold climates.

STORAGE AND PRESERVATION
If a large animal is killed or an abundance of smaller game is found, you should store or preserve some of the meat for future use. During cold weather, freezing fresh meat or fish preserves it. Freeze the meat as quickly as possible by spreading it around outside your shelter.

During summer months, meat and game should be kept in a cool shady place. A hole in the ground will substitute for a refrigerator. Cure meat by hanging it in strips in trees where the wind and sun can reach it. To be out of the range of most flies, meat should be hung at least 15 feet from the ground.

In some areas it may be necessary to protect your supplies from scavengers like bears or wolverines. This can be accomplished by hanging your supplies from a sapling that will stand about 15 feet from the ground, and pulling the sapling upright with a rope thrown over the branch of a nearby tree. The sapling will be too small for the bear to climb and the animal won't understand how to cut the rope tied some distance away so the weight of the cache will bring the sapling to the ground.

FISH
There are few poisonous fish in arctic waters. But some fish, like the sculpin, lay poisonous eggs; the black mussel may be poisonous at any season, and its poison is as dangerous as strychnine. Also avoid arctic shark meat. In coastal streams and rivers, salmon moving upstream to spawn may be plentiful and delicious, but their flesh deteriorates as they travel farther from the sea, making them poor food farther inland.

In the North Pacific and North Atlantic, extending northward into the Arctic Sea, the coastal waters are rich in all seafoods. Grayling, trout, whitefish, and ling are common to the lakes, ponds, and the arctic coastal plains of North America and Asia. Many larger rivers contain salmon and sturgeon. River snails or freshwater periwinkles are plentiful in the rivers, streams, and lakes of northern coniferous forests. All coastal waters are equally rich in sea life.

Fish can be speared, shot, netted, hooked, caught by hand, or

Fig. 9-4   An Automatic Fisherman

stunned by a rock or a club. Cod will swim up to investigate strips of cloth or bits of metal or bone. Cod may also be caught through a hole in the ice. A good net can be made out of stout twine or from the inner strands of parachute suspension lines (if available). For full-grown salmon or trout, the meshes should be about 2 inches square. A scoop net with very fine mesh is required for smaller fishes. This can be made out of a pliable willow branch and netting or twine.

Fish can be netted or clubbed more easily in a narrow part of the stream. You can narrow a shallow stream by building a fence of stones, stakes, or brush from either bank. Fish can be stranded by diverting a stream. To strand coastal fish when the tide goes out, pile up a crescent of boulders on the tidal flats, scooping out the area within.

LAND ANIMALS
Many large land animals, such as deer, caribou, wild reindeer, musk ox, moose, elk, mountain sheep, goat, and bear, are found in arctic and subarctic regions.

Small tundra animals that are found during winter and summer include rabbits, mice, lemmings, ground squirrels, and foxes. However, rodents generally hibernate in the winter. During the summer, squirrels are abundant along sandy banks of larger streams. Marmots, much like woodchucks, are found in the mountains among rocks, usually near the edge of meadows. Farther south, where there are trees, the porcupine is found and can be easily shaken from a tree and clubbed. This animal feeds on bark. Tree limbs stripped bare are good signs of its presence. Handle a porcupine with care and only after it is dead.

Hunting is generally better during the early morning and late evening when the animals are moving to and from feeding and bedding grounds and water. Use large-caliber rifles on large game. Large animals in the Arctic are fairly easy to stalk, and they supply much food and fuel. Their skins are also very useful. To successfully hunt land game, you should know some of their characteristics:

1) Caribou or reindeer may be very curious. It is possible to attract them near enough for a shot by waving a cloth and moving slowly toward them on all fours.

2) Imitating a four-legged animal may also cause a wolf to come closer to a hunter.

3) Moose are usually found in heavy brush. Cows with calves and rutting bulls may charge. In the winter, moose can be spotted by climbing a hill or tree and looking for the animal's "smoke" (condensed body vapor which rises like the smoke of a small campfire).

4) Mountain goats and sheep are wary and hard to approach. They can be surprised, however, by getting above them and moving quietly downwind while they are feeding with their heads lowered.

5) Musk oxen leave cattle-like tracks and droppings. When alarmed, they group together and remain in that position unless approached; then one or more bulls may feign a charge toward the intruder.

6) Bears are surly and dangerous. A wounded bear is extremely dangerous and should not be followed into cover. The polar bear is a tireless, clever hunter with good sight and an extraordinary sense of smell. Polar bears will hunt and eat people.

7) Rabbits often run in circles and return to the same place where they were frightened. If the animal is running, whistle. It may stop. Snares are efficient for catching smaller land game.

8) During winter and spring, marine mammals—seals, walruses, and polar bears—are found in the frozen pack ice and on floes in open water. Like land animals, these sea animals may supply food, implements, fuel, and clothing.

9) Seals should be stalked with care. Keep downwind and avoid sudden moves. A white camouflage suit helps. Advance only when the animal's head indicates that it is sleeping. If a bearded seal appears to move, stand up quickly and shout; the seal may become frightened and lie still, allowing you to shoot or spear it. This species rests on floe ice and is found in numbers where ice is broken by current holes and tidewater cracks. Do not eat large amounts of the liver of any marine mammal or shark; their high vitamin A content may cause illness.

10) Walruses are found on floe ice and generally must be approached by boat. However, they are among the most dangerous animals of the Arctic and should generally be avoided.

11) Polar bears are found in practically all arctic coastal regions, but they rarely appear on land. Avoid them if possible. *Never eat polar bear meat unless it is cooked.* It is usually riddled with parasites.

BIRDS

The breeding grounds of many birds are in the Arctic. Ducks, geese, loons, and swans build their nests near ponds on the coastal plains during the summer, and they provide an abundant source of food. Grouse and ptarmigan inhabit mountainous terrain and brush-covered areas in arctic and subarctic regions. Sea birds may be found on cliffs or small islands off the coast. Their nesting areas can often be located by their noisy flights to and from feeding grounds. Sea birds, as well as ravens and owls, can be used for food.

In winter, owls, ravens, and ptarmigans are the only birds available. Rock ptarmigans are easily approached, travel in pairs, and are very tame. Although hard to locate because of their white protective coloring in winter, they are an easy source of food because they can be killed with stones, a slingshot, or even a club. Willow ptarmigans, which gather in large flocks, are easily snared. They are found among willow clumps in creek bottoms and wetland edges.

All arctic birds go through a two- to three-week flightless period in the summer while they are moulting. When birds are moulting, they can be run down. Fresh eggs are among the safest of foods, and *they are edible at any stage of embryo development.*

Birds may be caught in a variety of ways—netted with an improvised net made from cord, with a baited hook attached to a fishing line, by a simple box trap, or, in the case of half-grown birds, by hand.

PLANT FOODS

Many plants in polar regions are edible. The water hemlock is virtually the only poisonous plant, but buttercups and some mushrooms should be avoided. Some of the more common edible plants found in cold climates are:

Lichens—Lichens have possibly the greatest food value of all arctic plants. Some lichens contain a bitter acid that may cause nausea and

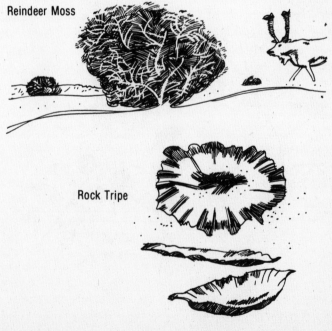

Reindeer Moss

Rock Tripe

Fig. 9-5 Lichens

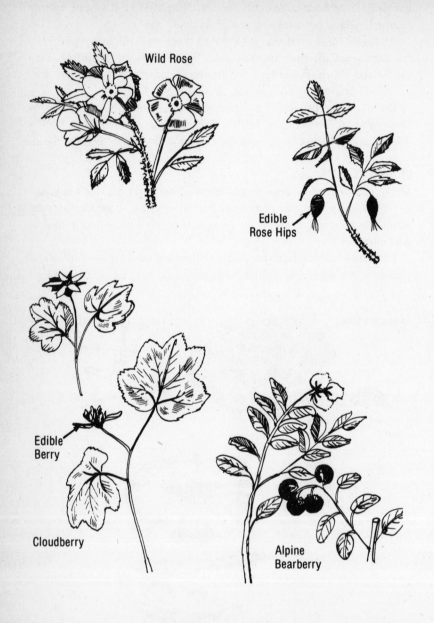

Fig. 9-6   Edible Berries

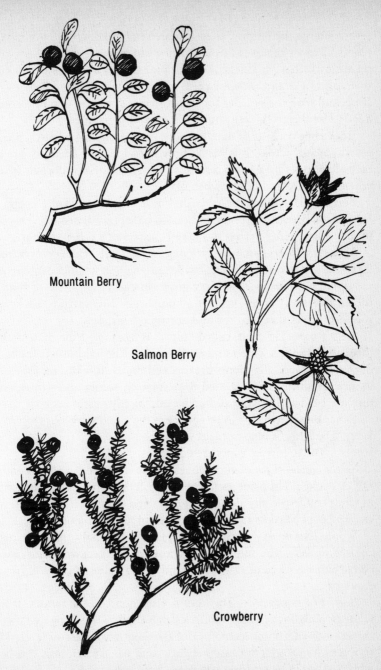

Mountain Berry

Salmon Berry

Crowberry

Fig. 9-6   Edible Berries

severe internal irritation if they are eaten raw. Soaking and boiling the plants in water removes the acid. They can be made crisp by roasting them slowly in a pan. Lichens can be prepared as a powder by soaking them overnight and allowing them to dry. Pound the dried lichen with stone and soak the powder for a few hours. Then boil it until it forms a jelly. Use this to thicken soups and stewed vegetables.

Rock tripe consists of thin, leathery, irregularly shaped discs, one to several inches across. It is black, brown, or grayish. The discs are attached to rocks by a short central stalk. This nutritious lichen is soft when wet, hard and brittle when dry.

Berries—The salmonberry is the most important of the northern berries. All berries except the poisonous baneberry are edible. This latter plant has its red berries in stalked clusters of a dozen or more.

Mountain berry—A low creeping shrub with leathery evergreen leaves. It has red, single berries which are high in vitamin content.

Alpine bearberry—This berry grows in clusters of three or four at the end of short stems, on a trailing shrub with shreddy bark and rounded leaves that turn red and are almost tasteless.

Wild Rose—The fruit, called "hips," is available from midsummer through fall (often winter and early spring). The wild rose is found in dry woods, especially along streams and bluffs. It is distinguished by its prickly shrub. Hips are red to orange. In spring and winter, rose hips are hard and dry but still edible and highly nutritious.

Other berries which can be eaten are the cloudberry and the crowberry. The latter is blue or black in color.

Roots   The following roots are edible:

Sweet vetch—This plant supplies the licorice root, which is edible raw or cooked. The plant itself is common in the north and can be found in sandy soil, especially along lake shores and streams. It has pink flowers. The cooked roots taste like carrots but are even more nourishing.

Wooly lousewort—This is a low plant with wooly spikes or rose-colored flowers. The sulphur-yellow root is a large, sweet root and is edible either cooked or raw. It is found in dry tundra regions of North America.

Bistort or knotweed—This root is also found on the tundra. It has white or pink flowers which form a slender spike. The elongated leaves are smooth-edged and come out of the stem near the soil level. The root is rich in starch but tastes slightly acid when eaten raw. It is best when soaked in water for a few hours and then roasted.

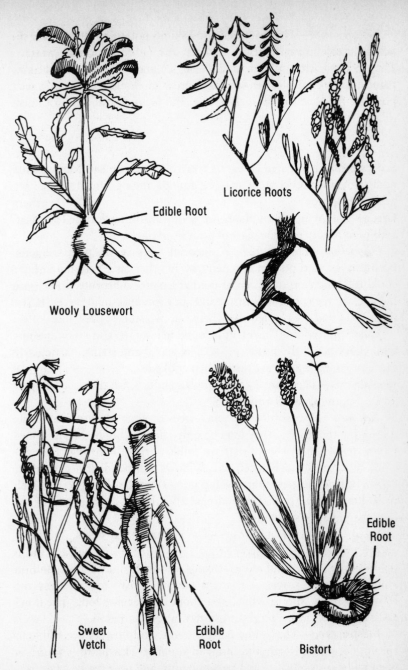

Fig. 9-7   Edible Roots

Licorice root—This root and the Eskimo potato have root-like tubers available in early spring, summer, and fall (occasionally winter). They become stringy and inedible in summer. The flowers of this plant are pink-purple, pea-like, and grow in elongated clusters; seed pods are flat, one to two inches long, and formed of several roundish joints.

Scurvy can be prevented by eating fresh plants and meat. Many plants high in vitamin C content may be found, among which are scurvy grass and spruce.

Greens   Many northern plants are good substitutes for the leafy vegetables normally eaten as part of your everyday diet.

Dandelion—This plant is a potential life-saver in polar regions. Both leaves and roots can be eaten raw, but they taste better after light cooking. Dandelion roots can be used as a coffee substitute. To prepare them, clean the roots, split them, and cut them into small pieces. Roast them and grind the roasted roots between two stones. Brew like coffee.

Marsh marigold—This plant is found in swamps and along streams and comes out early in the spring. The leaves and stems, particularly those of young plants, are tasty when cooked.

Seaweeds—These are a good supplement to a fish diet (see Chapter Ten, "Sea and Coastal Survival").

Willow—These shrubs or small trees are found throughout the world. On the tundra, they may be only a few inches high. They have young, tender, leafy shoots that are edible during the spring. They become bitter and tough when old. Willows can be identified by their flower or fruit clusters, that develop into caterpillar-like spikes an inch or so long. They are found in almost all habitats, and are one of the richest sources of vitamin C.

Dwarf fireweed (Rock Rose)—The young leaves, stems, and flowers are edible in spring, become tough and bitter in summer, and die in the fall. They are found along streams, sandbars, lake shores, and on alpine and arctic slopes. The stems are one to two feet tall, and the leaves are thick, almost white, and about three inches long. The flowers are rose to purple, large and showy, with four petals.

Tall fireweed—The young leaves, stems, and flowers are edible in spring, becoming tough and bitter in summer. This plant is found in open woods, on hillsides and stream banks, and near sea beaches. It is

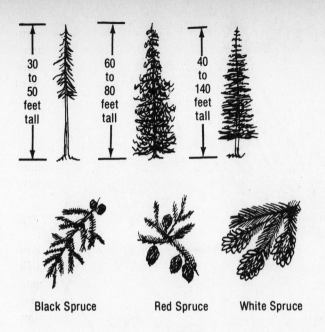

Black Spruce   Red Spruce   White Spruce

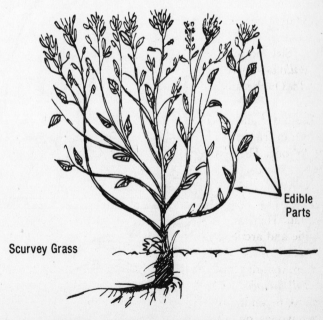

Edible Parts

Scurvey Grass

Fig. 9-8   Anti-Scurvy Plants

Dandelion

Willow

Tall Fireweed

Fig. 9-9   Edible Greens

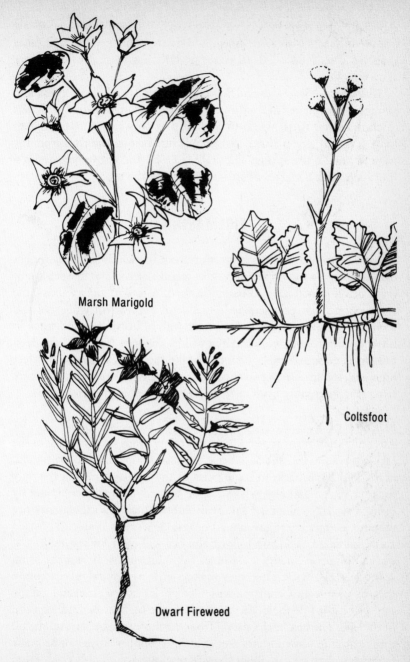

Marsh Marigold

Coltsfoot

Dwarf Fireweed

Fig. 9-9   Edible Greens

especially abundant in burned-over areas. It is similar to the dwarf fireweed, but its leaves are green, and its stems are reddish and taller than the dwarf fireweed. It grows as tall as a man; its flowers are showy pink.

Coltsfoot—The leaves and flowering shoots are edible in spring and summer. The plant is found in moist woods and wet tundra. It has thickish leaves, is triangular in outline, and grows three to ten inches long. It is dark green above and fuzzy white below, and rises from the ground only in the spring. The stalk is fleshy and cobwebby, about a foot high, with a cluster of creamy flowers at the top.

FIREMAKING

Select a site which affords protection from the wind. Standing timber or brush makes a good windbreak in wooded areas, but in open country protection will have to be improvised. A row of snow blocks, the shelter of a ridge, or a scooped-out side of a snowdrift will serve as a windbreak on the ice pack. A circular wall of brush, cut and stuck in the snow or ground, works well in willow country. A ring of evergreen boughs is good in timber country. Make the windbreak about 4 feet high and, except for an entrance, let it encircle the fire. Protect the fire from water dripping from melted snow on overhanging tree limbs.

FUEL
Anything that burns is good fuel, and many kinds are available in the far north: animal blubber, lichens, exposed lumps of coal, driftwood, grass, and birch bark. In some parts of the Arctic, however, the only fuel may be animal fats, which can be burned in a metal container by using a wick to ignite the fat. Seal blubber makes a satisfactory fire without a container if gasoline or heat tablets are available to provide an initial flame. A square foot of blubber will burn for several hours. Burned blubber cinders are edible. Eskimos burn seal blubber using seal bones as a wick. First, they make a little pyramidal pile of bones; then they saturate a small rag with oil from a piece of blubber, light the rag, place it inside the bone pile, and lay the blubber carefully on top of the pile. The heat melts the oil from the piece of blubber, and the oil drips onto the heated bones and ignites. A blubber stove can be made from an empty tin can about the size of a one-pound coffee tin. First,

punch the tin (including the bottom) full of small holes. Then build a wick from a piece of canvas, dry tundra moss, or a piece of sealskin with the hair side up. The wick is impregnated with the oil, lighted, and placed under the tin can, and blubber is placed on top of the tin can. The oil dripping from the blubber into the heated air inside the can will burn hotter than it does when blubber is placed directly on a wick without a tin can.

Fuel in subpolar regions is usually wood. The driest wood is found in dead, standing trees. In living trees, branches above snow level are the driest. In the tundra regions, split green willows and birch into pieces and burn them.

CLOTHING

The basic survival problem in polar regions is keeping warm. Cold allows no time for trial and error experimentations. *You must do the right thing first.* Your clothing and how it is worn may determine how long you survive.

In cold environments, body heat is lost to the surrounding air. Clothes in cold climates should serve one purpose—to keep the body heat from escaping by insulating it against the cold outside air. Clothing of the normal layer type, put on or removed as needed, helps to control body temperature. The inner layers of insulating clothing hold warm air in, while the wind-resistant outer clothing keeps cold air from penetrating the clothing and carrying heat away.

Some important facts about clothing and its relationship to you are:

1) Tight clothing reduces the zone of still air near the body and prevents free circulation of the blood.
2) Perspiration is dangerous because it reduces the insulating value of clothing by replacing air with moisture. As the moisture evaporates, it cools your body. Avoid overheating by removing layers of clothing and by opening your clothing at your neck, wrists, and front.
3) Hands and feet cool more quickly than other parts of the body and require special care. Keep your hands under cover as much as possible. They can be warmed by placing them next to the warm flesh under your armpits, between your thighs, or against

your ribs. Feet, because they perspire more readily, are difficult to keep warm. You can be comfortable, however, by wearing shoes large enough for at least two pairs of socks, and by keeping your feet dry. A warm, double sock can be made by putting one pair of socks inside another and filling the space between them with a layer of dry grass, moss, or feathers.

4) It may be necessary to improvise some articles of clothing like boots, especially if your hoots are too small to allow for extra socks. A piece of canvas and some cord are all you need. The canvas seat of a vehicle can be used when improvising boots; so can the seat pad cover of a pilot's parachute.

NATIVES

There are relatively few natives in the Arctic. Those found in North America and Greenland are friendly. Eskimos live mostly along the coasts. Indians are found along rivers and streams of the interior. Arctic natives, like yourself, have little enough to eat, so do not take advantage of their hospitality. Offer payment when leaving.

CHAPTER TEN

Sea and Coastal Survival

There are many reasons why you may find yourself faced with the problem of surviving at sea. The ship or aircraft that you are aboard may be sunk or downed by such hazards as storms, fire, or collision, or by war. Survival depends largely on the rations and equipment available, the use you make of them, and your skill and ingenuity.

Today all lifeboats, rafts, and aircraft contain equipment adequate for most emergencies at sea. Know this equipment, where it is stowed, and how to use it. Make certain that fishing tackle is included. Before and during a long ocean voyage, familiarize yourself with the lifeboat emergency equipment list, abandon-ship procedures, and command procedure aboard the lifesaving craft.

However, it is possible—even likely—that you will find yourself without a proper raft or equipment kit and in a position to improvise. In the case of a ditched plane or shipwreck, seek out the largest floating piece of wreckage material available. Once secured, attempt to transfer any salvageable life-sustaining articles such as containers of food, water, communications gear, etc.

SEA SURVIVAL: IMMEDIATE CONSIDERATIONS

DITCHING

If you are in an aircraft that lands at sea, do not try to inflate a raft or your life vest inside the plane. Once outside, with the raft inflated, attach a line between the raft and the aircraft as long as it floats. Transfer all useful and easily portable communications gear, and extra food and water, but keep one person stationed by the line at all times to cut the retaining line if and when necessary.

OIL ON WATER

If fire breaks out on the vessel or aircraft after it is ditched, and the oil spreads on the surrounding sea, swim or paddle the life raft quickly upwind of the fire zone. If you are in the water and surrounded by patches of burning oil, swim in the direction (generally upwind) most likely to lead you clear of the hazard. Dive and swim under narrow trails of burning oil. If confronted by a wide wall of fire, dive under and as you emerge, thrash your arms about to provide an "eye" in the storm, take a breath, submerge, and repeat this procedure until you are well clear of the hazard.

SURVIVAL SWIMMING

If you have a life preserver, you can stay afloat for an extended period. For easier swimming, some air can be released from the life preserver and the back stroke used for propulsion through the water. Even without a preserver, a man who knows how to relax in the water is in very little danger of drowning, especially in salt water. Trapping air in your clothes will help to buoy you up in the water and give you a rest. If you are in the water for long periods, you will have to rest from treading water. If you are an experienced swimmer and able to float on your back, do so if the sea conditions permit. Always float on your back if

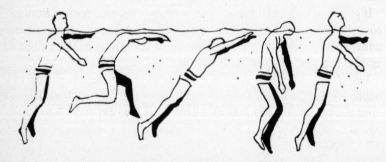

Fig. 10-1   Survival Swimming

238

possible. If you can't float on your back or if the sea is too rough, practice the following technique:

1) Resting erect in the water, inhale.
2) Put your head face down in the water and stroke with your arms.
3) Rest in this face-down position until you feel the need to breathe again.
4) Raise your head, exhale, support yourself by kicking your arms and legs, inhale, and then repeat the cycle.

TRAVEL AND SHELTER

THE RAFT

Knowledge of the care and proper handling of any raft is important, as it will be both your shelter and your mode of transportation until either you are rescued or you reach shore.

If you are in a rubber raft, proper inflation is important. If the main buoyancy chambers are not firm, use the pump or mouth inflation tube. Inflate cross seats if they are provided, unless there are injured men who must lie flat. Do not overinflate. Make chambers well-rounded but not drum-tight. On hot days, release some air to compensate for the expanding hot air.

Keep the raft as dry as possible. To keep the raft balanced, put weight in the center. If there are two or more persons aboard, let the heaviest sit in the middle. Leaks in rubber rafts are more likely to occur at valves, seams, and on underwater surfaces. They can be repaired with plugs provided with the raft.

If you've hoisted a sail or rigged an improvised one with canvas and cross sticks, never tie down both lower corners at the same time. A sudden gust of wind will tip the raft. Provide some method of releasing one corner of the sail, or hold it if necessary.

Take every precaution to prevent the raft from turning over. In a rough sea, keep an anchor off the bow (front) and sit low. Do not stand up or make sudden movements. In extremely rough weather, have a spare sea anchor available in case the first one is lost.

If the raft is capsized, toss the righting rope (on multi-place rafts) over the bottom. Move to the other side of the raft; place one foot on the flotation tube and pull. If there is no righting rope, reach across and grab the lifeline on the far side. Slide back into the water, pulling the raft back and over. Most rafts have righting handles on the bottom. Twenty-man rafts need no righting, since they are identical on both sides.

To board a one-man raft, climb in from the narrow end, remaining as nearly horizontal as possible. This is also the proper way to board multi-place rafts when alone.

If there are several rafts afloat, they should be tied together. Tie the stern of the first raft to the bow of the second and rig a sea anchor to the stern of the second raft. Use a line approximately 25 feet long between rafts; adjust the length of the line so that when the raft is at the crest of a wave, the sea anchor will stay in a trough.

All men in a raft should serve on watch except the injured or sick. Arrange that one man is on lookout duty at all times. Rotate this duty at intervals no longer than 2 hours. The lookout should watch for signs of land, evidence of potential rescuers, and signs of chafing or leaking of the raft. He should be lashed to the raft.

Wind and current will drift the raft. Use them if they are moving in the intended direction of travel. To use the wind, inflate the raft fully and sit high. Take in the sea anchor and rig a sail. Use an oar as a rudder. If the wind is against you, lower the sea anchor and huddle low in the raft to offer less wind resistance. Do not sail the raft unless you know land is near. Currents should not cause a problem, because in the open sea they seldom move more than six to eight miles a day.

SIGNALING

There are many ways to signal while surviving at sea—radios, flares, dye markers, mirrors, lights, whistles. Do not use your signaling device unless you are sure they will be seen or heard. In the absence of signaling equipment, churn the water with paddles or oars.

Radio—If the lifeboat or raft is radio-equipped, follow the instructions for signaling and operating that come with it.

Signaling mirrors—Especially useful for catching the eye of airborne rescuers.

Lights and flares—Instructions for the use of signal pistols, flares, smoke signals, and distress lights (normal lifeboat equipment) are found in the watertight containers holding this equipment. The lantern and flashlight are valuable night lights and can be used for signaling.

Signal flags—The best method of displaying the signal flag is for two men to stretch it taut by holding the ends and moving it to present a flash of color. Signal flags flown from a mast can be seen for great distances.

Boat cover—When using the tarpaulin or boat cover as a canopy, display it with the painted side up. Wave it when a rescue craft is in sight.

Whistle—Use the whistle during periods of poor visibility to attract surface vessels or people ashore or to locate other rafts when they become separated in the night.

SIGNS OF LAND

Indications by Clouds Clouds and certain distinctive reflections in the sky are the most reliable indications of land. Small clouds hang over atolls and may hover over coral patches and hidden reefs. Fixed clouds or cloud crests often appear around the summits of hilly islands or coastal land. They are recognized easily because moving clouds pass by them. Other aerial indications of land are lightning and reflection. Lightning from a particular region in the early hours indicates a mountainous area, especially in the tropics. In polar regions, a sharply defined patch of brightness in a gray sky is a sign of an area of ice floe or shore ice in the midst of open water.

Indications by Sound Sounds from land may originate from the continued cries of sea birds from a particular direction, from ships or buoys, and from other noises of civilization.

Other Indications of Land An increase in the number of birds and insects indicates nearby land. Leafy seaweeds, usually found in shallow water, may also indicate the nearness of land. Bay ice, which is usually smoother, flatter, and whiter than pack ice, indicates a nearby frozen inlet, especially if the pieces are close together. Land is also indicated by odors that may be carried on the wind for long distances. This fact is important when navigating in heavy fog or at night. An increase in floating driftwood or vegetation means nearby land.

ENVIRONMENTAL HAZARDS

SHARKS

These large aquatic predators are curious and will investigate objects in the water. It is unlikely they will attack unprovoked, but they *are* likely to attack a wounded and bleeding swimmer. Any flow of blood should be stopped as quickly as possible. If necessary to stop bleeding, make a tourniquet from a shoelace or a piece of clothing.

Sharks live in almost all oceans, seas, and river mouths. Records show, however, that most shark attacks have occurred in waters with temperatures ranging from 65°F upward. There is no shark problem in areas of colder water.

Actually, the chances of being attacked by a shark are very small. Even in warm oceans where attacks are possible, the risk can be reduced by knowing what to do and how to do it, and by the use of shark repellent, if available.

Protective Measures Against Sharks
In the water—

1) Keep clothing and shoes on.
2) If in a group threatened or attacked by a shark, bunch together and form a tight circle. Face outward so you can see an approaching shark. If the sea is rough, tie yourselves together. Ward off attack by kicking or stiff-arming the shark.
3) Stay as quiet as possible. Float to save energy and to expose less of your body. If you have to swim, use strong regular strokes; do not make frantic irregular movements.
4) Stay away from schools of fish.

If a shark moves in wide, elongated circles, it is only curious. If the circle tightens and the shark begins to move in a quick agitated fashion, he is preparing to attack. If a single shark threatens at close range:

5) Use strong regular swimming movements; try feinting toward the shark—it may be scared away.
6) Do not swim away directly in the shark's path; face the shark and swim quickly to one side or the other.
7) Make loud sounds by rhythmically slapping the surface of the water with cupped hands. Also, let out a loud and sharp yell with your head underwater. Sharks are attracted by noise and movement, but, once you are threatened, a shout may scare it away.
8) At close quarters, in a showdown, use a knife to stab the shark on the snout, eyes, gills, or belly.
9) As a last resort, kick or stiff-arm a shark to push it away, or grasp a side fin and swim with the shark until you can veer away from it.

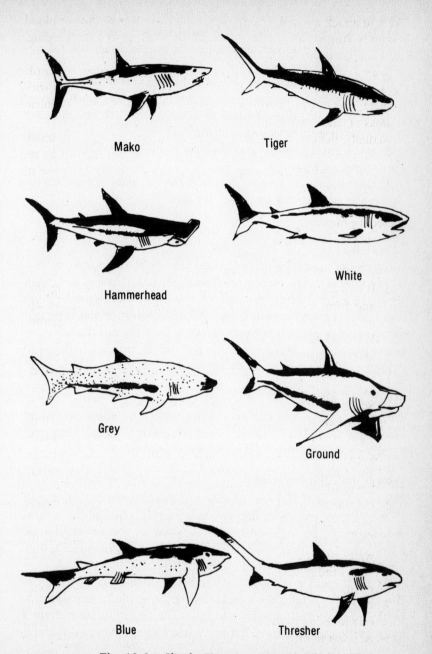

Mako

Tiger

Hammerhead

White

Grey

Ground

Blue

Thresher

Fig. 10-2   Sharks Known to Attack Man

On a raft—

1) Do not fish from the raft when sharks are nearby. Abandon hooked fish if a shark approaches. Do not clean fish over the water when sharks are sighted.
2) Do not throw waste overboard if sharks are around.
3) Do not dangle hands or feet in water, especially when fishing.
4) If a shark threatens to attack or to damage the raft, discourage it by jabbing snout or gills with the oar.
5) Fire a pistol (if one is available) above the shark—the noise may frighten it away.
6) Look for sharks around and under the raft before going into the water or attempting to beach the raft.

GIANT RAY

Giant rays or mantas, which are found in tropical waters, may be mistaken for sharks. A swimming ray curls up the tips of its fins, and, when seen from water level, the fins somewhat resemble the fins on the backs of two sharks swimming side by side. Closer observation will show that the animal is a ray and not two sharks; if both the fins disappear together periodically, it is a ray. In deep water, all rays are harmless to swimmers; however, some are dangerous if stepped on in shallow water.

ELECTRIC RAY

The electric ray is found both in open water and along sandy and muddy bottoms. The "torpedo," as it is sometimes called, can give a paralyzing shock; however, it is rarely encountered.

FISH POISONOUS TO EAT

There are hundreds of species of poisonous fish found in tropical waters. However, most poisonous fish have many similar physical characteristics. Generally they are odd-shaped—box-like or almost round—and have hard skin (often covered with bony plates or spines), tiny mouths, small gills, and small or absent belly fins.

Many tropical poisonous fish are described by their names. The cowfish, for example, has a rigid, boney, "cow-like" back and two horn-shaped protrusions above its eyes. The file fish is characterized by its sandpaper skin and a narrow, barbed spine that extends above its eyes.

Fish that are toxic may be inherently poisonous, or only poisonous when their diets include toxic materials.

Fish that should never be eaten are the puffers, the porcupine fish, and the molas or sunfish. All these are easily recognized, since the porcupines and puffers swell or puff up when disturbed, and the molas look like a large head with no tail section. Some Japanese consider certain species of puffers a delicacy when prepared in the proper manner; however, deaths occur in spite of all precautions taken. In the United States, from Georgia north, a species of puffer (*Spheroides maculatus*) is eaten with pleasure and without ill effects by many people. However, for all practical purposes, every puffer should be treated as poisonous.

Several species of fish secrete a foam or slime from glands in their skin. This is toxic if ingested or allowed to contact the eyes or other sensitive areas of the skin. Examples of *fish with poisonous secretions*

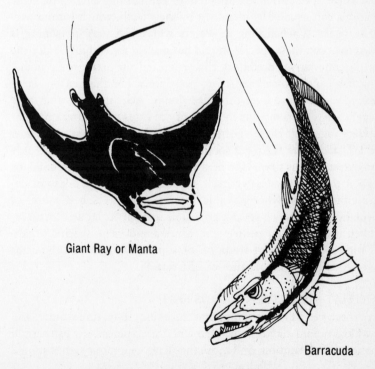

Giant Ray or Manta

Barracuda

Fig. 10-3   Dangerous Marine Life

are the soapfish, toadfish, hagfish, moray eel, and boxfish (or cowfish). These fish must be carefully skinned if they are to be used as food.

Finally, for a variety of reasons, the liver, intestines, gonads, brain, and associated visceral organs may be poisonous in otherwise edible species. Therefore, clean unfamiliar fish carefully to prevent any possible contamination of the edible flesh with visceral toxins. If these organs, or any part other than the flesh are to be eaten, they should be given the edibility test unless the particular species is known to be entirely nontoxic during *all* seasons. Never cook a poisonous fish expecting to remove the poison. No amount of boiling or cooking will remove the poison from the fish. Even broth or chowders made with poisonous fish can be extremely dangerous.

Ciguatera This toxin is thought to be caused by small blue-green bottom-growing algae which occur most often on tropical island reefs. Consequently, some algae-eating fish are occasionally found to be poisonous, especially around the tropical Indo-Pacific and Caribbean Islands. Those species that are adapted for eating small encrusting algae and corals can usually be identified by their teeth, which form a parrot-like beak. When fishing in waters where ciguatera poisoning is known to occur, these species should be checked for edibility. Since the toxin is cumulative, predators that have fed on many toxic algae-eating fish can become even more poisonous. For this reason, large barracuda (e.g. those over three feet long), jack, snapper, and large groupers are responsible for the majority of cases of ciguatera poisoning. Here, again, if these species are needed for food and *are taken from affected areas,* the meat should be tested before eating. The *only* positive test for this toxin is to feed some of the meat to a mammal, or to give it the edibility test yourself. Cooking or washing does not deactivate the poison. When possible, local people are the best source of information as to which species are edible in a particular area. Also remember, however, that people sometimes avoid using specific organisms for food because of tradition or superstitions; these organisms may be found to be edible after careful testing.

FISH THAT STING (VENOMOUS FISH)
Many species of fish have spines that can cause a puncture wound, and a few have venom glands associated with these spines. Any fish should be handled with caution, and those that have venomous spines should

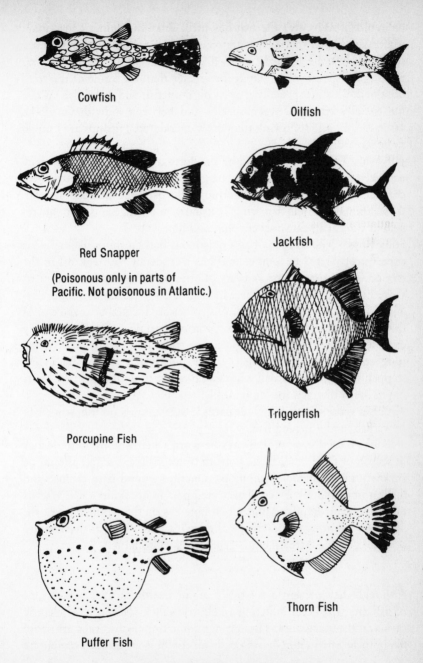

Cowfish

Oilfish

Red Snapper

(Poisonous only in parts of
Pacific. Not poisonous in Atlantic.)

Jackfish

Porcupine Fish

Triggerfish

Puffer Fish

Thorn Fish

Fig. 10-4   Fish Poisonous to Eat

be avoided even after the fish has died, since the spines can remain toxic. Venomous species are not toxic to eat if the poison glands are removed, but the hazards entailed in catching these species and removing the glands are likely to be greater than the value of the food obtained. This is especially true of the stonefish and zebra fish. While the toxicity varies between species and between individuals of the same species, the following frequently encountered groups are known to be hazardous.

Jellyfish   The jellyfish, including the Portuguese man-of-war, is characterized by its ability to sting. The greatest danger may develop from contact with the tentacles. Clothing affords some protection from these animals. A jellyfish sting is usually not dangerous, though repeated stings can cause severe pain and illness.

Sting Rays   The sting ray has a poisonous barbed spine. This spine is consequently hard to remove and has a tendency to break off in the wound, increasing the probability of infection. These animals are flat, skate-like fish, often several feet in length. They are similar in appearance to the giant ray; the poisonous spines are located near the end of the tail. They are found in shallow, warm, coastal waters. Waders may clear a path in the water by poking a stick as they advance. When touched or poked, the sting ray will quickly dart away. But when stepped on squarely, it will whip its tail upward with great fury, driving its spine through the leg or ankle.

Other venomous fish include catfish, weever, surgeon fish, stonefish, zebra fish, and scorpion fish.

Foot protection should always be worn when wading in the water in search of food, and, if the bottom is not visible, the feet should be shuffled. First aid for a venomous puncture wound is to cleanse and flush it immediately. Place the affected part in hot water (120°F or as hot as you can stand) or put hot compresses on the wounded area for 30 to 60 minutes to deactivate the toxins. Since few antivenins are available, medical treatment is generally symptomatic.

Although they present a relatively minor health hazard, two groups of fish are capable of inflicting an electric shock. They are the electric rays and the stargazers. Though not common, electric rays are more likely to be encountered and occur on the bottom of both temperate

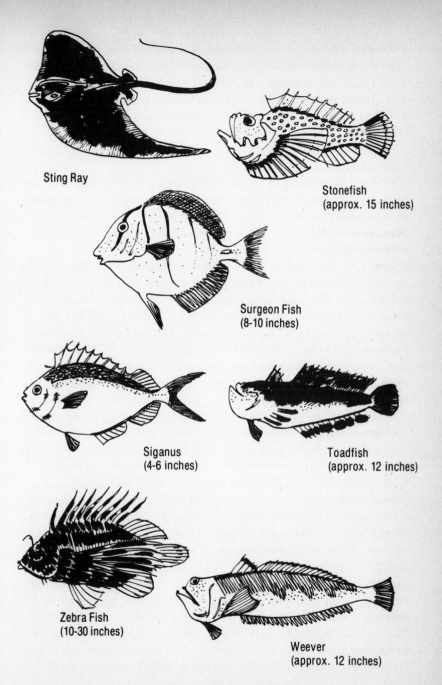

Sting Ray

Stonefish
(approx. 15 inches)

Surgeon Fish
(8-10 inches)

Siganus
(4-6 inches)

Toadfish
(approx. 12 inches)

Zebra Fish
(10-30 inches)

Weever
(approx. 12 inches)

Fig. 10-5   Venomous Fish

and tropical oceans. A large electric ray, if touched, can deliver a shock sufficiently strong (up to 220 volts) to knock over and temporarily daze a man. Electric rays may be recognized by their nearly circular, disk-shaped body and the typical fish-like tail and caudal fin, as opposed to the whip-like tail and triangular-shaped body typical of the stingrays.

FISH THAT BITE

Although one is less likely to be attacked by a fish in the ocean than to be hit by lightning, the grotesque consequences of such an attack make this possibility of major concern to most people. The three groups of animals which are primarily responsible for this concern are moray eels, barracuda, and sharks (see p. 241).

Moray eels   Any eel, if sufficiently provoked, may bite. Moray eels have earned a reputation for being a most aggressive family, however, and they are the most dangerous to man. These eels, which live in holes and crevices in tropical reefs or rocks, will defend their homes if a foot or arm is placed too near. When searching for food in the sea, examine each hole carefully before attempting to reach in and remove a fish or lobster. If bitten by a moray eel, the recurved teeth may remain embedded, and sometimes the only way of detaching the eel is to cut off its head.

Barracuda   Barracuda have acquired an often undeserved reputation for aggressiveness. While they are known to have inflicted severe wounds, their savage appearance and curious nature are frequently more responsible for this reputation than are their actual number of attacks on man. Those species of barracuda found off Australia are reported to be more aggressive than those species found around the Caribbean and Pacific islands. Large schools of barracuda are usually more dangerous than one encountered singly, much as is true of a pack of dogs. Many species will display a vertically striped color pattern just prior to feeding or attack. Barracuda frequently take freshly caught fish away from fishermen and, in murky waters, they may strike at a reflective object, possibly mistaking it for a smaller fish. At night, barracuda, as well as hound fish and several other species, are likely to charge a bright light source. Unless a barracuda is displaying definite aggressive behavior or freshly killed fish are nearby, their typically curious behavior patterns are not sufficient reason for alarm.

OTHER WATER HAZARDS

The dangerous and toxic water animals discussed earlier by no means exhaust the list of hazards that may be encountered. Tropical boneshell and long, slender, pointed tereba snails are also poisonous. Handle big conchs with caution; large abalones and clams can be dangerous if gathered by hand instead of pried loose with a bar or wedge. They may clamp onto your fingers and hold you until you drown. Coral, dead or alive, can inflict painful cuts. There are hundreds of water hazards that can cause deep puncture wounds, severe bleeding, and the danger of infection.

HEALTH HAZARDS

For protection against specific weather extremes, see individual chapters dealing with those extremes. The following is a list of health problems and hazards more directly attributable to the sea environment.

1) *Immersion Foot*—This is a physical ailment that can become serious aboard a raft. This condition is caused by exposure to cold, immersion in water, cramped quarters, and restricted circulation. You will notice tingling, numbness, redness, and swelling. Blotchy red areas and blisters eventually appear. Keep your feet warm and dry, maintain circulation by exercising toes and feet, and loosen footgear. Elevate feet and legs for 30-minute periods several times a day. If you are suffering from immersion foot, stay off your feet after reaching shore.

2) *Saltwater Burns or Boils*—These may be caused by continued exposure to salt water. Do not prick or squeeze these boils; keep them dry.

3) *Seasickness*—Do not eat or drink if seasick. Lie down and change the position of your head frequently.

4) *Sore Eyes*—This condition is caused by glare from the sky and water. Prevent this by wearing sunglasses or improvising an eyeshield from a piece of cloth or bandage. If no medicines are available, moisten a bandage or cotton cloth with seawater and place this over the eyes before you bandage them.

5) *Constipation*—This is normal aboard liferafts. Do not take any laxatives. Exercise as much as possible.

6) *Difficulty in Urinating or Dark Urine*—This problem is also normal under such conditions.

WATER

Rain, ice, and the bodily fluids of other creatures are the only natural sources of water at sea. *Seawater is not drinkable.* It aggravates your thirst and increases water loss by drawing fluids out of the tissues to be eliminated by way of the kidneys and intestines.

RAINWATER
Use buckets, cups, tin cans, sea anchors, boat covers, sails, strips of clean clothing, and all canvas gear in the boat to collect rainwater. Devise catchments before there is an actual need. If a shower promises to be light, wet the receptacle in the sea. The salt contaminating the rainwater will be slight, and the dampened cloth will prevent the fresh water from becoming absorbed in the fabric. The body can store water; therefore, drink all you can hold.

ICE
Sea ice loses its salt after a year and becomes a good source of water. This "old" ice is identified by rounded corners and its bluish color.

SEAWATER
In freezing weather, fresh water can be obtained from seawater. Collect this water in a container and allow it to freeze. Since the fresh water freezes first, the salt concentrates as a slush in the core of the frozen fresh water. Remove this salt, and the remaining ice will be sufficiently salt-free to keep you alive.

Chemical kits may be available in your raft or lifeboat. These kits can be used to remove the salt and alkaline substances from seawater. Directions accompany the kits.

FOOD

The sea is rich in different forms of life. The challenge is to obtain them for food. If fishing equipment is available, chances are excellent that you will have food, but, even if there is no equipment, the situation is not hopeless.

FISH

Practically all freshly caught sea fish are palatable and wholesome, cooked or raw. In warm regions, gut and bleed fish immediately after catching them. Cut fish that are not eaten immediately into thin narrow strips and hang them to dry. A well-dried fish stays edible for several days. Fish not cleaned and dried may spoil in half a day. Never eat fish that have pale, shiny gills, sunken eyes, flabby skin and flesh, or an unpleasant odor. (Such sick and diseased fish are rarely found in the open sea.) Good fish should show the opposite characteristics. Sea fish should have a salt water or clean fishy odor. Eels may be mistaken for sea snakes, which have an obviously scaly body and strongly compressed, paddle-shaped tail. Both eels and sea snakes are edible, but the latter must be handled with care because of their poisonous bites. The heart, blood, intestinal wall, and liver of most fishes are edible. The intestines should be cooked. Also edible are the partly digested smaller fishes which might be found in the stomachs of large fish. In addition, sea turtles are good food.

Although medical research sponsored by the U.S. Navy has learned that under certain circumstances a broad range of sea foods from sea turtles and barracuda to shark and whale livers can be toxic, there is certain evidence to suggest otherwise. Much depends on where the creatures are caught—for example, only a few turtles from the western Pacific or Indian Ocean have ever indicated toxicity—or the amount you eat, as in the case of vitamin-A-enriched shark and marine mammal livers.

On the high seas, ichthyotoxin or fish poisoning is more likely to occur due to improper handling or spoilage of the fish than any other cause. Fish are particularly susceptible to bacterial decomposition. For this reason, they should be gutted immediately and either eaten or preserved. Fish can be preserved by cutting in thin strips, then salting and drying. Dark-meated fish are particularly susceptible to scromboid bacterial poisoning, and if they cannot be cleaned and kept in a cool place, they should be cooked or eaten raw and the leftovers used for bait rather than being set aside for another meal. Although bacterial poisoning can be treated with antibiotic drugs, you may have none or not enough aboard a raft to risk eating two-day-old tuna.

Fishing Aids   The following are useful fishing aids:

Fishing line—Make a strong fishing line from pieces of tarpaulin or canvas by raveling the threads and tying them together in very short lengths in groups of three or more threads. Also use parachute suspension lines, shoelaces, or thread from clothing.

Fish hooks—No one at sea should ever be without fishing equipment, but even without fishing tackle, you can improvise enough to survive. Hooks may be made from items with points or pins, such as nail files, collar insignia, and belt buckle tangs or, from bird bones, fish spines, and pieces of wood. To make a wood hook, shape the shaft and cut a notch near the end to hold the point. Sharpen the point so that the hardest part of the grain forms the tip of the hook. Use strands of canvas to lash the barb and shaft together.

Fish lures—Improvise fish lures by using a coin or snap hook, or a dime fastened to a double hook.

Grapple—Gather seaweed by using an improvised grapple made of wood from the raft or boat. Use the heaviest piece of wood as the shaft, and cut three notches in which to fit three grapples. Lash them in place at a 45° angle. Tie a line to the shaft and drag the grapple behind the raft. This grapple can sometimes be used to snag small fish for food or bait or to snag clumps of seaweed from which shrimp, crabs and occasionally small fish can be shaken for food or bait; the weed itself can be eaten to provide essential minerals and vitamins. However, raw Sargassum weed (a brown algae with small gas floats to provide buoyancy)—the most commonly found weed on the high seas—is tough, salty, and difficult to digest. Sargassum weed is better when eaten pickled, but even then it absorbs much body fluid, and should be eaten only if you have plenty of drinking water aboard the lifeboat or raft.

Sea Anchor/Plankton Tow—Most lifeboats and rafts come equipped with a sea anchor. If not, one can be improvised from a bailing bucket or shirt. Its purpose is to provide an underwater drag to help maintain direction and location, especially if you plan to stay close to the wreckage of the ship or aircraft. In the case of a storm, a sea anchor will help the lifeboat or raft stay bow to the wind. Do not allow the anchor rope to chafe the sides of the raft. In case you have to improvise a sea anchor, a shirt is better than a canvas bucket because a permeable fabric like cotton can be used to strain plankton and small fishes from the sea. Plankton includes both minute plants and animals that drift about or swim weakly in the ocean. These basic organisms in the marine food chain are generally more common near land than in the middle of the oceans, since their occurrence depends upon the nutrients dissolved in the water. However, a combination sea anchor/plankton tow in the open sea can passively strain a remarkable quantity of small marine life.

Plankton Considerable debate surrounds the value of plankton to supplement survival diets. Proponents, including the Air Force's Environmental Training Division, point out that the average protein content of plankton is 30 to 60 percent; fat content, 4 to 31 percent; and carbohydrates, 18 to 23 percent. If all spiny material and stinging tentacles are removed, plankton is an excellent food source. It is already widely consumed as a "shrimp paste" or condiment in China, India, and Japan. Opponents, including some respected voices in the Army and Navy Medical Corps, argue that because you ingest a great deal of salt water with the plankton, and because you may run the risk of consuming poisonous dinoflagellates, you should not eat plankton under any circumstances.

Shark Shark meat is a good food source, raw, dried, or cooked, and is a common item in the markets of many countries. Some species of sharks are preferred over others and consumption of the liver of all sharks should be limited, due to the possible high vitamin A content. The flesh, as well as the liver, of the Greenland shark can also be toxic due to its high concentration of vitamin A. Shark meat spoils rapidly due to the high urea content of the blood. Therefore, the meat is best if bled immediately or soaked in several changes of water.

Bait Use small fish as bait for catching larger fish. Use the dip net from your fishing kit to scoop up these small fishes. If no kit is available, make a net from a mosquito headnet, parachute cloth, or clothing fastened to oar sections. Hold the net underwater and scoop upward. Save guts of birds and fish for bait. Use a piece of colored cloth, bright tin, or even a button from your shirt. Keep the bait moving in the water to make it appear alive. Try it at different depths.

The following are helpful guidelines for fishing at sea:

1) Handle spiny fish and those with teeth *carefully*.

2) Do not attach the line to anything solid; a big fish might break it. Do not wind the line around any part of your body.

3) If a large fish is hooked, it is wiser to cut it off than risk capsizing the raft or boat.

4) Take care not to puncture a rubber raft with hooks, knives, or spears.

5) Fish for small fish. Avoid fishing when near large sharks.

6) Watch for schools of fish which can be seen breaking water. Move closer to such a school if possible.

7) Shine a flashlight on the water at night, or use a piece of canvas or cloth to reflect moonlight. The light will attract fish and squid which may leap into the raft.

8) Shade by day attracts many varieties of small fish. A lowered sail or tarpaulin may gather fish.

9) The flesh of all fish caught in the open sea (except jellyfishes and the liver of a few fish species) is edible, cooked or raw. Raw fish are neither salty nor unpleasant.

10) Make a spear or harpoon for catching large fish by tying a knife to an oar. (Get your quarry into the boat quickly as the fish will wriggle and slip off an unbarbed blade.)

11) If your fishing equipment is lost, try dangling a piece of fish or bird gut in the water. One survivor reported that he caught eighty fish in one day by allowing them to swallow a piece of gut and snatching them into his raft.

12) Care for your equipment. Allow lines to dry, and make certain that hooks do not stick into and damage the line. Clean and sharpen the hooks.

BIRDS

Eat any birds caught. They sometimes settle on a raft or boat, and survivors have reported instances where birds landed on their shoulders. If birds are shy, try dragging a baited hook in the sea or throwing a baited hook into the air. More birds are seen far at sea in the Southern Hemisphere than in the Northern. However, don't be discouraged. You never know when a bird might show up.

Many sea birds can be attracted within certain shooting distance by a bright piece of metal or shell dragged behind the raft. (Be careful not to shoot a hole in an inflatable raft!) It is possible to catch a bird if it lands within reach. Most birds, however, are shy and will settle on the raft out of reach. In this case, try a bird noose. Make it by tying a loose knot with two pieces of line. Bait the center with fish entrails or similar bait. When the bird settles, tighten the noose around its feet. Use all parts of the bird, even the feathers, which can be stuffed inside your shirt or shoes for insulation, or used to make fishing lures.

COASTAL SURVIVAL:
TERRAIN AND IMMEDIATE CONSIDERATIONS

A drifting raft or swimmer is not always spotted by searching planes and ships. You may have to land along the coast before being rescued. When approaching the shore, try to avoid coral and rocks. Land in the daylight with the sun behind you, if possible. If you must land on a rocky shore, avoid abrupt cliffs and ridges where the waves break with much spray. If you're in a raft or lifeboat, swim into the beach or shore, towing a line behind you. When you land, pull in the raft or boat and drag it well up the beach. It can provide temporary shelter or form the roof of a more permanent shelter. If you must cross coral, keep your shoes and clothes on to avoid severe cuts. If you must float or swim, let the surge of the waves carry you with your legs tucked up but relaxed to cushion blows.

TRAVEL

If you decide to travel, it is better to move along the coast than to go inland. Don't leave the coast except to avoid obstacles such as swamps and cliffs, unless you find a trail which you know leads to human habitation.

SHELTER

Information on shelters in Chapter Six ("Basic Survival Skills") is applicable for a coastal shelter.

ENVIRONMENTAL HAZARDS

REPTILES

Turtles Sea turtles have long been considered such a good source of food that their numbers have been steadily decreasing. Most are endangered species and should be used for emergency food only. A few cases of turtle poisoning have been reported from Indo-Pacific reefs; however, these are rare and sporadic, with symptoms similar in nature to ciguatera poisoning. Turtle eggs are always nutritious, and the liver and fat are also edible.

Sea Snakes Sea snakes are found only in the Pacific and Indian Oceans, and their bites are highly toxic (over ten times more deadly than any other snake). Species of sea snakes vary widely in color pattern and can best be identified by their vertically flattened tail and scaled body. They are generally not aggressive toward swimmers, although their docile nature can vary between species, and they are said to become more aggressive during the mating season. Since their grooved fangs are short and a chewing action is necessary to inject the toxin into the victim, relatively few bites occur. As is frequently the case with venomous snakes, in the majority of bites that do occur, no serious envenomation results.

Sea snakes are frequently attracted to a light at night, and the most likely victims are fishermen who are pulling in nets. Since sea snakes must breathe air, they are often seen on the surface, and, during spring, sightings are reported of vast numbers of some species forming aggregations several miles in length. The initial bite usually produces little or no local pain, and paralysis (normally the first noticeable symptom) may not develop for hours. The mortality rate is believed to be less than 17 percent, and death can occur up to a week or more after the bite. First aid is similar to treatment for other poisonous snakebites, but cutting the wound is not recommended, and sucking is believed to be of less value than a restricting band and immediate immobilization of the victim.

Sea snakes are edible after the head containing the venom glands is removed. They are sold in the markets in China, and some fish hatcheries in the Philippines specialize in the culture of sea snakes, for their meat and skins. The Japanese are also said to be successful culturists of sea snakes. Only six to eight of the many species are generally eaten, since the remaining species are too small for commercial markets.

Crocodiles   The crocodile inhabits tropical saltwater bays and mangrove-bordered estuaries, and ranges up to 40 miles into the open sea. Few remain near inhabited areas, and they are most commonly found in the remote areas of the East Indies and Southeast Asia. Specimens over seven feet long should be considered dangerous, especially females guarding their nests. Crocodile meat is an excellent source of food when available.

SEA URCHINS, SEA BISCUITS, SPONGES, AND ANEMONES

Though seldom fatal, sea urchins and their aquatic cousins can cause extreme pain. Usually found in tropical shallow water near coral formations, sea urchins resemble small, round porcupines. If stepped on, they slip fine needles of lime or silica into the skin, where they break off and fester. If possible, the spines should be removed and the injury treated for infection. For fuller discussion of sea urchins, see the "Food" section of this chapter.

HEALTH HAZARDS

Exposure to extremes of weather is a significant health hazard for coastal survival. See the "Health" sections in chapters dealing with specific climate extremes.

WATER

See Chapter Six ("Basic Survival Skills") as well as the "Water" section earlier in this chapter.

FOOD

SEAWEEDS

Leafy green, brown, and red seaweeds contain up to 25 percent protein and 50 percent carbohydrates and are a valuable source of iodine and vitamin C.

Select seaweeds attached to rocks, or floating free, because those lying on the beach are often spoiled or decayed. Dry the thin, tender varieties over a fire or in the sun until they are crisp; then crush and use them to flavor soups and broths. Wash the thick leathery species, and then soften by boiling. Seaweeds are ideal for supplementing your diet. Eat them with other seafoods.

Leafy green algae or sea lettuce (Ulva)—grows below the low tide line along the North Pacific and North Atlantic coasts. Wash it in fresh water and use it as you would garden lettuce.

Sugar wrack—tastes sweet. A brown algae, it is found on both sides of the Atlantic and along the coasts of China and Japan.

Kelp—is a large brown or olive green algae, which lives offshore, attached to the bottom, and may grow more than a dozen feet in a single week. Boil before eating. Mix with vegetables or soup.

Irish moss—is found on both sides of the Atlantic and looks like a stunted or leathery form of bib lettuce. Boil before eating.

Dulse—is a red algae with a short stem but a broad, thin, fan-shaped leaf, often divided by several clefts into peculiar round-tipped lobes. It is found in the Atlantic and Mediterranean. The plant is sweet and can be eaten fresh or dried. Some people use it as a kind of chewing gum.

Laver—is common in the North Atlantic and Pacific and is either red, dark purple, or purplish brown with a satin or filmy luster. Use it as a relish. Boil it briefly until tender, then pulverize. Add it to crushed cereal grains; it also makes a superb pancake. Look for this plant below the high tide line.

OTHER EDIBLE PLANTS

Salt marsh grasses (Spartina)—found on both sides of the North Atlantic, produce an edible grain in the autumn.

Sea Orach—in the Mediterranean has small, edible, gray-colored leaves about an inch long. Found along the coast, it is recognized in the spring by its narrow, densely compartmented flower spikes at the tips of the branches.

St. John's Bread—is a tree reaching a height of fifty feet and growing in the arid wastes bordering the Mediterranean as well as the Sahara across Arabia and Iran, and into India. It is an evergreen with leathery, glistening leaflets paired two or three on a stem. Its flowers are small and red. Its seed pod has a sweet edible pulp. Pulverize the seeds of St. John's Bread and cook them as a porridge.

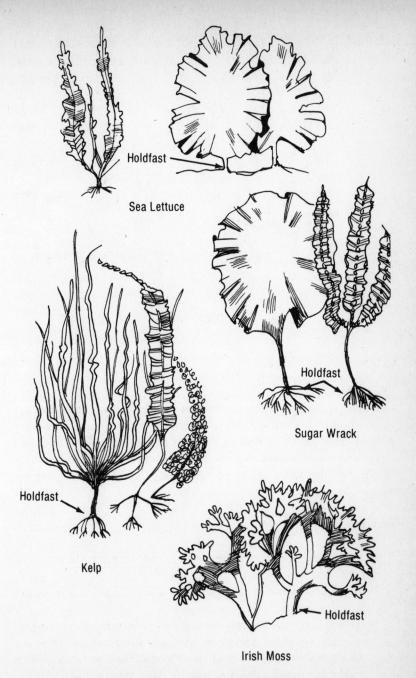

Holdfast

Sea Lettuce

Holdfast

Sugar Wrack

Holdfast

Kelp

Holdfast

Irish Moss

Fig. 10-6   Algae and Seaweed

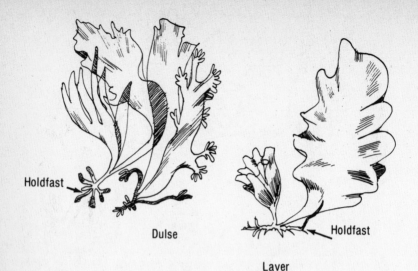

Holdfast

Dulse

Holdfast

Laver

Fig. 10-6   Algae and Seaweed

INVERTEBRATES

Generally speaking, sponges, jellyfishes, corals, and sea anemones are to be avoided, both to eat and to touch, for many species are able to sting or cause rashes on human skin. If you are low on food and need to eat anemones, handle them with gloves and boil them in seawater. Ideally, run them through an edibility test to make sure they are not toxic.

Edibility Test

1) Taste a small portion of the seafood, and if it stings the mouth or tastes bad, spit it out.
2) If it is acceptable to taste, swallow a small portion and wait 1 hour for results.
3) If there is no reaction, the food is relatively safe since most poisons (except those caused by spoilage) will produce symptoms within a short time. A small serving may then be eaten. (When spoilage is suspected this procedure should not be used.)

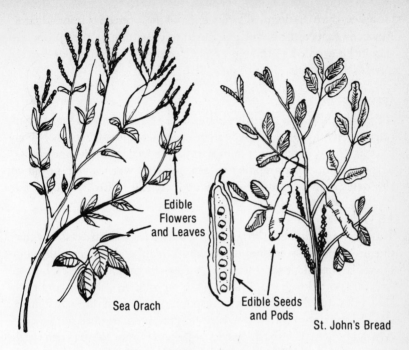

Edible
Flowers
and Leaves

Sea Orach

Edible Seeds
and Pods

St. John's Bread

Fig. 10-7   Edible Coastal Vegetation

4) If no symptoms occur within 12 hours after eating a small serving of the seafood, the flesh can be considered edible. If ciguatera (see above) is suspected, the test must be applied to each fish, since one cannot assume that all fish of the same species are edible.

MOLLUSKS

Mussels, limpets, clams, sea snails, octopuses, squids, and sea slugs are all edible and (with the exception of the blue-ringed octopus of the southwestern Pacific reefs, whose bite can be fatal, and the occurrence of "red tides" which may make mollusks poisonous) shellfish will usually supply the bulk of the protein consumed by coastal survivors. However, apply the edibility test on each species in an area before consuming large quantities. **Warning:** When collecting cone shells, pick them and hold the tapered end away from you. Never store live shells next to your body. Only fifteen Pacific and Indian Ocean cones are poisonous out of a family comprising approximately four hundred species.

However, the hypodermic-like injection of these fifteen is fast and fatal. Any cone-shaped shells with a textured color pattern or a red proboscis should be avoided. Although edible if the cone's poison gland is removed, the risk is not worth the effort.

WORMS
Although edible, it is probably better to use coastal worms for fish bait rather than for food. Especially to be avoided are bristle worms (which look like fuzzy caterpillars) and the sharp-edged tubes of tubeworms. Arrowworms, alias amphioxus, are not true worms, but primitive chordates found in the sand. They are excellent to eat fresh or dried.

ARTHROPODS
This phylum includes crabs, lobsters, barnacles, and insects. The marine arthropods are seldom dangerous to man, and are generally considered an excellent food source. One species of horseshoe crab from Asia is reported to be toxic during the reproductive season, and both land and sea crabs can become poisonous if they feed on toxic materials. This occurs so rarely, however, that the survivor need not be concerned about it. The sharp pincers of larger crabs or lobsters can crush a man's finger, and many species have spines on their shells, which make it desirable to wear gloves when catching them. Barnacles have been responsible for many a scrape or cut, and although they are sometimes difficult to detach, the larger species are a good source of food.

ECHINODERMS
The echinoderms are exclusively marine and generally bottom-dwellers. Sea urchins, starfish, sea cucumbers, and sand dollars are some of the frequently seen members of this group.

Sea urchins   These are often abundant and are a common cause of painful injuries. Although they are not aggressive, any sea urchin can be hazardous if it is accidentally stepped on or brushed against. The long-spined species that inhabit the tropics (e.g., *Diadema*) are especially hazardous. These species often have thin secondary spines that can cause more damage than the thicker primary spines, all of which are serrated—making removal nearly impossible. If a puncture wound is incurred, extract those spines which can be removed and the rest can be left to dissolve, or they may be surgically removed if an infection

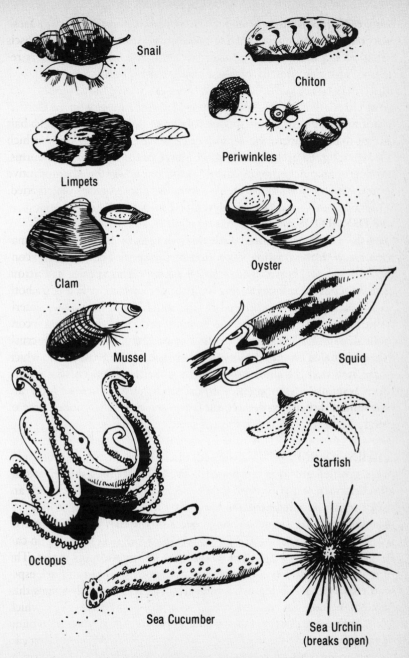

Snail

Chiton

Periwinkles

Limpets

Oyster

Clam

Mussel

Squid

Starfish

Octopus

Sea Cucumber

Sea Urchin
(breaks open)

Fig. 10-8   Edible Coastal Marine Life

occurs. The application of ammonia, alcohol, or citrus juice has been reported to hasten the dissolving process. Most of the short-spine varieties of sea urchins can be carefully gathered with gloves or bare hands. The ripe gonads of these species are considered a delicacy which may be cooked, but are most often eaten raw. Large numbers of sea urchins are currently being shipped from the northwestern United States to the Orient, where the roe is in great demand. The edibility of several species during the reproductive season has been questioned, but generally sea urchins are a good source of food. A few sea urchins have cup-like pincer organs called "pedicellaria" scattered among the spines, which can be moderately venomous. Those species which have venomous pincers sufficiently developed to be hazardous to man are so infrequently encountered that no clinical data are available.

Starfish The starfish offers little nourishment to man and poses few hazards, with the possible exception of the species commonly called the "Crown of Thorns" *(Acanthaster planci)*. This species has many arms and a thick spiny covering on its upper surface, which is considered toxic. A wound produced by the tough, briar-like spines is extremely painful, similar to the wound produced by a venomous mollusk or fish. This species should not be eaten. Very little information is available on the edibility of other species of starfish, although it is reported that the slime produced by some may cause a skin irritation. Generally, it is impractical to use starfish as a source of food except possibly during the reproductive season, when more edible material is contained inside the arms and body cavity.

The sea cucumber This tube-like animal is essentially harmless to man. Some species, when disturbed, discharge their minimal internal organs, which are soon regenerated. The visceral fluids should not be allowed to contact your eyes. Other species can discharge long, white, sticky strings as a defensive measure when disturbed. These strings are usually only bothersome, although occasionally they cause a slight irritation. Several species are an important food source in the Indo-Pacific regions. They are used whole after evisceration (as in the case of the genus *Stichopus*), or the five muscular strips that run the length of the body may be removed, and are usually eaten either smoked, pickled, or cooked.

CHAPTER ELEVEN

Survival Under Unusual Conditions

EMERGENCY PROCEDURES FOR PLANE CRASH

ON LAND

1) Stay away from the airplane until the engines have cooled and spilled gas has evaporated.
2) Check injuries. Give first aid. Make the injured people comfortable. Be careful when removing casualties—particularly people with injured backs—from the airplane.
3) Get out of the wind and rain. Throw up a temporary shelter. If you need a fire, start it at once. In cold weather, make hot drinks.
4) Get your emergency radio operating on schedule and have other signaling equipment handy.
5) Now, relax and rest until you are over the shock of the crash. Leave extensive preparations and planning until later.
6) After you have rested, organize the camp. Appoint individuals to perform specific duties. Pool all food and equipment, putting one person in charge. Prepare a shelter to protect yourself from rain, hot sun, snow, wind, cold, or insects. Collect all possible fuel. Try to have at least a day's stock of fuel on hand. Look for a water supply. Look for animal and plant food.
7) Prepare signals so that you will be recognized from the air.
8) Start a log book. Include date and cause of crash; probable loca-

tion; roster of personnel; inventory of food, water, and equipment; weather conditions; and other pertinent data.

9) Determine your position by the best means available, and include this position in your radio messages. If position is based on celestial observations, transmit the observations also.

10) If you have bailed out, try to make your way to the crashed plane. Rescuers can spot it from the air even when they cannot see a man.

11) Stay with the airplane unless briefed to the contrary. Do not leave the airplane unless you know that you are within easy walking distance of help. If you travel, leave a note giving planned route (except in hostile territory). Stick to your plan so rescuers can locate you.

12) In the Arctic, use the aircraft for shelter. Cover openings with netting or parachute cloth to keep insects out. Do your cooking outside to avoid carbon-monoxide poisoning. Make your fire at a safe distance from the plane. Don't plan to live in the airplane for an extended period; it will be too cold. Try to improvise a better, insulated shelter outdoors.

13) In the desert, don't use the inside of the airplane for shelter in the daytime; it will be too hot. Get under the shade of a wing if you have no other shelter. If you stay with the airplane, you can make a good shade-shelter by tying a spread-out parachute to the wing to make an awning. Leave the lower edge at least 2 feet clear of the ground for air circulation. Use sections of airplane tubing for tent poles and pegs.

14) Conserve power of electronic equipment.

15) Sweep the horizon with your signal mirror at frequent intervals.

Remember: You are the key man in the rescue. Help the search parties to find you, and follow their instructions when they sight you. They can use all the assistance you can give. Don't take chances which might result in injury.

ON SEA (ALSO FOR SHIPWRECK)

1) Do not inflate rafts or life jackets inside the aircraft.

2) Get yourself and emergency equipment out of the plane or off the sinking ship as quickly as possible.

3) Keep a line tied between the plane or ship and the liferaft(s) until all people are aboard or until the plane or ship starts to sink. Assign one man to cut the line as soon as the plane or ship goes under.

4) If possible, load liferafts directly from the ship or plane without going into the water. Even a temporary dose of cold water can create adverse impacts for days following.

5) Keep the raft properly balanced at all times, but be prepared to right it if it tips or flips over.

6) Stay clear of the plane or ship (out of gas- or oil-saturated waters) but in the vicinity until it sinks. Stay up-current.

7) Search for missing passengers, especially in the direction toward which waves are moving.

8) Salvage floating equipment; stow and secure all items and check rafts for inflation, leaks, and points of possible chafing. Bail out your raft. Be careful not to snag it with shoes or sharp objects.

9) In cold oceans, rig a windbreak, spray shield, or canopy. If you are with others, huddle together; exercise regularly.

10) Check the physical condition of all aboard. Give first aid. Take seasickness pills. Wash gasoline or oil off yourself.

11) If there is more than one raft, connect rafts with at least 25 feet of line. Connect rafts only at the lifeline around the outer periphery of the raft. Unless the sea is very rough, shorten the line if you hear or see an airplane. Two or more rafts tied close together are easier to spot than scattered rafts.

12) Get the emergency radio into operation. Directions are on the equipment. Use emergency transceivers only when aircraft are known to be in the area. Prepare other signaling devices for instant use.

13) Position the liferaft repair plugs along the side of the raft as soon as possible.

14) Keep compasses, watches, matches, and lighters dry. Place them in waterproof containers.

15) In warm oceans, rig a sunshade or canopy. Keep your skin covered. Use sunburn cream and lip balm. Keep your sleeves rolled down and your socks pinned up over your trousers. Wear a hat and sunglasses.

16) Make a calm estimate of your situation and plan your course of action carefully.

17) Ration water and food; assign duties; use the canopy or tarpaulins for catching and storing rainwater.

18) Keep a log. Record the navigator's last fix, time of ditching, names and physical condition of personnel, ration schedule, winds, weather, direction of swells, times of sunrise and sunset, and other navigation data. Inventory all equipment.

19) Keep calm. Save water and food by saving energy. Don't shout unnecessarily. Don't move around unnecessarily. Keep your sense of humor sharp; use it often. Remember that rescue at sea is a cooperative project. Search aircraft contacts are limited by the visibility of survivors. Increase your visibility by using all possible signaling devices. Keep your mirrors handy; use your radio whenever you can; use your signal panel and dye marker when you think an aircraft can see them.

20) If you are wearing a life jacket, but cannot reach a raft, you should be able to survive in temperate or tropical seas for several days. Since a swimmer is less visible from the air than a raft, be prepared at all times to use your sea-marker dye and signal mirror.

NUCLEAR ATTACK

IMMEDIATE ACTION
Most likely your first warning of a nuclear blast will be an alarm or an attack warning signal. Follow local Civil Defense Procedures; otherwise, seek out shelter immediately.

If this is not the case and your first warning is the blast itself, instantly seek out any shelter.

If you are in the immediate vicinity of the nuclear blast your chances of survival are virtually non-existent. If you are a few miles away you may have 10 to 15 seconds before the heat wave hits you, and possibly longer before the arrival of the shock wave.

If shelter is impossible to reach, seek any depressed area in your immediate vicinity and drop to the ground. Cover your face with your hands and lie face down, exposing as little flesh to the blast as possible. (Even at a distance of fifteen to twenty miles, the heat can burn the skin off the body.) **Do not at any time look at the flash of the fireball.**

RADIATION

If you have survived the nuclear blast, protection from the effects of residual radiation will be your immediate and most important task. Unless countermeasures are employed against this hazard when it exists, other survival techniques will be of little value. Residual radiation is potentially lethal and must be dealt with as soon as you arrive on the ground.

Protection in Rural Areas   The most effective means of protection against penetrating gamma radiation is shelter. If you are away from a town or city, find a natural shelter which can be used with the least improvement. Find the shelter quickly (not more than 5 minutes) after arrival on the ground. Some ideal locations are caves, overhanging rocks, deep defiles, or large, downed logs.

Improve the shelter while taking advantage of the shielding it provides. On level ground, sweep the ground clean and lie down. Dig a slit trench from the prone position, and stack the earth around the trench. A shielding cover (roof) should be considered only if materials to build it are available without undue exposure. A cover of parachute cloth, although it does not provide shielding, will prevent entry of particles into the shelter. It must be struck (shaken) frequently to remove the particles that have alighted on it.

Under marshy conditions or in areas of permafrost, sod blocks may be stacked on the surface to make a shelter. If you are surrounded on all sides, including the top, the following thicknesses will provide ideal shielding to protect from "sky-shine"—the radiation scattered back by air molecules from radiation originating from fallout particles on the ground. However, a lesser amount of shielding may be life-saving.

Steel	½ ft.	Earth	3 ft.
Rock	2 ft.	Ice	5 ft.
Concrete	2 ft.	Snow	20 ft.

Once you have entered the shelter, continue to work on it from the inside to make living in it more comfortable. You will need as much comfort as possible to allow for rest and increased recovery from radiation. Take steps to be as warm and dry as possible. Your parachute may be used as insulating material after it has been decontaminated by shaking, or by rinsing and drying.

The radiation hazard dissipates fairly rapidly, provided that no new detonations add to the contamination. After 7 hours from the time of maximum contamination, only 1/10th of the hazard will remain. After 49 hours from the time of maximum contamination, only 1/100th of the hazard will remain. Two weeks after the time of maximum contamination, only 1/1000th of the hazard will remain. If new contaminating events take place (more weapons exploded), the contamination will be renewed and you must wait out the decay of the fresh radioactive material. Stay in the shelter for a minimum of 200 hours after you estimate the last weapon has exploded; longer, if possible. You should not go outside the shelter except to satisfy a critical need for water. The shelter should be camouflaged and movement held to a minimum to preclude compromise of your position.

Processed foods (rations) will be safe to eat as long as containers are intact. The same will be true of any processed foods located in the area. Animal foods will be usable even when taken from an area contaminated by radiation. The animal must be carefully skinned and the heart, liver, and kidneys discarded. Meat close to the bone should not be eaten, since a large percentage of the radioactivity in the body of the animal is found in the skeleton.

Plant foods are, in general, safe to eat. Plants with the edible portion below ground are best. Smooth-surfaced plant foods that can be easily washed are next best. Rough-surfaced plant foods are difficult to wash, but may be used as a last resort. All plant foods should be peeled and the edibility test applied.

Open water in an area that has received fallout may contain harmful particles. Water from an underground source (spring, covered well, etc.) is your best supply. Water from other sources (lake, pond, river, stream, etc.) is next best. A filter can be made by digging a hole approximately 1 foot from the bank of the water source. The water will seep into the hole where it may be collected for drinking. The water may be cloudy or even muddy, but will settle out if allowed to remain still. This water should be purified from bacteria before drinking.

Keep your clothing on. This includes hat and gloves. This will prevent beta burns which will occur on exposed skin. Clothing and equipment should be decontaminated by shaking. Washing clothing in any available water will remove radioactive particles.

Washing dust from exposed skin areas will assist in preventing burns. Keep as warm and dry as possible. If beta burns develop, treat as regular burns except that the burned areas should be washed.

Radiation sickness is most prevalent among the very young, the infirm or the old. It disrupts or alters the body's chemistry, but mildly contaminated people in otherwise good health will recover. Remember that radiation sickness is not a contagious disease. You can help a contaminated individual at no risk to yourself.

Protection in Towns and Cities   If you are in a town or city, you may be warned of a nuclear attack or other major threat to life and property by a 3- to 5-minute wavering siren or a series of short blasts on horns, whistles, or other devices. This will enable you to get to a public fallout shelter, if you are a civilian at work (always know where your nearest shelter is; if your employer is vague on this point, remind him that it's a federal offense not to have a nuclear attack contingency plan) or into your home or apartment fallout shelter. Keep a battery-powered radio for official information. Do not use your telephone to try to obtain information or advice.

Fallout Shelters—Home fallout shelters can be improvised from an existing cellar. If, like many homeowners, particularly in sunbelt states and newer developments, you do not have a cellar, you should consider constructing a community shelter, or even a personal shelter in your backyard. Most existing home basements will require additional shielding material to protect occupants from fallout radiation.

Minimal standards of shielding involve:

4 inches of concrete,
5 to 6 inches of brick,
6 inches of sand (packed in bags or boxes),
7 inches of earth,
8 inches of hollow concrete blocks (6 inches if filled with sand),
10 inches of water,
14 inches of books or magazines, or
18 inches of wood.

Plans for home basement modifications and backyard shelters can be obtained free from The Department of Defense, Office of Civil Defense, The Pentagon, Washington, D.C. 20310.

Food and Water—Sufficient food, water, and sanitation facilities should be stored in the shelter to last at least fourteen days. The following list supplies sample food items and their approximate shelf life. They should be replaced within the periods specified:

Food	Months
Milk:	
Evaporated	6
Nonfat dry or whole dry milk, in metal container	6
Canned meat, poultry, fish:	
Meat, poultry	18
Fish	12
Mixtures of meats, vegetables, cereal products	18
Condensed meat-and-vegetable soups	8
Fruits and vegetables:	
Berries and sour cherries, canned	6
Citrus fruit juices, canned	6
Other fruits and fruit juices, canned	18
Dried fruit in metal container	6
tomatoes, sauerkraut, canned	6
Other vegetables, canned (including dry beans and dry peas)	18
Cereals and baked goods:	
Ready-to-eat cereals:	
in metal container	12
in original paper package	1
Uncooked cereal (quick-cooking or instant)	
in metal container	24
in original paper package	12
Hydrogenated (or antioxidant-treated) fats and vegetable oil	12
Sugars, sweets, nuts:	
Sugar	will keep indefinitely
Hard candy, gum	18
Nuts, canned	12
Instant puddings	12
Miscellaneous:	
Coffee, tea, cocoa (instant)	18
Dry cream product (instant)	12

Bouillon products	12
Flavored beverage powders	24
Salt	will keep indefinitely
Flavoring extracts (e.g., pepper)	24
Soda, baking powder	12

Water must be kept in tightly sealed plastic containers. (Glass may break, and metal tends to corrode or rust.) There should be enough water to provide each person with at least one quart daily. Other sources of liquid are ice cubes or ice cube water (if you had a working freezer in the shelter before conventional power sources gave out), milk, soft drinks, juices, water from the hot-water tank (if in the cellar/shelter), and water already in your plumbing system. To use this water if the main water valves have been turned off or destroyed, turn on the faucet at the highest point of your home to allow air into the system. Then draw water, as needed, from the faucet located at the lowest point in your house, usually in the cellar/shelter. Treat this water as you would water from any other potentially contaminated source: boil. If you are unable to boil the water, add water purification tablets (available without prescription from any druggist), 12 drops of 2 percent tincture of iodine per gallon of water, or 8 drops of liquid chlorine bleach (provided the label says that hypochlorite is its only active ingredient) per gallon of water.

Radiation will pass through food and water without permanently contaminating it. The danger is in your swallowing fallout particles that may be on the food (or spread to the food during the handling of a contaminated container.)

Any container of suitable size with a tight-fitting lid can serve as a toilet. Another pail, plastic-lined, can hold the garbage. Also, have sufficient disinfectant, toilet paper, soap, washcloths and towels, pails or basins, and sanitary napkins. A well-stocked first-aid kit, in addition to any special family medicines, is essential.

NATURAL DISASTERS

PREPARATION

Disasters and emergencies affecting large areas and many people can sometimes develop quickly. Flash floods and earthquakes, for example, can strike with little or no advance warning.

Other types of disasters and emergencies are preceded by a buildup period that provides more time for taking effective protective measures. For example, the path of a hurricane is traced for days, and people in likely danger areas are notified several hours before the storm is expected to strike land. In many cases, floods also can be predicted so as to provide considerable warning time for people in the danger areas. Even in cases of tornadoes, the forecast of weather conditions frequently permits some warning of possible disaster. Winter storms—blizzards, heavy snows, ice storms, or freezing rains—also may pose hazards of disaster proportions, which lend themselves to reasonable prediction.

You should find out now, before any emergency occurs, what warning signals are being used in your community: what they sound like, what they mean, and what actions you should take when you hear them. Keep your radio or television set turned on to hear weather reports and forecasts, as well as other information and advice that may be broadcast by your local government.

Know how to disconnect your gas, electricity, and water supplies. (Obtain this information from your local utilities.) Check home fire extinguishers periodically to make sure there is adequate pressure behind the valve, that the chemicals haven't settled, and that the equipment will function properly. Keep a first-aid kit well stocked and in some central location, such as the kitchen. Smaller kits can be kept in the bathrooms. (Your local American Red Cross will supply you with medical handbooks instructing you on how to deal with nearly all medical emergencies that may arise.) Maintain a supply of canned or sealed-package foods that do not require refrigeration or heat for cooking, a stopped plastic jug of water, medicine needed by family members, blankets or sleeping bags, flashlights or lanterns, a battery-powered radio, and a covered container, with several rolls of toilet paper, to be used as an emergency toilet. In addition, an automobile in good running condition, with an ample supply of gasoline, may be necessary in case you have to leave your home. In parts of the country subject to hurricanes or floods, keep plywood sheeting and other lumber to board up windows and doors, and plastic sheeting or tarpaulins to protect furniture and appliances.

If you are warned to evacuate your home or move to another location, do so promptly and follow instructions given by the local authorities. If certain travel routes are specified or recommended, use those routes rather than trying to find shortcuts on your own. If you are told to leave, turn off your water, gas, or electric service before leaving the house. Find out on the radio where emergency housing and mass feeding stations are located in case you need to use them.

Floods In the event of a flood, the following procedures should be followed:

1) Find out how many feet your property is above or below possible flood levels so when predicted flood levels are broadcast, you can determine if you may be flooded.
2) If flooding is imminent, do not stack sandbags around the outside walls of your house to keep flood waters out of your basement. Water seeping downward through the earth may collect around the basement walls, or else raise the entire basement and cause it to "float" out of the ground. In most cases it is better to permit the flood waters to flow freely into the basement (or flood it yourself with clean water, if you are sure it will be flooded anyway). This will equalize the water pressure on the outside of the basement walls and floors, and thus avoid structural damage to the foundation and the house.
3) Store drinking water in closed, clean containers.
4) If flooding is likely, and time permits, move essential items and furniture to upper floors. Disconnect any electrical appliances that can't be moved—but don't touch them if you are wet or standing in water. Lock house doors and windows. If you are leaving a vehicle behind, put it in the garage or driveway, close its windows, and lock it.
5) When driving through flood waters put the car in low gear and drive very slowly, to avoid splashing water into the engine and

causing it to stall. Remember that brakes may not work well after the wheels have been in deep water.

6) If you are caught with a flood rising around your house, get to the roof. If the roof is on the verge of going under, find some large, *stable* floating object on which to ride with the flood.
7) Help others to share your haven if it will support them.
8) Don't be in a hurry to enter a building after the flood waters subside. Its foundations may have been weakened, and it could collapse.
9) If you are engaged in rescue operations after the flood, always wear a safety vest.
10) Avoid direct contact with a desperate victim who could jeopardize your life as well as his own. Always throw a buoyed rope or extend an oar, depending on circumstances, before going overboard after the victim.
11) In winter, extend a pole or piece of clothing to someone who has fallen through ice, while you remain flat on the ice to distribute your weight with less stress on any one small area. If other people are willing to help, form a human chain across the ice (on your stomachs) to reach the victim, with people on shore pulling (sliding) the chain to safety once the victim is secured.

Tornadoes In the event of a possible tornado, these procedures should be followed:

1) Listen for advice on the radio or television.
2) Watch the sky, especially to the south and southwest. When a "tornado watch" is announced during the approach of a hurricane, however, keep watching the sky to the east.
3) If you see any revolving, funnel-shaped clouds, report them by telephone to your local police or weather bureau. Do not use the telephone to ask for additional information.
4) Seek shelter inside, if possible.
5) If in the open, move away from a tornado's path at a right angle.
6) If there is no time to escape, lie flat in the nearest depression, such as a ditch or ravine.
7) In office buildings, the basement or an interior hallway on a lower floor is safest. Upper stories are unsafe. If there is not time

to descend, a closet or small room with stout walls, or an inside hallway will give some protection against flying debris. Otherwise, get under heavy furniture.

8) In homes with basements, seek refuge near the basement wall in the most sheltered and deepest below-ground part of the basement. A storm cellar, or a reinforced portion of the basement, can be planned and constructed; or the safest portion of the basement can be selected and the family drilled to use it.

9) In homes without basements, take cover in the smallest room with stout walls, or under heavy furniture or a tipped-over upholstered couch or chair in the central part of the house. The first floor is safer than the second (or third).

10) If there is time, partly open windows, on the side away from the direction of the storm's approach—but *stay away from windows when the storm strikes.*

11) Mobile homes are particularly vulnerable to overturning and destruction during strong winds, and should be abandoned in favor of a preselected shelter, or even a ditch in the open. Damage can be minimized by securing the trailer with cables anchored in concrete footing.

12) Factories, auditoriums, and other large buildings with wide, free-span roofs, should have preselected, marked shelter areas in their basements, smaller rooms, or nearby.

Hurricanes   In the event of an imminent hurricane, follow these procedures:

1) If your house is on high ground and you haven't been instructed to evacuate, stay indoors.

2) Before the storm hits, secure outdoor objects that might be blown away. Garbage cans, garden tools, toys, signs, porch furniture, and a number of other harmless items become missiles of destruction in hurricane winds.

3) Board up windows or protect them with storm shutters or tape. Danger to small windows is mainly from wind-driven debris. Larger windows may be broken by wind pressure.

4) If the center, or "eye," of the hurricane passes directly over you, there will be a temporary lull in the wind, lasting from a few

minutes to perhaps a full hour or more. Stay in a safe place during this lull. The wind will return—perhaps with even greater force—from the opposite direction.

5) Parked cars are unsafe as shelter during a hurricane or severe windstorm. However, as a last resort, if no ravine or ditch is nearby they may provide some shelter from flying debris to those who crawl under them.

6) Review the safety rules for floods and tornadoes. Most of the same common sense procedures apply to all natural disasters.

Earthquakes In the event of an earthquake, follow these procedures:

1) Keep calm. Don't run or panic. If you take the proper precautions, chances are you will not be hurt.

2) Stay where you are. If outdoors, stay outdoors. If indoors, stay indoors. Most injuries occur as people are entering or leaving buildings.

3) If the shaking catches you indoors, take cover under a desk, table, or bench, or against inside walls or doorways. Stay away from glass, windows, and outside doors.

4) Don't use candles, matches, or other open flames either during or after the tremor. Douse all fires.

5) If the earthquake catches you outside, move away from buildings and utility wires. Once in the open, stay there until the shaking stops.

6) Don't run through or near buildings. The greatest danger from falling debris is just outside doorways and close to outer walls.

7) If you are in a moving car, stop as quickly as safety permits, but stay in the vehicle. A car may jiggle fearsomely on its springs during an earthquake, but it is a good place to stay until the shaking stops. When you drive on, watch for hazards created by the earthquake, such as fallen or falling objects, downed electrical wires, or broken or undermined railways.

Tidal Waves (Tsunami, pronounced soo-nam´-ee)

1) All earthquakes do not cause tidal waves, but many do. When you hear that an earthquake has occurred, stand by for a tidal wave emergency.
2) Do not stay in low-lying coastal areas after a local earthquake.
3) A tidal wave is not a single wave but a series of them. Stay out of danger areas until an "all clear" is issued by a competent authority.
4) Never go down to the beach to watch for a tidal wave. When you can see the wave you are too close to escape it.
5) During tidal wave emergency, follow the instructions of local authorities on what to do and what not to do, with respect to the emergency.

Lightning   Safety rules and procedures:

1) When a thunderstorm threatens, get inside a home or large building, or inside an all-metal (not convertible) vehicle.
2) Inside a home, avoid using the telephone, except for emergencies.
3) If outside, with no time to reach a safe building or an automobile, follow these precautions:

- Avoid projecting above the surrounding landscape, as you would do if you were standing on a hilltop, in an open field, or on the beach, or fishing from a small boat. Stay "indoors" in large boats.
- Get out of and away from open water.
- Get off of and away from motorcycles, scooters, golf carts, and bicycles. Put down your golf clubs.
- Stay away from wire fences, clotheslines, metal pipes, rails, and other metallic parts which could carry lightning to you from some distance away.
- Avoid standing in small, isolated sheds or other small structures in open areas.
- In a forest, seek shelter in a low area under a thick growth of small trees. In open areas, go to a low place such as a ravine or valley. Be alert for flash floods.

- If you're hopelessly isolated in a level field or prairie and you feel your hair stand on end—indicating that lightning is about to strike—drop to your knees and bend forward, putting your hands on your knees. Do not lie flat on the ground.

4) Persons struck by lightning receive a severe electrical shock and may be burned, but they carry no electrical charge and can be handled safely. Even someone "killed" by lightning can be revived by prompt action. When a group has been struck, the seemingly dead should be treated first.

5) The American Red Cross says that if a victim is not breathing, first aid should be rendered immediately to prevent irrevocable damage to the brain. Give mouth-to-mouth resuscitation once every 5 seconds to adults and once every 3 seconds to children, until medical help arrives.

6) Victims who appear to be only stunned or otherwise unhurt may also need attention. Check for burns, especially at fingers and toes, and next to buckles and jewelry.

Forest Fires   Safety rules:

1) When traveling through dry, forested country, periodically check your local radio news broadcast to determine whether any major fires are reported in your area.

2) If you are without a radio, keep a watch toward distant mountains for black clouds that stay in one area or undulate and flow upward, unlike ordinary rain clouds or thunderheads. If downwind, you can often smell the smoke long before seeing it. Try to determine the course of the fire and detour accordingly.

3) If on foot, don't try to outrun a forest fire when it is already close. Make for the nearest stream or river, even if you must risk crossing in front of the fire. Get into the stream and away from flammable portions of the shore. Make sure all portions of your clothing and body are wet. Rocks along the shore may get extremely hot, and the water will get warm.

4) Don't panic. Only an exceptionally large fire would cause exceptionally shallow or stagnant streams to get so hot as to scald you.

5) Avoid smoke inhalation by breathing through dampened cloths, a handkerchief, or an undershirt.

6) The fire may absorb much of your local oxygen supply, so lie still and maintain, as much as possible, normal respiration.

7) If you are unable to reach water of any kind (even low, marshy ground might help), depending on the depth and intensity of the fire, you may want to try to clear a firebreak around you. Frankly, this may work for a minor brush fire, but it won't do you much good if you are surrounded by an enormous wall of fire.

8) Whatever you do, avoid shallow caves. If the inhalation of smoke doesn't kill you, the heat and loss of oxygen will.

AFTER A DISASTER

1) Enter all buildings with care. They may have been damaged or weakened by the disaster, and they may collapse without warning.

2) Do enter buildings to find gas leaks or electrical short circuits.

3) Don't bring lighted cigarettes or other burning objects into any enclosed spaces because of the threat of leaking gas lines.

4) Stay away from fallen or damaged electric wires.

5) Check for leaking gas in your home. If you smell gas, open all windows and doors, turn off the main gas valve at the meter, and leave the house immediately. Notify the gas company or the police or fire department, and don't re-enter the house until you have been told it is safe to do so.

6) If electrical appliances are wet: First, turn off the main power switch in your house; then, unplug the wet appliance; dry it out; reconnect it; and—only then—turn on the main power switch. (Caution: Don't do any of these things while you are wet or standing in water.)

7) If fuses blow when the electric power is restored, turn off the main power switch and inspect the area and appliances for short circuits.

8) Check your food and water supplies. Foods that require refrigeration may be spoiled if electric power has been off for some time. Don't eat food that has come in contact with flood waters. Follow the instructions of local authorities concerning the use of food and water supplies.

9) If needed, get food, clothing, medical care, or shelter at Red Cross stations or from your local government.
10) Don't go sightseeing. You could interfere with first-aid or rescue work, and it may be dangerous as well.
11) Don't use the roads unless absolutely necessary.
12) Report the local hazards you find to your local authorities.
13) Write, telegraph, or telephone your relatives when the emergency is over. Otherwise local authorities may waste time and money trying to locate you. Do not tie up the telephone.
14) Do not pass on rumors.

Poisonous Snakes of the World

FACTS ABOUT SNAKES

Poisonous snakes should be respected and avoided, but they should not be feared. The following facts will help dispel many of the unfounded fears people have about snakes.

Most snakes are harmless. Even many poisonous snakes that have not reached maturity are only marginally dangerous. There are many small snakes, however—maximum length of about five feet—that are very poisonous from the time of birth. Some of the more prevalent are listed below:

Snake	Average Size (ft.)	Location
Asiatic Cobra	5	India
Asp—Egyptian Cobra	3½	Egypt and South Africa
Tic Pologna	4	India
Puff Adder (African)	3½	Morocco and Arabia
Mamba	5	West, central South America
Tiger Snake	4	Australia
Sand Viper	2	North Africa

Gaboon Viper	3–4	Tropical Africa
Urutu	4	Brazil
Coral	1–2	United States, south-western Pacific

A variety of poisonous snakes exists in the tropics, but the danger from these snakes is actually less than in rattlesnake- or moccasin-infested areas of the United States. Some areas of the world are free of poisonous land snakes, including New Zealand, Cuba, Haiti, Jamaica, Puerto Rico, and the Polynesian islands.

Some snakes may be aggressive and attack without apparent provocation. The king cobra of Southeast Asia, the bushmaster and the tropical rattlesnake of South America, and the mamba of Africa have been reported to do so on occasion. But aggressiveness is the exception. Nearly all snakes are timid and docile and will go out of their way to avoid man.

Snakes cannot tolerate weather extremes. In temperate regions, they are active day and night during the warmer months; they hibernate or become inactive in cold weather. In desert and semi-desert regions, snakes are most active during early morning and seek shade during the day. Many snakes are active only at night.

Snakes normally are slow travelers, but can strike with astonishing rapidity. *They cannot outrun a man, and only a few can leap clear of the ground.*

The striking distance of a snake is often exaggerated. It is seldom more than half the snake's length; of a large snake, about a third of its length. Some of the small vipers, however, have been known to strike from a distance equal to their full length. Also, in a full coil, some snakes can strike from a distance equal to two-thirds their length.

The distance a cobra can strike is easy to judge since the part raised is never bent into deceptive S-curves, but is merely jabbed forward and downward. The distance is commonly about one foot, but the striking distance of a twelve-foot king cobra may be as much as three feet.

GENERAL GROUPINGS OF POISONOUS SNAKES

POISONOUS LONG-FANGED SNAKES

Among the group of very venomous snakes are the vipers and adders of Europe, Asia, and Africa; the rattlesnakes, copperheads, and cottonmouth moccasins of North America; and the bushmaster, fer-de-lances, and several other species of tropical America.

The true vipers and pit vipers are mostly thick-bodied with flattened heads. Well-known species of the true vipers, found only in the Old World, are Russel's viper of India; the Cape viper of southern Africa; the puff adder of dry areas of Africa and Arabia; and the gaboon viper of tropical Africa.

The bite of a snake belonging to this group is very painful, and is followed by local swelling which increases as the venom spreads throughout the tissue.

POISONOUS SHORT-FANGED SNAKES

Because of the relatively short fangs of snakes belonging to this group, even light clothing reduces their danger to man. Their venom is the most deadly among poisonous snakes. Snakes included in this short-fanged group are the cobras, kraits, and coral snakes. They comprise the majority of snakes in Australia, and many species are found in India, Malaya, Africa, and New Guinea.

There are ten or more species of cobras, all found in Africa or Asia. All are more or less able to form a "hood." The king cobra is the largest of poisonous snakes.

The venom of the cobra and its relatives chiefly affects the nerves, and the cobra bite is not painful until some time later. Since the venom is absorbed into the victim's bloodstream, it is distributed rapidly to all parts of the body.

SEA SNAKES

Venomous sea snakes are not found in the Atlantic, but occur in large numbers off the shores of the Indian Ocean and the southern and western Pacific. They are usually encountered in tidal rivers and near the coast but may be seen far out at sea. Usually they do not disturb swimmers, so there is little danger of being bitten. They are identified by their flat, vertically compressed paddle tail.

THE CONSTRICTORS
Though nonpoisonous, it is worth mentioning some facts about pythons, boas, anacondas, and other constrictors—snakes that use their powerful musculature to strangle their prey. Some of these are large snakes which may grow to twenty-five feet in length. These reptiles are timid and rarely attack man. Boas are found in the American tropics; pythons in the tropics of Africa and Asia. They sometimes attack small children but will not deliberately tackle anything that is too large to swallow. A man is too big for even the largest python. They are slow-moving and shy, but if caught or cornered, these snakes may fight back by wrapping their coils around the attacker. Their sharp teeth and power of constriction can make them vicious and dangerous.

IDENTIFICATION OF POISONOUS SNAKES

There is *no single characteristic* which distinguishes a poisonous snake from a harmless one except the presence of poison fangs and glands. *The idea that all poisonous snakes have lance-shaped or triangular heads or some other warning feature is wrong and a dangerous misconception.*

The only positive way to identify dangerous snakes is to learn to know and recognize the poisonous kinds on sight in different regions of the world. The illustrations on the following pages describe the important kinds found in any given locality. The ability to distinguish a poisonous snake from a harmless one will minimize the danger of snakebite and help eliminate fear.

POISONOUS SNAKES OF NORTH AMERICA

RATTLESNAKE
There are about twenty-seven species of rattlesnake in the United States and Mexico. Except in those localities where they have been exterminated, one or more types are found in every locality. The rattle on the end of the tail is the best and most positive means of identification. If the rattle is hidden, the thick body and the wide head are good danger signs. Some rattlesnakes are small, and their bite is not likely to result in death. Others, such as the diamondbacks, may grow to lengths

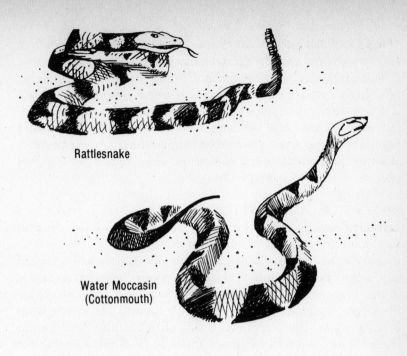

Rattlesnake

Water Moccasin
(Cottonmouth)

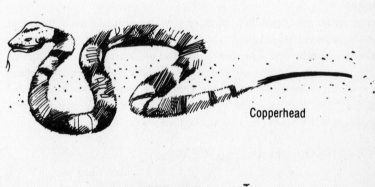

Copperhead

Coral Snake

Fig. I-i Poisonous Snakes of North America

of eight feet, and are very dangerous. In color, rattlesnakes vary from gray to black and may or may not have spots or blotches.

Rattlesnakes may be found in practically any type of terrain, but they prefer open, sandy places or rocky ledges. They do not always give a warning rattle; when surprised, they may strike first and rattle afterward. Rattlesnakes will almost always try to escape without a fight. The danger from a bite depends upon the size of the snake: A small rattlesnake will make a normal man sick; the bite of a large one (three to five feet long) may be fatal.

WATER MOCCASIN (COTTONMOUTH)

The water moccasin has a thick body and a head which is wider than the neck. It averages three to four feet in length, but may grow to as long as six feet. It is usually dull brown or olive in color and is marked with indistinct bands or blotches; the markings sometimes disappear in the larger snakes. The belly is yellowish, blotched with darker markings. Young moccasins are brilliantly colored. The mouth, when open, is white. The water moccasin is often confused with various species of harmless water snakes, many of which closely resemble it in color and shape. Unidentified snakes found in or near water should be avoided.

The water moccasin lives in or near water and is a good swimmer. It is often seen basking on branches and logs along sluggish streams, bayous, and swamps. The snake usually will retreat when disturbed, but it may stand its ground, holding its mouth wide open in a threatening gesture. For this reason, it is sometimes called a "cottonmouth," "gapper," or "trapjaw." The venom of the water moccasin is very poisonous, and the bite of a large snake is often fatal.

COPPERHEAD (UPLAND MOCCASIN)

This is a thick-bodied snake with a head wider than the neck. It reaches an average length of two and a half feet, but some specimens may be as long as four and a half feet. The color is usually pale brown, with a number of darker crossbands narrowing at the midline of the back. The markings may be few and inconspicuous on the larger snakes. The head is copper-red in color. The belly is generally light in color and somewhat mottled.

In the northern areas, the copperhead is usually found in thick forests. In the south, it may be found almost anywhere in the fields or woods. It prefers high dry ground. These snakes are rather timid; they usually stay hidden and try to escape when discovered. If cornered, they may vibrate the tail and produce a distinct buzzing sound in vegetation. Bites from copperheads are rare, even where the snakes are quite numerous. The venom is weak and not particularly dangerous to adults. Only a few fatal cases have been recorded. The copperhead is also known as "upland moccasin," "chunk-head," "death adder," or "pilot snake."

CORAL SNAKES

These snakes are actually members of the cobra family. They have bright red or pink bellies and brightly colored bands on the back. There are three or four kinds of coral snakes generally averaging under two feet in length; one species may grow to be four feet long.

Coral snakes are found only in the subtropical regions of North America—southern Florida and parts of Mexico—preferring to live near low-lying swamps and marshes.

When the short-fanged coral strikes it literally must "chew" through the skin, thus making it virtually impossible for the snakes to strike through any form of clothing.

Coral snakes are inoffensive and timid. They are seldom seen and cause very few fatalities.

POISONOUS SNAKES OF CENTRAL AND SOUTH AMERICA

CORAL SNAKES

See Poisonous Snakes of North America.

RATTLESNAKES

Of the five kinds of rattlesnakes in Central and South America, only the tropical rattlesnake is widely distributed. This snake and its close relatives are large snakes, averaging about five feet in length. The characteristic tropical rattlesnake has a pair of dark stripes extending along the neck, with geometrical body markings. The Mexican rattlesnake is similarly marked, but without dark stripes. A smaller rattlesnake, found on Aruba Island, has a pale gray back and a white belly. The rattle on the tip of the tail is sufficient identification for all rattlesnakes.

The tropical rattlesnake is a vicious reptile. It is large and aggressive, and its venom is highly poisonous. This snake may strike with very little warning rattle and before coiling. If teased, it may advance toward the tormentor. It is found only in dry, hilly country, not in thick forests. The tropical rattlesnake is also known as the "cascabel" in Mexico and Central America and as the "cascavel" in Brazil.

BUSHMASTERS

These are large snakes with moderately slender bodies and heads much wider than their necks. They average from seven to nine feet in length, but may grow longer than eleven feet. They are light brown with a pinkish hue, and have a series of dark blotches which are wide on the back and narrow down the sides. The scales are extremely rough and raised like the teeth of a rasp.

The bushmaster is found mostly in forests at low altitudes. It prefers dry ground and often hides in animal burrows. When lying on the forest floor, its camouflage makes it difficult to spot. The snake may either remain motionless until touched, or it may attempt to escape when cornered. It may strike viciously—sometimes it may even edge toward an intruder. The tail is vibrated when the snake is irritated, and if it vibrates among dry leaves, the snake may be mistaken for a rattlesnake. The bushmaster is a savage and dangerous snake, but is seldom seen. The best precaution is to wear hoots, and to keep hands out of holes and brush that are close to the ground.

FER-DE-LANCE GROUP

There are several closely related species in this group. The fer-de-lance and about six of its relatives are gray to brown or reddish in color, with dark geometrical blotches which generally are narrow on the back and broad at the sides. It is moderately thick, with a head much wider than the neck. The fer-de-lance averages about three to four feet in length, but may grow to as long as eight or nine feet. Some members of the group are smaller and display almost any color, including green or yellow; some have thick bodies. The fer-de-lance is also known as the "barba amarilla."

Tropical Rattlesnake

Fer-de-Lance Group

Bushmaster

Sea Snake

Fig. I-ii Poisonous Snakes of Central and South America

The fer-de-lance group is widespread throughout Central and South America. The large species are ground snakes; some of the small ones, known as palm vipers, live in trees, especially at the base of the leaves of a palm tree. The larger types in the group are dangerous, and are often found in cane fields or around dwellings where they catch rats. They all loop their bodies before striking.

The rattlesnake, the bushmaster, and the fer-de-lance group are all related to pit vipers. All have two long fangs in the upper jaw and no other teeth of comparable size. The two long fangs may be covered with a curtain of flesh, or they may be folded back in the mouth. Another characteristic of these snakes is the presence of a deep pit between the eye and the nostril.

SEA SNAKES

The sea snake is found only in brackish or salt water along the Pacific Coast, from the Gulf of California to Ecuador. It is sometimes very abundant in the Gulf of Panama. It is not found in the Atlantic Ocean. The sea snake of the Americas has a brown to black back and a yellow belly. These snakes may average two to three feet in length.

There are no poisonous snakes in all of the Caribbean Islands, except Martinique, St. Lucia, and Trinidad. Chile and the Andean highlands above 10,000 feet have no poisonous snakes.

POISONOUS SNAKES OF SOUTHEASTERN ASIA

COBRAS

The typical combat attitude of the raised head and spread hood is the easiest characteristic by which cobras can be identified. The most common species, the Indian cobra, may grow to as long as six feet. The "spectacle" mark on the hood is typical of this species; the mark may consist of only one spot, or of two without the bridge. Cobras usually (but not always) form a hood when angered. The king cobras are the largest of all poisonous snakes: They average ten to twelve feet; some may reach eighteen feet. In proportion to its body, the hood formed by the king cobra is narrower than that of other cobras.

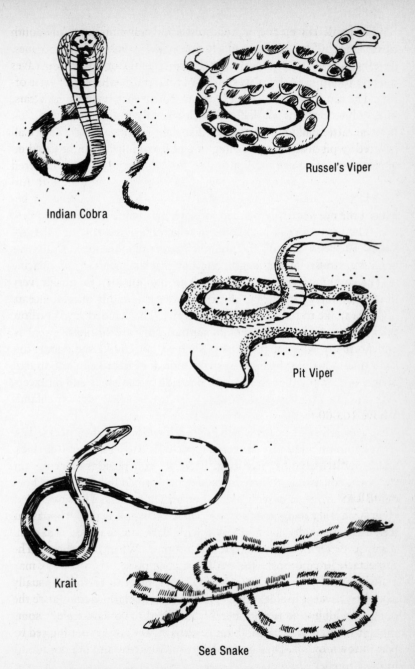

Indian Cobra

Russel's Viper

Pit Viper

Krait

Sea Snake

Fig. I-iii   Poisonous Snakes of Southeastern Asia

Cobras are the most common poisonous snakes in much of south-eastern Asia. They are particularly numerous in India where, because of religious beliefs, natives do not destroy them. Cobras are most frequently found in rocky places, or in old buildings where they feed on rats. The most common species are not particularly vicious; however, king cobras may attack deliberately, especially if guarding eggs. Cobras are slow snakes; they always raise their heads to strike. They can be killed with a stout stick swung in a plane parallel with the ground, aimed at the head or raised part.

KRAITS

Most kraits are brightly banded in black and white or black and yellow. They have a rigid backbone on which there is a row of enlarged scales. The head is small, and not much larger than the neck. Kraits average four to five feet in length, but may reach six feet.

The common krait of India moves around mostly at night. It lives in open country rather than thick jungle brush, and is often found at night near inhabited places and on trails. The handed krait prefers thick jungle. All kraits are very poisonous. They are inoffensive snakes and normally will not bite unless stepped on. Unlike the cobra, the krait does not raise the head to strike, nor does it strike in a loop like a viper—it simply flips the head to one side or the other and bites.

VIPERS

Vipers usually have heads which are much wider than their necks. The most common and most dangerous species is Russel's viper. It is thick and grows to up to five feet long. There are conspicuous markings on the back, consisting of three rows of spots formed by black rings bordered with white, and with reddish or brown centers. The saw-scaled viper is another dangerous species. These are small snakes, about two feet long, generally light in color with dark quadrangles. The side scales are rough and somewhat saw-toothed. When disturbed, these snakes writhe vigorously and make a hissing noise.

Russel's viper prefers open, sunny spots, but can be found almost anywhere, except in thick jungle. It is not particularly vicious and will not strike unless it is considerably irritated. The saw-scaled viper, though small, is vicious and bites readily; vipers only a foot long have been known to kill. They prefer desert or dry areas and are not found in thick jungle.

PIT VIPERS

Pit vipers may be slender or thick-bodied. They usually have heads which are much wider than their necks. These snakes commonly are brown with dark blotches; some types are green. They are named for the deep pit located between the eye and nostril.

India has about a dozen species of this snake. Pit vipers are found in all types of terrain, and may be found in the trees or on the ground. The tree snakes are slender; the ground snakes are thicker and heavy-bodied. Only the larger ones are dangerous. One of the pit vipers of China is a moccasin similar to those found in North America; it is found in the rocky areas of the remote mountains of southern China. It attains a length of four and a half feet but is not vicious unless irritated. A small pit viper, about one and a half feet long, is often found on the plains of eastern China; it is too small to be dangerous to a man wearing shoes.

SEA SNAKES

These snakes have a flattened, oar-like tail and are distinguished from eels in that snakes have scales and eels do not. Sea snakes vary widely in color and shape; they average four to five feet in length, but sometimes reach a length of eight to ten feet.

Sea snakes are found along the coasts, and at the mouths of some of the larger rivers. The bite of these snakes is dangerous but rare. Sea snakes sometimes may be seen in large numbers, particularly during mating season, but they will seldom bite unless they are handled. No cases of a deliberate attack of a man in the water are known.

POISONOUS SNAKES OF EUROPE, AFRICA, AND THE NEAR EAST

In Europe, west of the Volga, vipers are the only poisonous snakes found. There are no poisonous snakes in Ireland or Madagascar.

CORAL SNAKES
See Poisonous Snakes of North America.

SEA SNAKES
See Poisonous Snakes of Southeastern Asia.

EUROPEAN VIPERS
These snakes have a short, thick body and a wide head which is much broader than the neck. There is usually a zigzag stripe down the back; colors may be gray, olive-brown, reddish, or yellowish. The European viper averages two to three feet in length. There are eight species on the European continent. They are also known as adders or asps.

Vipers generally are found in the wilder areas, particularly in rocky planes, such as the Pyrenees, the Apennines, and in the Balkan mountains, where they may be found at heights up to 5,000 feet. They are found as far north as 67° latitude in Scandinavia and across Siberia. Sunlit slopes, moors and heaths, grain fields, and trash piles are favorite prowling places. Some of the European vipers are aggressive and savage, causing occasional deaths.

AFRICAN VIPERS
The vipers of North Africa are similar to those of Europe, except for the puff adder. This is a large brownish or sand-colored snake with striking markings, a heavy body, and a very short tail. The puff adder grows to a length of five feet. Central and South Africa have several additional kinds of vipers; among the largest is the rhinoceros viper. Found in West Africa, it has horns on its nose, a very wide head, and a thick body covered with colored marks down the back; it reaches a maximum length of four feet. The gaboon viper has one horn on the nose, a wide head, and a thick body with oblong markings on the back and triangular colored spots on the sides; it has been known to reach a length of six feet. There are a number of other African vipers, most of them small.

The puff adder prefers open forest or grasslands near streams. The rhinoceros viper is found in or near streams. The gaboon viper lives in heavy forest. The bite of any of these snakes is extremely dangerous. However, they are not aggressive nor are they inclined to bite. The smaller vipers, found in sandy country, open brush, grassland, or light forests, are likely to be aggressive and dangerous in spite of their small size. One of the smaller kinds buries itself in the sand and may strike at a passing man; its presence is disclosed by a characteristic coiling pattern in the sand.

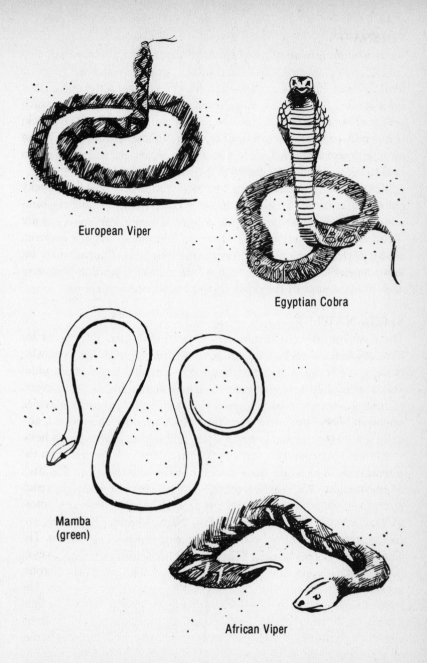

European Viper

Egyptian Cobra

Mamba
(green)

African Viper

Fig. I-iv   Poisonous Snakes of Europe, Africa, and the Near East

COBRAS

There are several varieties of cobras in Africa and the Near East. The cobras of this area may be black, brown, gray or yellowish, with or without markings. Cobras are often six to seven feet long; one kind—the water cobra—may attain eight feet.

The cobras of Africa and the Near East can be found in almost any habitat. One variety lives in or near water; another climbs trees. Some of the cobras in this area are reported to be aggressive and savage. The fairly common Egyptian cobra of North Africa and the adjacent regions is often found around rocky places and ruins. The distance the cobra can strike in a forward direction is equal to the distance the head is raised above the ground. Some cobras, however, can spit venom a distance of ten to twelve feet; this venom is harmless unless it gets into a man's eyes, in which case it may cause blindness if not washed out immediately. It is particularly dangerous to poke around in holes and rock piles because of the possibility of encountering a spitting cobra.

MAMBAS

These snakes are very slender and have small heads. They generally have a green or dark, uniform color without conspicuous spots or markings. The scales are smooth, symmetrical, and large. Mambas attain lengths of up to twelve feet. An eight-foot mamba is about half the thickness of an ordinary broomstick. It is difficult to identify mambas positively. The fangs in an eight-foot snake are only about one and a half inches long, the thickness of a pin, and almost covered with flesh.

Mambas are found throughout Africa, except in the extreme northern portions. The South African mamba may be found from Tanzania in the east, to West Africa south of the Congo; it undergoes two changes in color—one black and one green. The green mamba is found in West Africa, from the Senegal to the Niger. Mambas live in trees or on the ground, and have been known to enter houses in search of rats. They are very quick snakes. They may attack deliberately during their breeding season but otherwise are quite timid. The bite of the mamba is very dangerous.

POISONOUS SNAKES OF AUSTRALIA, NEW GUINEA AND THE PACIFIC ISLANDS

In Australia, New Guinea, New Hebrides, the Carolinas, the Solomons, and adjacent islands *nearly all snakes are poisonous*. In islands east of New Zealand, there are no poisonous land snakes.

SEA SNAKES
See Poisonous Snakes of Southeastern Asia.

COPPERHEADS
See Poisonous Snakes of North America.

DEATH ADDERS
This snake has a short, thick, clumsy body with a head much wider than the neck, and a short, thin tail. It seldom grows to more than two feet in length. It may be gray, brown, pink, or brick-red, depending on the sandstone of the region in which it lives and into which its camouflage skillfully blends. There are bands of darker color across the body, particularly in the young snakes. The death adder has rough scales, and a spine on the tail.

This snake is found in sandy localities over most of Australia except Victoria, and in southern New Guinea and the Maluccas. Because the death adder resembles the ground it inhabits, it is not likely to be seen. While the snake is not quick to strike, it can be dangerous if irritated or stepped on. The venom of this snake is highly poisonous.

TIGER SNAKES
The tiger snake has dark bands on a tawny background of green, gray, orange, or brown: Sometimes the bands are indistinct. It has a stout body with a rather wide head. It averages about four to five feet long when full grown, but may reach six feet. The tiger snake spreads its neck when angry.

The tiger snake lives in dry country, ranging extensively throughout Australia and Tasmania. It is a savage and dangerous reptile *which causes more deaths in Australia than all the other snakes combined.* Tiger snakes are quick to bite, spreading the neck and lunging with a

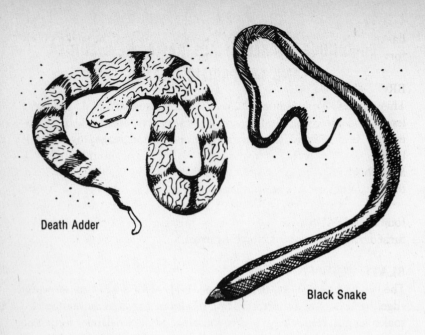

Death Adder

Black Snake

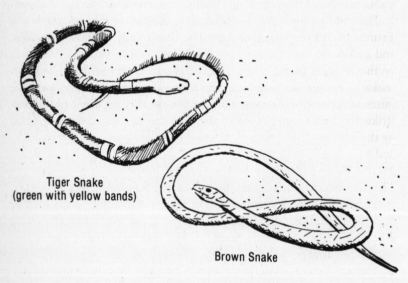

Tiger Snake
(green with yellow bands)

Brown Snake

Fig. I-v   Poisonous Snakes of Australia, New Guinea,
and the Pacific Islands

flashing stroke that is so vigorous it sometimes moves the snake's body forward so that the snake seems to be making a short jump.

BROWN SNAKES

This is a slender snake with a small narrow head; it usually attains a length of four or five feet. The eyes are large. The color is light yellow to brown or gray above, and white underneath; the young are pale brown and have a pretty, ringed pattern. There are about a dozen relatives of this snake, some of which are called whip snakes. In spite of the small size of the head, the venom of this snake is highly poisonous.

The brown snake is widely distributed throughout Australia and is found also in New Guinea. It is not an aggressive snake unless disturbed. It strikes from a looped position.

BLACK SNAKES

The black snake is blue-black on top and brilliant scarlet underneath, edged with black. The scales are symmetrical and satiny-smooth. This snake averages six to seven feet in length, and has a slender body and a small, narrow head. It spreads its neck at the least feeling of alarm.

This snake is found throughout Australia, except in the north and Tasmania. It prefers marshy places or streams; it dives and swims well, and can stay under water for long periods of time. Because it lies still on the bottoms of streams, it may be dangerous to bathers. The black snake will not attack unless stepped on or cornered. When angry, it raises its head a few inches from the ground on a slanting plane, and strikes from that position. While more people in Australia are bitten by the black snake than any other kind, its venom is relatively weak, and very few victims die of the bite.

Survival Kit (Recommended List)

New nylon back packs with aluminum frames are light in weight, but can carry many indispensable items besides bedrolls (in cold climates, use down bags; in jungles, use a hammock) and small tents or parachute panels.

- Lightweight, roll-up rainsuit
- In hot climates, a broad-brimmed, lightweight hat
- In cold climates, a knitted cap to cover head and ears, and extra gloves or mittens
- A change of underwear and socks
- Roll-up 4-foot seine (Poles can be fashioned from available sticks or other wood found near a stream.)
- Waterproof, strike-anywhere matches
- Waterproof, batteryless flashlight
- Candle stub (Besides light, candle wax is sometimes useful for plugging and patching.)
- Fire starter
- Toilet paper (Don't use poison ivy!)
- Insect repellent (in plastic squeeze bottle)
- Sunscreen lotion or cream
- Sunglasses
- Signal mirror
- Two smoke signals
- Two flares

- Compass
- Appropriate topographic maps
- Halazone tablets for purifying water
- Two dozen assorted fishhooks
- Fifty feet of 50-lb. test monofilament line
- Brass swivels and 25 feet of light wire for rigging snares
- Swiss Army-style pocket knife
- Needle and thread
- Twenty-five feet of parachute cord, or other heavy-duty nylon line
- Short file or whetstone
- Axe or hatchet
- A strong saw—easily stored yet sturdy enough to take down trees many inches in diameter
- Plastic pack of bouillon cubes and chocolate packs to mix with water
- One square yard of aluminum foil
- Antiseptic cream
- Small pad and pencil

First-Aid Kit

The following first-aid pack is recommended by the U.S. Army. It represents "barebones" emergency items, with an emphasis on ministering to major wounds and shock:

- Individual dressings (4 by 7 inches) or sterile gauze dressings in tightly sealed plastic packs
- Compress and bandage, 2 by 2 inches, 4 strips
- Gauze compress-type bandages (3 inches by 6 yards)
- 3 six-yard rolls of 1- and 2-inch gauze bandage
- Muslin-type compressed bandage (37 by 37 by 52 inches)
- Gauze, petrolatum (3 by 26 inches, 3 strips)
- Adhesive tape (1 inch by 1 yard, 100 strips)
- Adhesive bandage (¾ inch by 3 inches, 300 strips)
- Eye wash and dressing
- Ammonia inhalation solution, aromatic ampules, ⅓ cc, 10 units
- Povidone-iodine solution, non-ferrous, 10 percent, ½ fl. oz. (14.8 cc)
- Sodium chloride (salt)-sodium bicarbonate mixture
- Surgical preparation razor blade
- Instruction sheet and list of contents

A civilian should not plan an extensive trip to or over a wilderness area, unless he or she has a complete physical checkup with the family physician, including a chest X-ray, respirator test, and exercise cardiogram.

A civilian first-aid kit can be improvised from an Army-Navy surplus ammunition box painted white with a Red Cross. It should be kept on prominent display in camp at all times and never packed so deeply among other supplies that the first-aid equipment can't be reached in a matter of seconds.

The following items (suggested by wilderness medical expert, Dr. George H. Hulsey of Norman, Oklahoma) should be carried in addition to the Army recommended list inside Zip-Loc freezer bags in the converted ammo box:

- Assortment of adhesive bandages
- Roller bandages
- Tweezers
- Elastic bandages
- Ethyl chloride spray
- Small can of foot powder
- Plastic bottle of aspirin
- Snakebite kit (for non-arctic and non-subarctic areas)

Special conditions and suggested types of medications (Some of these items will need a doctor's prescription):

- Motion sickness—Bonine
- Nausea and vomiting—Compazine suppositories
- Diarrhea—tincture of opium
- Indigestion—antacid tablets
- Minor pain—aspirin
- Major pain—a narcotic
- Insect bites, poison ivy, nettles, etc.—Calamine lotion with 1 percent Phenol, 1 percent Menthol, and 1 percent hydrocortisone, or meat tenderizer. (The latter is especially effective in soothing bee stings. For people who suffer severe allergic reactions to bees or wasps, get a prescribed drug from your physician.)

Tips and Other Items:

- Garlic extract capsules (found at health-food stores) discourage mosquitoes and other biting insects for many people.
- Salt tablets are essential for desert travel; antimalaria tablets for jungle travel.
- Always carry water purification tablets. If available, 1 capful of liquid bleach per 5 gallons of water will help.
- Germicidal soap
- Sunscreen lotion for sunny climates; lip balm (or, if nothing else, lipstick) to prevent chapping.
- For sunburns, use cortisone aerosol spray.
- Insect repellent, with 40 percent or more NN diethyl-meta-toluamide, is recommended.

Survival Weapons

Cutting tools are *essential* to survival.

- Make sure you have a sturdy sheath knife with about a 6-inch blade, even if you don't have an axe or hatchet. Care for these tools properly.
- If you don't have a file or whetstone, any sandstone will sharpen tools. A gray, somewhat clayey sandstone gives better results than a pure quartz one. Quartz is the only *common* mineral that will bite into steel, cutting a bright groove with every grain.
- If you don't find sandstone, look for granite or any glittering, crystalline rock except marble. If you use granite, rub two pieces of the stone together until they are smooth before you use one as a grindstone.
- Axes can best be sharpened by using both file and whetstone, but a stone alone will keep the axe usable. Use the file every few days; the whetstone after each use of the axe. Always push the file away from the blade, wetting the axe with water.
- Put a finer edge on your axe with the whetstone. Move the stone, with a circular motion, from the middle of the blade to the edge.
- A snow knife can be sharpened with a file alone. Other knives are sharpened with the whetstone alone. Hold the blade at a slight angle on the stone. Push the blade away from you.

Sharpen the blade alternately on one side and then the other. You can get a keener edge by gradually decreasing the pressure on the blade.

- When you use an axe, don't try to cut through a tree with one blow. Rhythm and aim are more important than force. Too much power behind a swing interferes with your aim. When the axe is swung properly, its weight will provide all the power you need.
- Before chopping, clear away all obstructions. A branch, vine, or bush can deflect an axe onto your foot or leg. Remember— an axe can be a wicked weapon.
- A broken handle is difficult to remove from the head of the axe. Usually the most convenient way is to burn it out. For a single-bit axe, bury the blade in the ground, up to the handle, and build a fire over it. For a double bit, dig a small trench, lay the middle of the axe over it, cover both bits with earth, and build the fire.

  If you have to improvise a new handle, save time and trouble by making a straight handle instead of a curved one like the original. Use a young, straight hardwood without knots. Whittle it roughly into shape and finish it by shaving. Split the end of the handle that fits into the axe head. After it is fitted, pound a thin dry hardwood wedge into the split. Use the axe awhile; pound the wedge in again, then trim if off flush with the axe.

Firearms are *useful* to survival.

- Several companies manufacture combination .410-gauge shotgun/.22 rifle weapons. One such weapon has a hollow stock so the barrels can be inserted for storage along with room for shells and basic cleaning equipment.

  However, the .410 shotgun load has an effective range of twenty to twenty-five yards against small birds and an effective range of ten to fifteen yards against small animals. Don't waste ammunition on long shots, especially long wing shots.

  The .22 rifle can kill at ranges over one hundred yards, but your chances of hitting game in a vital spot at ranges over fifty yards are very slight.

- Remember, most game is actually killed at ranges under fifty yards. Unless it is impossible to secure a clean kill by closer stalking, never attempt to kill by shooting over seventy yards. Make sure of your first shot, for it may be your last one at that particular animal, and your ammunition supply is limited.
- Don't shoot rapid-fire. One shot will do the job if aimed properly.
- Fire from as steady a position as possible. Remember, survival rifles are light, and any unsteadiness on your part due to exertion or excitement will set the barrel to trembling. The prone position is best for a steady shot, but sitting or kneeling positions may have to be used. Use a rest, such as a log or stone, for the barrel whenever you can, but put your hand between the rest and the gun barrel, or the gun may fire wild. Never shoot offhand unless time prevents your taking another position.
- Aim at a vital spot. The shoulder or chest is probably the best spot for medium and large game. Do not shoot unless a vital spot is open.
- Do not trust your first shot even if the game appears to have fallen dead. Reload immediately but keep your eye on the game.
- Look for blood if the game runs away after the first shot. If blood is found, wait 30 minutes before following. Wounded game may lie down and stiffen if given time.
- Survival-type firearms are built to withstand survival conditions, but they do require intelligent care if they are to function when you need them. Keep your weapon clean. If possible, cover it when it's not in use. Keep the action, receiver walls, bolt and assembly, and especially the barrel clean and free from oil, dirt, snow, or mud. If the barrel is obstructed by mud, snow, or any foreign substance, clean it out before shooting. Never try to shoot out an obstruction—the barrel will burst.
- Don't use your weapon as a club, hammer, or pry bar. It is a precision-made instrument on which your life may depend.
- Don't over-oil your weapon. Only a few drops on moving parts are needed.
- A piece of cloth on a string, pulled through the barrel, is a handy substitute for a ramrod and cleaning patch.

- If you must give the barrel a thorough cleaning and have no powder solvent, pour boiling water through it from the breech. Mop up the excess water by pulling a cloth on a string through the barrel, and the hot barrel will dry itself.
- During the winter, remove all lubricants and rust prevention compounds from your weapons. Strip them completely and clean all parts with a dry solvent. Use gasoline or lighter fluid. Normal lubricants thicken in cold weather and slow down the action. In cold weather, weapons function best when absolutely dry.
- A major problem is keeping snow and ice out of the working parts, sights, and barrel. Even a small amount of ice or snow may disable your weapon, so careful handling is essential, especially in snow. Improvise muzzle and breech covers, and use them. Carry a small stick in your pocket to clean the sights and breech block.
- Weapons sweat when they are brought from extreme cold into a heated shelter; when they are taken out again into the cold, the film of condensation freezes. This ice may seriously affect their operation, so leave them outdoors or store them in unheated shelters. If your shelter is not greatly warmer than the outside temperature, you may bring your weapons inside, but place them at or near floor level, where the temperature is lowest. When you take them into a heated shelter for cleaning, remove all the condensed moisture before cleaning. They may sweat for an hour.
- If a part becomes frozen, do not force it. Warm it slightly, if possible, and move it gradually until unfrozen. If it cannot be warmed, try to remove all visible ice or snow and move it gradually until action is restored.
- Before loading your weapon, always move the action back and forth a few times to insure that it is free and to check your ammunition.
- If your weapon has a metal stock, pad it with tape or cloth, or pull a sock over it to protect your cheeks.

Orientation Charts and Diagrams

DIRECTION FROM THE SUN
AT SUNRISE AND SUNSET

If you know your latitude and longitude, you can find north by observing the sun when it rises or sets. Figure V-i shows the true azimuth (true bearing) of the rising sun and the relative bearing of the setting sun for all the months in the year in the Northern and Southern Hemispheres.

An example of how to find north from the rising sun is as follows: On January 26, your position is 50°00′ N and 165°06′ W. Entering the table at the date and under 50° N latitude, you find the azimuth of the sun to be 120°. Since the sun is rising, you know that this is the true azimuth of the sun from north. Therefore, north will be to your left 120° when you are facing the sun.

To find north from the setting sun, consider the same problem as above. However, in this case, the azimuth of the sun is not the true azimuth. Instead, it is a relative bearing. Since the sun sets in the west, north must be to the right of the sun. Therefore, north will be 120° to your right when you face the sun.

Angle to North from the rising or setting sun (level terrain)

DATE		0°	5°	10°	15°	20°	25°	30°	35°	40°	45°	50°	55°	60°
JANUARY	1	113	113	113	114	115	116	117	118	121	124	127	133	141
	6	112	113	113	113	114	115	116	118	120	123	127	132	140
	11	111	112	112	113	113	114	115	117	119	122	125	130	138
	16	111	111	111	112	112	113	114	116	118	120	124	129	136
	21	110	110	110	111	111	112	113	115	117	119	122	127	133
	26	109	109	109	109	110	111	112	113	115	117	120	124	130
FEBRUARY	1	107	107	108	108	108	109	110	111	113	115	117	121	126
	6	106	106	106	106	107	107	108	109	111	113	115	118	123
	11	104	104	105	105	105	106	107	108	109	110	112	116	120
	16	103	103	103	103	103	104	105	106	107	108	110	112	116
	21	101	101	101	101	101	102	102	103	104	105	107	109	112
	26	99	99	99	99	100	100	100	101	102	103	104	106	108
MARCH	1	98	98	98	98	99	99	99	100	100	101	102	104	106
	6	96	96	96	96	96	97	97	97	98	98	99	100	102
	11	94	94	94	94	94	94	95	95	95	96	96	97	98
	16	92	92	92	92	92	92	92	92	93	93	93	93	94
	21	90	90	90	90	90	90	90	90	90	90	90	90	90
	26	88	88	88	88	88	88	88	88	87	87	87	87	86
APRIL	1	86	86	86	86	85	85	85	85	84	84	83	82	81
	6	84	84	84	83	83	83	83	82	82	81	80	79	77
	11	82	82	82	82	81	81	81	80	80	79	77	76	74
	16	80	80	80	80	79	79	78	78	77	76	74	72	70
	21	78	78	78	78	77	77	76	76	75	73	72	69	66
	26	77	77	76	76	76	75	75	74	72	71	69	66	63
MAY	1	75	75	75	74	74	73	73	72	70	69	66	63	59
	6	74	74	73	73	73	72	71	70	68	67	64	61	56
	11	72	72	72	72	71	70	69	68	67	64	62	58	52
	16	71	71	71	70	70	69	68	67	65	63	60	55	49
	21	70	70	70	69	69	68	67	65	63	61	58	53	47
	26	69	69	69	68	68	67	66	64	62	60	56	51	44
JUNE	1	68	68	68	67	66	66	64	63	61	58	54	49	41
	6	67	67	67	67	66	65	64	62	60	57	53	48	40
	11	67	67	67	66	65	64	63	62	59	56	53	47	39
	16	67	67	67	66	65	64	63	62	59	56	53	47	39
	21	67	67	67	66	65	64	63	62	59	56	53	47	39
	26	67	67	67	66	65	64	63	62	59	56	53	47	39

Azimuth of the Rising and Setting Sun

Month	Date														
JULY	1 / 6	39/40	47/48	53/53	56/57	59/60	62/62	63/64	64/65	65/66	66/66	67/67	67/67	67/67	67/67
	11 / 16	41/43	49/50	54/55	58/59	61/62	63/64	64/65	65/66	66/67	67/68	68/68	68/68	68/69	68/69
	21 / 26	45/48	52/54	57/59	60/62	63/64	65/66	66/67	67/68	68/69	69/70	69/70	69/70	69/70	69/70
AUGUST	1 / 6	51/55	57/60	61/63	64/66	66/68	68/69	69/71	70/71	71/72	71/73	72/73	72/73	72/73	72/73
	11 / 16	58/61	63/65	66/68	68/70	70/72	71/73	72/74	73/75	74/75	74/76	74/76	75/76	75/76	75/76
	21 / 26	65/68	68/71	71/73	72/75	74/76	75/77	76/78	76/78	77/79	77/79	78/79	78/79	78/79	78/79
SEPTEMBER	1 / 6	73/77	75/78	77/80	78/81	79/81	80/82	80/82	81/83	81/83	81/83	82/83	82/83	82/83	82/83
	11 / 16	81/84	82/85	83/85	83/86	84/86	84/86	85/87	85/87	85/87	85/87	85/87	85/87	85/87	85/87
	21 / 26	88/92	88/92	88/92	89/91	89/91	89/91	89/91	89/91	89/91	89/91	89/91	89/91	89/91	89/91
OCTOBER	1 / 6	96/100	95/99	95/98	94/97	94/97	94/96	93/96	93/96	93/95	93/95	93/95	93/95	93/95	93/95
	11 / 16	104/108	102/105	101/104	100/102	99/101	99/101	98/100	98/100	97/99	97/99	97/99	97/99	97/99	97/99
	21 / 26	112/115	109/112	107/109	105/108	104/106	103/105	102/104	102/104	101/103	101/103	101/103	101/102	101/102	101/102
NOVEMBER	1 / 6	120/123	116/119	113/115	110/113	109/111	108/110	107/109	106/108	105/107	105/107	105/106	104/106	104/106	104/106
	11 / 16	126/130	121/124	117/120	115/117	113/115	111/113	110/112	109/111	108/110	108/109	108/109	107/109	107/109	107/110
	21 / 26	133/135	126/128	122/124	119/120	116/118	114/116	113/114	112/113	111/112	111/112	110/111	110/111	110/111	110/111
DECEMBER	1 / 6	138/140	130/132	125/126	122/123	119/120	117/118	115/116	114/115	113/114	113/113	112/113	112/112	112/112	112/112
	11 / 16	141/141	133/133	127/127	124/124	121/121	118/118	117/117	116/116	115/115	114/114	113/113	113/113	113/113	113/113
	21 / 26	141/141	133/133	127/127	124/124	121/121	118/118	117/117	116/116	115/115	114/114	113/113	113/113	113/113	113/113

NOTE: When the sun is rising, the angle is reckoned from East to North.
When the sun is setting, the angle is reckoned from West to North.

Fig. V-i   Azimuth of the Rising and Setting Sun

Figure V-i does not list every day of the year nor does it list every degree of longitude. If you want accuracy to within one degree of azimuth, you may have to interpolate between the values given in the table. However, for all practical purposes, using the closest day and the closest degree of latitude listed in the table will give you an azimuth which will enable you to hold your course. For example: If you are at 32° north latitude on the 13th of April, the azimuth of the rising sun is actually 79°22′; however, by entering the table with the closest day listed, 11 April, and the closest latitude, 30°, you get 81° as the azimuth of the rising sun. This value is accurate enough for field purposes.

LATITUDES BY LENGTH OF DAY

(See figure V-ii) When you are in any latitude between 60°N and 60°S, you can determine your exact latitude within 30 nautical miles (½°), if you know the length of the day within 1 minute. This is true throughout the year except for about ten days before and ten days after the equinoxes—approximately 11–31 March and 13 September–2 October. During these two periods, the day is approximately the same length at all latitudes. To time sunrise and sunset accurately, you must have a level horizon. A land horizon cannot always be used.

OBSERVATIONS FOR LATITUDE

Find the length of the day from the instant the top of the sun first appears above the ocean horizon to the instant it disappears below the horizon. This instant is often marked by a green flash. Write down the times of sunrise and sunset. Don't count on remembering them. Note that only the length of day counts in the determination of latitude; your watch may have an unknown error and yet serve to determine this factor. If you have only one water horizon, as on a seacoast, find local noon by the stick and shadow method (Chapter Three). The length of day will be twice the interval from sunrise to noon or from noon to sunset.

Knowing the length of day, you can find the latitude by using the nomogram, figure V-ii.

LONGITUDE FROM LOCAL, APPARENT NOON

To find longitude, you must know the correct time. You should know the rate at which your watch gains or loses time. If you know this rate and the time you last set the watch, you can compute the correct time. Correct zone time on your watch to Greenwich time; for example, if your watch is on eastern standard time, add 5 hours to get Greenwich time.

You can find longitude by timing the moment when a celestial body passes your meridian. The easiest body to use is the sun. Put up a stick or rod as nearly vertical as possible, in a level place. Check the alignment of the stick by sighting along the line of a makeshift plumb bob. (To make a plumb bob, tie any heavy object to a string and let it hang free. The line of the string indicates the vertical.) Sometime before midday, begin marking the position of the end of the stick's shadow. Note the time for each mark. Continue marking until the shadow definitely lengthens. The time of the shortest shadow is the time when the sun passed the local meridian or local apparent noon. You will probably have to estimate the position of the shortest shadow by finding a line midway between two shadows of equal length, one before noon and one after. If you get the times of sunrise and sunset accurately on a water horizon, local noon will be midway between these times.

Mark down the Greenwich time of local apparent noon. The next step is to correct this observed time of meridian passage for the equation of time—that is, the number of minutes the real sun is ahead of or behind the mean sun. (The mean sun was invented by astronomers to simplify the problems of measuring time. It rolls along the equator at a constant rate of 15° per hour. The real sun is not so considerate; it changes its angular rate of travel around the earth with the seasons.)

Figure V-iv gives the values in minutes of time to be added to or subtracted from mean (watch) time to get apparent (sun) time.

Now that you have the Greenwich time of local noon, you can find the difference of longitude between your position and Greenwich by converting the interval between 1200 Greenwich and your local noon from time to arc. Remember that 1 hour equals 15° of longitude, 4 minutes equal 1° of longitude, and 4 seconds equal 1' of longitude.

Example: Your watch is on eastern standard time. It normally loses 30 seconds a day. You haven't set it for four days. You time local noon at 15:08 on your watch on 4 February.

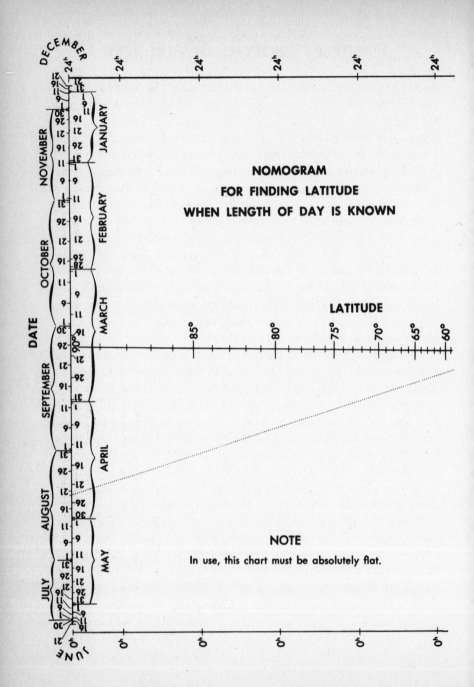

NOMOGRAM
FOR FINDING LATITUDE
WHEN LENGTH OF DAY IS KNOWN

LATITUDE

NOTE

In use, this chart must be absolutely flat.

Fig. V-ii Nomogram

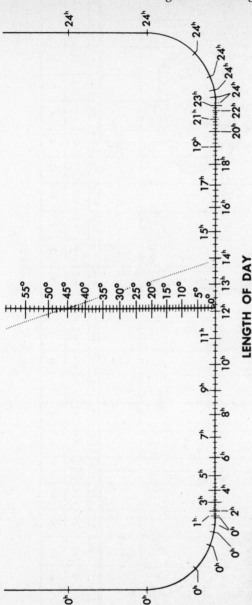

LENGTH OF DAY

INSTRUCTIONS

To find your latitude:

In Northern Latitudes:

1. Find length of the day from the instant the top of the sun appears above the ocean horizon to the instant it disappears below the horizon. This instant is often marked by a green flash.

2. Lay a straight edge or stretch across the Nomogram, connecting the observed length of the day on the Length of Day Scale with the date on the Date Scale.

3. Read your latitude on the Latitude Scale.

EXAMPLE: On August 20, observed length of the day is 13 hours and 54 minutes. Latitude is 45°30'N.

In Southern Latitudes:

Add six months to the date and proceed as in northern latitudes.

EXAMPLE: On 11 May observed length of day is 10 hours and 4 minutes. Adding 6 months gives 11 November. Latitude is 41°30'S.

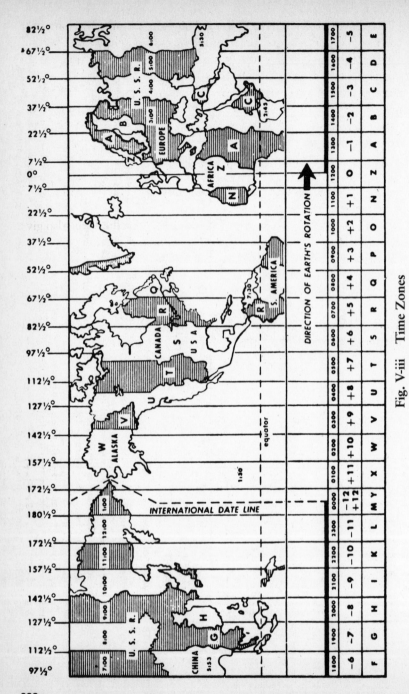

Fig. V-iii Time Zones

Watch correction is 4 x 30 seconds or plus 2 minutes. Zone time correction is plus 5 hours. Greenwich time is 15:08 plus 2 minutes plus 5 hours, or 20:10. The equation of time for 4 February is minus 14 minutes. Local noon is 20:10 minus 14 minutes, or 19:56 Greenwich. Difference in time between Greenwich and your position is 19:56 minus 12:00, or 7:56. 7:56 of time equals 119° of longitude. Since your local noon is later than Greenwich noon, you are west of Greenwich. Your longitude then is 119°W.

DIRECTION FROM THE SUN AT NOON

Determining local noon by the stick and shadow method will also give you direction. The line of the shortest shadow is also the line of the local meridian or north–south line. Whether the sun is north or south of you at midday will depend on your latitude. North of 23.4°N, the sun will always be due south at local noon; and the shadow will point north. South of 23.4°S, the sun will always be due north at local noon; and the shadow will point south. In the tropics, the sun can be either north or south at noon, depending on the date, and your position.

Date	Eq. of Time°	Date	Eq. of Time°	Date	Eq. of Time°	Date	Eq. of Time°	Date	Eq. of Time°	Date	Eq. of Time°
Jan. 1	-3.5 min.	Mar. 4	-12.0	May 2	+3.0 min.	Aug. 4	-6.0	Oct. 1	+10.0 min.	Dec. 1	+11.0
2	-4.0	8	-11.0	14	+3.8	12	-5.0	4	+11.0	4	+10.0
4	-5.0	12	-10.0	May 28	+3.0	17	-4.0	7	+12.0	6	+9.0
7	-6.0	16	-9.0	June 4	+2.0	22	-3.0	11	+13.0	9	+8.0
9	-7.0	19	-8.0	9	+1.0	26	-2.0	15	+14.0	11	+7.0
12	-8.0	22	-7.0	14	0.0	Aug. 29	-1.0	20	+15.0	13	+6.0
14	-9.0	26	-6.0	19	1.0	Sept. 1	0.0	Oct. 27	+16.0	15	+5.0
17	-10.0	Mar. 29	-5.0	23	-2.0	5	+1.0	Nov. 4	+16.4	17	+4.0
20	-11.0	Apr. 1	-4.0	June 28	-3.0	8	+2.0	11	+16.0	19	+3.0
24	-12.0	5	-3.0	July 3	-4.0	10	+3.0	17	+15.0	21	+2.0
Jan. 28	-13.0	8	-2.0	9	-5.0	13	+4.0	22	+14.0	23	+1.0
Feb. 4	-14.0	12	-1.0	18	-6.0	16	+5.0	25	+13.0	25	0.0
13	-14.3	16	0.0	July 27	-6.6	19	+6.0	Nov. 28	+12.0	27	-1.0
19	-14.0	20	+1.0			22	+7.0			29	-2.0
Feb. 28	-13.0	Apr. 25	+2.0			25	+8.0			Dec. 31	-3.0
						Sep. 28	+9.0				

* Add plus values to mean time and subtract minus values from mean time to get apparent time.

Fig. V-iv   Determining Time

LATITUDE BY NOON ALTITUDE OF SUN

On any given day there is only one latitude on the earth where the sun will pass directly overhead or through the zenith at noon. In all latitudes north of this, the sun will pass to the south of the zenith; and in those south of it, the sun will pass to the north. For each 1° change of latitude, the zenith distance will also change by 1°.

Figure V-vi gives, for each day of the year, the latitude where the sun is in the zenith at noon.

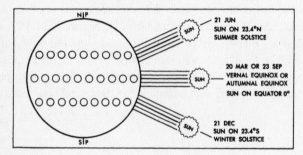

Fig. V-v   Positioning of the Sun at Equinox and Solstice

DECLINATION OF SUN

(IN DEGREES AND TENTHS OF A DEGREE)

Declination is tabulated to the nearest tenth of a degree rather than to the nearest minute of arc. To convert 1/10° (0.1°) to minutes, multiply by 6. (ie. 27.9° = 27° 54')

DAY	JAN	FEB	MAR	APR	MAY	JUN	JUL	AUG	SEP	OCT	NOV	DEC
1	S 23.1	S 17.5	S 7.7	N 4.4	N 15.0	N 22.0	N 23.1	N 18.1	N 8.4	S 3.1	S 14.3	S 21.8
2	23.0	17.2	7.3	4.8	15.3	22.1	23.1	17.9	8.1	3.4	14.6	21.9
3	22.9	16.9	6.9	5.2	15.6	22.3	23.0	17.6	7.7	3.8	15.0	.22.1
4	22.9	16.6	6.6	5.6	15.9	22.4	22.9	17.3	7.3	4.2	15.3	22.2
5	22.8	16.3	6.2	5.9	16.2	22.5	22.8	17.1	7.0	4.6	15.6	22.3
6	S 22.7	S 16.0	S 5.8	N. 6.3	N 16.4	N 22.6	N 22.7	N 16.8	N 6.6	S 5.0	S 15.9	S 22.5
7	22.5	15.7	5.4	6.7	16.7	22.7	22.6	16.5	6.2	5.4	16.2	22.6
8	22.4	15.4	5.0	7.1	17.0	22.8	22.5	16.3	5.8	5.7	16.5	22.7
9	22.3	15.1	4.6	7.4	17.3	22.9	22.4	16.0	5.5	6.1	16.8	22.8
10	22.2	14.8	4.2	7.8	17.5	23.0	22.3	15.7	5.1	6.5	17.1	22.9
11	S 22.0	S 14.5	S 3.8	N 8.2	N 17.8	N 23.1	N 22.2	N 15.4	N 4.7	S 6.9	S 17.3	S 23.0
12	21.9	14.1	3.5	8.6	18.0	23.1	22.0	15.1	4.3	7.3	17.6	23.1
13	21.7	13.8	3.1	8.9	18.3	23.2	21.9	14.8	3.9	7.6	17.9	23.1
14	21.5	13.5	2.7	9.3	18.5	23.2	21.7	14.5	3.6	8.0	18.1	23.2
15	21.4	13.1	2.3	9.6	18.8	23.3	21.6	14.2	3.2	8.4	18.4	23.3
16	S 21.2	S 12.8	S 1.9	N 10.0	N 19.0	N 23.3	N 21.4	N 13.9	N 2.8	S 8.8	S 18.7	S 23.3
17	21.0	12.4	1.5	10.4	19.2	23.4	21.3	13.5	2.4	9.1	18.9	23.3
18	20.8	12.1	1.1	10.7	19.5	23.4	21.1	13.2	2.0	9.5	19.1	23.4
19	20.6	11.7	0.7	11.1	19.7	23.4	20.9	12.9	1.6	9.9	19.4	23.4
20	20.4	11.4	0.3	11.4	19.9	23.4	20.7	12.6	1.2	10.2	19.6	23.4
21	S 20.2	S 11.0	N 0.1	N 11.7	N 20.1	N 23.4	N 20.5	N 12.2	N 0.8	S 10.6	S 19.8	S 23.4
22	20.0	10.7	0.5	12.1	20.3	23.4	20.4	11.9	0.5	10.9	20.1	23.4
23	19.8	10.3	0.9	12.4	20.5	23.4	20.2	11.6	N 0.1	11.3	20.3	23.4
24	19.5	9.9	1.3	12.7	20.7	23.4	20.0	11.2	S 0.3	11.6	20.5	23.4
25	19.3	9.6	1.7	13.1	20.9	23.4	19.7	10.9	0.7	12.0	20.7	23.4
26	S 19.0	S 9.2	N 2.1	N 13.4	N 21.1	N 23.4	N 19.5	N 10.5	S 1.1	S 12.3	S 20.9	S 23.4
27	18.8	8.8	2.5	13.7	21.2	23.3	19.3	10.2	1.5	12.7	21.1	23.3
28	18.5	8.5	2.9	14.0	21.4	23.3	19.1	9.8	1.9	13.0	21.3	23.3
29	18.3	8.1	3.2	14.4	21.6	23.3	18.8	9.5	2.3	13.4	21.4	23.3
30	18.0	...	3.6	14.7	21.7	23.2	18.6	9.1	2.7	13.7	21.6	23.2
31	S 17.7	...	N 4.0	...	N 21.9	...	N 18.4	N 8.8	...	S 14.0	...	S 23.1

EXAMPLE: On 10 December the declination of the sun is 22.9°S., so an observer who measures the zenith distance as 0° would know that he is at latitude 22.9°S. If he measures a zenith distance of 5° with the sun south of this zenith, he is 5° north of 22.9°S, or at a latitude 17.9°S; and if the sun is north, he is 5° south of 22.9°S, or in latitude 27.9°S.

Fig. V-vi   Declination of the Sun in Degrees

❂ INDEX ❂

Page numbers in *italics* refer to separate illustrations

Ditching, plane, 237–238
Dock, wild, 150
Dogs
  bites, 112
  cooking, 127
  danger from, 112
Down, plant and bird, as fuel, 120
Dressings, wounds, 74–75, 80
Drowning, 92
Drying food, 132
Ducks, 224
Dulse, 260
Dunes, 116
Dung, firemaking with, 119
Dwarf fireweed, 230
Dye
  fluorescent, 104
  sea-marker, 270
Dysentery, 49, 114, 165

Ear, foreign body in the, 92
Earthquakes, 280
Echinoderms, 264, 266
Edible plants. *See* Plants, edible
Eggs
  cooking, 131
  in cold climates, 224
  tropical, 189
Eels, 131, 253
  electric, 164, 186
Elderberry rushes, water near, 117
Electric eels, 164, 186
Electric lines, 35
Electric rays, 244, 250
Electric shock, 92–93
Elephants, danger from, 111
Elks, 222
Emergencies. *See* Natural disasters and
  First aid
Emotional problems and survival, 1–2
Encephalitis, 165
Energy, 2, 3, 33
Environmental hazards
  at sea, 242, *243*, 244, *245*, 246, *247*,
    248, *249*, 250–251
  coastal areas, 257–259
  cold climates, 213–214, *215*
  desert areas, 194–197
  tropics, 161, *162*, *163*, 164–165
Equal shadow method for determining
  direction, *28*, 30
Ergot poisoning, 143

Eskimos, 236
Europe, 103
  poisonous snakes of, 297–298, *299*
Exhaustion, 166
  heat, 199
Exposure to the sun, 199
Extension scale, 13
Eyes
  applying bandages, 77, 91
  foreign body in, 92
  sore, 251–252

Face wounds, 80
Fallout shelters, 273
Fanged snakes,
  long, 287
  short, 287
Fear, 2, 3, 4, 5
Feathers, 126, 257
Feet, taking care of, 51–52, 158, 205, 235
  See also Immersion foot
Fer-de-Lance Group, snakes, 292–293
Ferns
  bed of, 109
  edible, 148, *149*
  fuel, 120
Fever, louse-borne relapsing, 54
Fiddleheads, 150
Field dressing, 75–76
Figs, wild, 143, 157, 183
Fingers, applying bandages to, 77
Firearms, 135, 310–312
Fireball, nuclear attack, 271
Firemaking, 119
  cooking fires, *123*, 124
  fuel, tinder and location, 119–120
  in cold climates, 234–235
  in desert area, 203
  tropical, 189
  without matches, *121*, 122
Fireman's carry, 95, *96–97*, 98, 99
Fireplace, underground, 124
Fire saw, 122
Fire thong, 122
Fireweed, tall, 230
Firewood, 119–120
  See also Fuel
First aid, 3, 49–101
  basic hygiene, 49–52
First aid, emergencies
  common first aid for drowning, 92
  electric shock, 92–93

Friction, wood, firemaking, 122
  bow and drill, 113, 115
  fire saw, 122
  fire thong, 122
Frogs, 186–187
Frostbite, 216–217
Fuel, firemaking, 119–120, 208, 234–235
Fruit, 50
  cooking, 130
  edible, 154, *156*, 157
  edible, tropical, 178, 180, *181–182,* 183, 184
  in cold climates, 214, *226–227,* 228
Fungi, 143

Game, hunting
  finding, 134
  shooting, 135
  weapons, 134, 310–312
Game, small, cooking, 130
Gamma radiation, 271–272
Gangrene, 217
Garbage, 50
Gas cans as swimming aid, 40
Gasoline, 53
  firemaking with, 120
Gastritis, 50
Gastrointestinal allergy, 50
Gauze, 75
Geese, 224
Geographical coordinates, 14, *15,* 16
Giant ray, 244
Glacier travel, 38
Glare, sun, 199, 218
Glass and sun, firemaking with, 120
Goa beans, 184
Goats, 222, 223
Goosefoot, 154
Gorge hook, 140
Gourd, wild, 174
Government Printing Office, vii, 9
Grad, 17
Grains
  cooking, 130
  edible, 154
  edible, tropical, 184, *185,* 186
  parching, 130
Granite, 116
Grapevine, wild, 157
Graphic (bar) scale, 12, *13*
Grapple, 254

Grass
  fuel, 119
  weather indicator, 110
Grasshoppers, 131, 187
Grayling, 221
Greasewoods, water near, 117
Greens, in cold climates, 230, *232–233, 234*
  See also Plants
Greenwich Prime Meridian, 13–14, *15–16*
Grid
  azimuth, 17
  north, 17
Ground, preparing for beds, 109
Ground-to-air body signals, *47*
Group survival, 2, 3, 6–7
Grouse, 224
Grubs, 131, 187
Gulls, catching, 135
Gum tree, sweet, 75
Gun powder, firemaking with, 122

Hagfish, 246
Hand, fishing by, 140
Handling the wounded, *95*
Hands, applying a bandage to, 77
Hasty rappel, 36, *37*
Hazards
  at sea, 241–252
  coastal areas, 258–259
  danger from mammals, 111–112
  danger from plants, 112, *113,* 114
  in cold climates, 213–214, *215,* 216–219
  in desert areas, 194–197
  in the tropics, 161–165
  poisonous snakes, 111
  See also First aid
Hazelnut (Filbert), 153
Headaches, 80
Head injuries, 61, 63, 74, 77, 80
Head-tilt method, 58
Health hazards
  at sea, 252
  in cold climates, 216–219
  in desert areas, 198–199
  tropical, 165–167
  See also First aid
Heartbeat, maintaining, 73
Heartburn, 50
Heart massage, closed-chest, *64,* 65–67
Heat
  cramps, 199
  exhaustion, 199

New Guinea, poisonous snakes of, 301, *302,* 303
Newts, 187
Night
    determining direction at, *29,* 30
    steering marks, 32
Nimbus clouds, indicating weather conditions, 110
Nipa palm boughs, 131
Nonpotable water, danger of drinking, 114–115
North
    grid, 17
    magnetic, 17, 18
    true, 17, 18
North America
    poisonous plants of, *113*
    poisonous snakes of, 288, *289,* 290–291
North Star, finding, 30
Norwegian itch, 54
Nose, foreign body in the, 92
Notched raft, building, 42
Nuclear attack
    immediate action, 270–271
    radiation, 271–275
Nut grass, 144
Nuts
    cooking, 130
    edible, tropical, 153–154, *155*
    parching, 128

Oak, English, 153–154
Octopus, 263
Odors, indicating land, 241
Oil, 54
    on water, 238
Ointment on burns, 82
Onion, wild, 147–148
Open fracture, 83
Orientation, 16, 34
    direction from the sun at noon, 321
    direction from the sun at sunrise and
        sunset, 313, 316
    latitude by length of day, 316
    latitude by noon altitude of sun, 322
    observations for latitude, 316, *318–319*
Owls, 224
Oxygen, lack of, first aid measures
    artificial respiration, 58–59, *60,* 61, *62,*
        63
    closed-chest heart massage, *64, 65,* 66–67
    enlarging airway passage, *57,* 58

Pace as unit of measure, 31–32
Pacific Islands, *56*
    poisonous snakes of the, 301, *302,* 303
Packstrap carry, 98
Padding for a fracture, 85
Pain, 1, 2, 3
Palms, 177–178
Pangi, 161
Panic, 3, 4, *5–6*
Papaya, 143, 180, 183
Parachutes, 104, 160
    shelters, 99, 102, *256*
    suspension lines, 36
Paraffin, waterproofing matches, 119
Parallels, 14
Parasites, 126
Parateepee shelter, 106
Parboiling, 130
Parching, 128
Pearl millet, 184
Pedicellaria, 266
Periwinkles, 221
Philippines, *56*
Physic nut, 164
Piggyback carry, 98
Pigs, wild, danger from, 112
Pine tree, 75, 120
Piranha, 164, 186
Pistachio nut, wild, 201
Pistol-belt carry, 101
Plague, 49
Plane crash, 33, 103, 120, 160
    ditching, 237–238
    on land, 267–268
    on sea, 268–270
Planimetric maps, 9, 11
Planks as swimming aids, 40
Plankton, *255*
Plankton tow, 254–255
Plantains, 180
Plant foods
    cooking, 130
    preserving, 132, 272
Plants, danger from, 112, *113,* 114
    poisonous in cold climates, 214, *215*
    poisonous to eat, 114
    poisonous, to touch, 112–113
    poisonous tropical, 112–114
Plants, edible
    guidelines, 143–144
    in coastal areas, 259–260, *261, 262,*
        263